Notes

Tendency to quote large passages of
text as evidence of points without
unpacking them

Most historical research seems
second hand.

use of secretar... writers.

Central argument ... ...
the settlement of the ...
that "this ...
The ... fact that so many
of the texts are comparatively
...
the ... of ... the
marks of length.

"the narrative of ... play"

Fails to pick up on textual allusions. p191 example of same.

Lack of contextual material. He is only interested in ...

The Literary Quest for an American National Character

Routledge Transnational Perspectives on American Literature

EDITED BY SUSAN CASTILLO, *King's College London*

1. New Woman Hybridities
Femininity, Feminism, and International
Consumer Culture, 1880–1930
Edited by Ann Heilmann and
Margaret Beetham

2. Don DeLillo
The Possibility of Fiction
Peter Boxall

3. Toni Morrison's *Beloved*
Origins
Justine Tally

**4. Fictions of the Black Atlantic in
American Foundational Literature**
Gesa Mackenthun

5. Mexican American Literature
Elizabeth Jacobs

6. Native American Literature
Towards a Spatialized Reading
Helen May Dennis

**7. Transnationalism and
American Literature**
Literary Translation 1773–1892
Colleen Glenney Boggs

**8. The Quest for Epic in
Contemporary American Fiction**
John Updike, Philip Roth and
Don DeLillo
Catherine Morley

**9. The Literary Quest for an
American National Character**
Finn Pollard

Related:

Fictions of America
Narratives of Global Empire
Judie Newman

The Literary Quest for an American National Character

Finn Pollard

Routledge
Taylor & Francis Group
New York   London

First published 2009
by Routledge
270 Madison Ave, New York, NY 10016

Simultaneously published in the UK
by Routledge
2 Park Square, Milton Park, Abingdon, Oxon OX14 4RN

Routledge is an imprint of the Taylor & Francis Group, an informa business

© 2009 Taylor & Francis

Typeset in Sabon by IBT Global.
Printed and bound in the United States of America on acid-free paper by IBT Global.

Library of Congress Cataloging in Publication Data
Pollard, Finn.
  The literary quest for an American national character / by Finn Pollard.
      p. cm. — (Routledge transnational perspectives on American literature ; 9)
  Includes bibliographical references and index.
  1. American literature—Revolutionary period, 1775–1783—History and criticism. 2. National characteristics, American, in literature. 3. American literature—1783–1850—History and criticism. 4. United States—Intellectual life—18th century. 5. United States—Intellectual life—1783–1865. 6. Group identity in literature. I. Title.
  PS195.N35P65 2008
  810.9'35873—dc22
                              2008025412

ISBN10: 0-415-96373-7 (hbk)
ISBN10: 0-203-88591-0 (ebk)

ISBN13: 978-0-415-96373-2 (hbk)
ISBN13: 978-0-203-88591-8 (ebk)

Contents

Acknowledgements

This book, which began life as my PhD thesis, has been a long project and I have incurred debts to many people, which an acknowledgement here can only partially repay.

Without Owen Dudley Edwards, this book would never have been written. Owen first inspired me to undertake a PhD in American history, and never lost faith in me or the project. He has always given his time, support, and love unstintingly.

The other members of the American History section at the University of Edinburgh, Frank Cogliano and Alan Day (who also acted as supervisors of my graduate thesis at different stages), Rhodri Jeffries-Jones, Robert Mason, Benjamin Carp and Mark Newman. Also at Edinburgh Susan Manning and Andy Taylor in English Literature and Richard Mackenney and John Gooding.

My former colleagues at the University of Glasgow, in particular Sam Maddra, Susan Castillo, Simon Newman, Marina Moskowitz, Thomas Munck, Don Spaeth, Alison Peden and Margo Hunter.

My students at Edinburgh, Glasgow and Newcastle.

My present colleagues at Friends House, London, who have given much needed support during the final revisions.

My postgraduate colleagues Keith Mears, Jeff Nelson, Kirsten Phimister, Jenny Litster, Jim Fog, Dean Williams, James Inglis and Natasha.

My family—Garth and Lucy Pollard, my brothers Tam and Liam, and many other relatives. Tam's technical and proofreading support at an earlier stage went beyond the call of brotherly duty.

My flatmates—Johny Clelland, Florence Berland and Pauline Lemaigre.

Central Edinburgh Quaker Meeting, in particular Pat and Phil Lucas and Alan Sayle.

The members of the Edinburgh University Savoy Opera Group.

The Scottish Association for the Study of America Conference, the British Association for American Studies Conference, the NY State History Conference, and Scotland's Trans-Atlantic Relationship Postgraduate Seminar in American Studies—all friendly environments in which ideas were tried out. I am also grateful to the anonymous readers of my book proposal and the article from which part of Chapter 3 is drawn for their comments.

The International Center for Jefferson Studies at Monticello whose award of a Short-term Fellowship enabled me to conduct research in the States.

The Staff of the Edinburgh University Main Library; the National Library of Scotland; Cambridge University Library; the Special Collections Department at the University of Virginia; the Rare Books Room at the Library of Congress and the Jefferson Library at Monticello.

Christopher Phipps for providing the excellent index very rapidly and with very little notice.

Laura MacDonald for love and faith.

During the last year of work on this book in its earlier incarnation as my graduate thesis, three members of my family died—my grandfather Martin Robertson, my uncle Neil, and my cousin Muriel. I would have loved them all to have seen the final result.

I extend my thanks to the following individuals and publishers for permission to reproduce the following material. Quotations from James Fenimore Cooper, *The Spy: A Tale of the Neutral Ground*; historical introduction by James P. Elliott; explanatory notes by James H. Pickering etc. (AMS Press, New York, 2002) are reproduced by kind permission of AMS Press. Quotations from Benjamin Franklin, *The Autobiography of Benjamin Franklin: A Genetic Text*, eds. J. A. Leo Lemay and Paul M. Zall (Knoxville: University of Tennessee Press, 1981) by kind permission of J. A. Leo Lemay. Quotations from *The Pioneers* are reprinted by permission from *The Pioneers or the Sources of the Susquehanna: A Descriptive Tale* by James Fenimore Cooper (State University of New York Press, 1980, State University of New York. All rights reserved). Quotations from *The Prairie* are reprinted by permission from *The Prairie: A Tale* by James Fenimore Cooper (State University of New York, 1985, State University of New York. All rights reserved). Material from the letters of Benjamin Franklin is reproduced by kind permission of the *American Philosophical Society* and *The Papers of Benjamin Franklin*. Part of Chapter 3 first appeared as an article in *American Nineteenth Century History*.

Introduction

In 1782, forced by revolution back to his native France, J. Hector St. John,[1] published the work which asked, with an attractive simplicity, the question on which this thesis starts, "What then, is the American, this new man?"[2] As an imaginative writer, he enjoyed a luxury denied to the historian, that of being allowed to ask such a question, leaving it to the evidence he produced, and to the decision of his readers, to determine whether it was a reasonable, or indeed an accurate, question. One can only wish that the same simplicity might be allowed to attend the opening of this study.

Since Crèvecoeur, the pursuit of the American has become an object of some interest to historians, literary critics, and other interested parties. The National Library of Scotland produces, under "National characteristics, American," 166 titles covering American history from first colonisation to the present day.[3] This abundance is the more striking considering its historian's first problem: Does such a thing as national character actually exist? Michael Kammen, in his masterly *People of Paradox* (1980) devoted much of his introduction to this difficulty. He produced statements from thinkers as diverse as Alexis de Tocqueville and Isaiah Berlin[4] to support his contention of its existence, and the value of studying it, but these remain contentions.

Other studies, more in the "straight history" genre, simply assume its existence as a matter of course. Gordon Wood's superb brief history, *The American Revolution*, opens in precisely this manner, "The Revolution, in short, gave birth to whatever sense of nationhood and national purpose Americans have had."[5]

This study seeks a middle way between these two reputable extremes. It hopes to persuade the reader that a quest for and different definitions of national character existed, but offers documentary evidence, rather than imposing a theoretical framework. It explores how certain Americans tried to construct versions of America in the period of the Revolution and the early Republic, and suggests that the evidence will show that they, at least, were seeking a unique quality, which they could not always clearly define any more than we can. Some of these versions of America were known and (sometimes) revered by many contemporaries in whole or part; others, to their authors' dismay, were little known. Henry Adams's *History of the United States* (1884–1890) holds as its central theme the search for an American character over a shorter period. I follow in its great footsteps.[6] Adams opened his survey with a detailed consideration of America in the year 1800. Adams recognised the significance of that moment of refashioning. He did not impose this from outside, but acknowledged the claim of Thomas Jefferson. For, Jefferson, on his election to the presidency in 1800–1801, proclaimed that the proper character of the nation was restored by that act and that a glorious future lay ahead for the Republic:[7]

> The tough sides of our Argosie have been thoroughly tried. Her strength has stood the waves into which she was steered with a view to sink her. We shall put her on her Republican tack, and she will now show by the beauty of her motion the skill of her builders.[8]

This moment, and Henry Adams' recognition of it, displays the key issues of this study: first, the assertion that a national character existed; second, the sense that the nature of national character was closely bound to the political system; third, the belief that a glorious future awaited the people possessed of that character. Jefferson's accession mirrored similar moments: the act of Revolution in 1776, the ratification of the Constitution in 1789, Monroe's First Inaugural in 1817.

But Henry Adams also recognised, as Jefferson disputed, the other side of the coin. For Jefferson claimed a national unity in this journey, despite his close and bitter election victory. He implied that the other side (in this case John Adams, and perhaps even George Washington) had tried to sink the country. He did not, in so many words, strip his opponents of their claim to be Americans and name them traitors, but the effect was much the same. Again, he reflected other moments, in 1776 the dismissal of the Loyalists, in 1789 the dismissal of the Anti-Federalists, in 1817 the dismissal of the die-hard Federalists. These groups, by their very existence, denied such assertions of unity. They also asserted rival visions of national character which the expressed beliefs behind the republic required should be recognised.[9]

These repeated restatements of national character demonstrate a further point. National character is both something fixed, by the ascendant forces at particular moments, and something in flux, as those outside the dominant section question and challenge. Yet, constant is the awareness among all the writers that this "national character" exists, whether they believe it has been fully forged or whether their quest continues.

Both the fixed and the flux are explored here through the works of a sequence of imaginative writers. A relationship is presumed between their writings and their lives, based on the central theme, of importance to each, of what their ideas of America and Americans were in general terms, and what that meant to them personally. Or, how they thought America and

Americans should be, and how they acted as Americans themselves. The study attempts to give some sense of the complexities of the debate, to stress that there is not simply one dominant line of development. Yet, a pattern does emerge of a series of writers passionate about their idealised country and its people, but unable to escape the recognition that too often, and in too many ways, that ideal was a sham.

Our focus is the encompassing quest for America and Americans fuelling the early answers to Crèvecoeur's question. This complex search, for the writers considered here, embraced certain recurring issues. These include: the place in America of the excluded—African-Americans, Indians, and the poor;[10] whether the democrat or the aristocrat is to rule; whether America is civilised or savage; whether it is British or American. The writers concerned sometimes lost sight of their overall quest: we must not.

Finally the United States and its people were, centrally, a political creation. As Wood, from a slightly different angle perceived, politics impinged upon everything else from the moment of Revolution. But the Revolution was also more than a mere political act. The Republican ascendancy, as Henry Adams saw, repeated this, being both a political movement and an aspect of national character. Key documents, the Declaration, the Constitution, and the Inaugural Addresses, performed the same dual role. The writers examined here operated within this nexus.

These writers are, in order of consideration, Michel-Guillaume Jean de Crèvecoeur, Benjamin Franklin, Hugh Henry Brackenridge, Washington Irving, James Kirke Paulding, Jonas Clopper, John Neal, and James Fenimore Cooper. This is not an arbitrary selection, but grows from a much more extensive survey of the considerable body of literature produced in the period 1760–1826.[11] It is asserted, and the body of the study must prove, that these writers were especially concerned with the broader question of American national character, and its critical political dimension.

But this is only one of a series of possible explanations, an unsatisfactory limitation. It joins a body of literature of this type, each volume of which explores facets of America, for example the optimistic strain, stressed in the previous Wood quotation and best defined as "the rising glory dream,"[12] the hopeless,[13] the excluded.[14] This angle is new and deserves this exploration, but there is also a need for a new comprehensive literary history of the era, asking these questions, and basing its response on close critical readings of the whole gamut of texts.

The framing dates are also distinctive and have evolved in the course of research. We begin in 1760 with the Seven Years War drawing towards its American conclusion. There are several reasons for this. That war transformed the British Empire in the New World, a transformation which would ultimately precipitate Revolution, a Revolution which is central to our story.[15] Both historians (see for example Palmer, Wood, Cogliano[16]) and contemporaries, including John Adams[17] noted its significance. Finally, it was an important moment in the relationship of our first two witnesses

to America: in 1760, Benjamin Franklin produced an extended consideration of the possible future of the Empire (the Canada Pamphlet), while
the start of the conflict also saw Crèvecoeur set foot in the New World for
the first time.

The project's original intention was to begin the study in the post-Revolutionary period. This proved unsustainable, for, as Wood saw, it was the
Revolution that made the question of American national character vital.
The Revolution forged an America. It was the moment of definition. But it
was also the moment of challenge, demonstrating that at the very founding
there was no agreement on what America was.

The study concludes in 1826, a date more easily explained. Again, we
recall the contemporary perspective, witnessing in the deaths of Thomas
Jefferson and John Adams on the same day that a national era had closed.
But this changing dynamic is also mirrored in the situation of the key writers examined, as will be shown.

This introduction began by dismissing imposed theoretical structures.
Because this research operates on the borders between history and literature, this may seem doubly culpable. It is useful to pause here and reflect on
why this study might be considered history, and the general way it proposes
to advance the thesis detailed. The essential aim is very simple, to build
a narrative framework in which the writers' work may speak for itself as
voices from the past every bit as compelling as the voices of such founders
who, unsurprisingly, also appear. Thus, it is content and not structures
or form or style which is at the heart of the story. Content as art and its
relation to later writers: the history of literature purely as literature is a
separate question. It may be a facet of our story but it is not the central
one. This study is concerned with content as history, as a reflection on the
period in question, and of the experiences of the author. In essence, this
is about literature as a window on the past, which we ignore at our peril.
Finally, there is also a case for clarity. Many theorists create a world of literary criticism in which the original sources are drowning, in works which
do not speak outside a restricted field of experts. The voice of the writers
needs to be recovered and to be framed with narrative which can address
a wider audience.

One other potential point of criticism must be dealt with. In developing
this research, I have encountered the argument on several occasions that
literature is inadmissible as an historical source.[18] In so far as this argument
has a theoretical basis, it appears to be that much literature is fictional and,
therefore, cannot be considered as accurate historical evidence. Such an
argument obviously presupposes that one can define what fiction is, which
runs into immediate problems in the era in question (to give one, provoca-
tive, example, we might start with that initial hypothesis in the Declaration
of Independence that "all men are created equal"). We might also interro-
gate the potential factual accuracy or inaccuracy of newspapers or private
correspondence. As with the question of "what is national character," it

seems counterproductive to get hung up on a theoretical dispute of this point. These texts are a key part of the historical record. For a number of these writers, comparatively little correspondence survives. To simply ignore their literary productions would make for a significantly poorer historical story. This study does not claim that every word they wrote was factually true, that, for example, every Irishman in America, or indeed any Irishman in America in the 1790s, behaved precisely as Teague does in Brackenridge's *Modern Chivalry*. But, to take a much older case, these writers sought to mirror the society in which they found themselves.[19] And, the stories they produced are revealing, if not about that society (although I argue that they are also that), then about how they saw that society. The evidence must serve to persuade the reader on this point.[20]

1   A Farmer Asks a Question and a Scientist Creates a Model

PRELIMINARIES

The Revolution was in the Minds of the People, and this was effected, from 1760 to 1775, in the course of fifteen years before a drop of blood was drawn at Lexington.[1]

It is *right*, O ye Americans! for us to charge you . . . with *dreaming* that the seat of government will . . . be transported to America, and Britain dwindle to one of its provinces. And because Joseph's brethren hated him for a dream he *really* dreamed, we for a dream you never *dreamed*, and which we only *dream* you *dreamed*, are to hate you most cordially.[2]

The American Revolution created the dynamic making explorations of American national character of crucial relevance. Without the separation from Britain and their establishment as an independent nation, who the Americans might be, or who they might claim to be, would have been a very different question. But the Revolution also provided the stage for the first clash about that identity, which is the central theme of this narrative. Even as the Patriots evolved their visions of American national character, centred on the severing of ties with Britain, other writers, who considered themselves equally American, were questioning these developments and advancing visions of their own. This conflict is vital, not only because the Patriot vision became the dominant identity of the new nation, but also because the response to this challenge created a critical fissure in its own self-image. The American republic, without which the question would have had little relevance, was born in a vicious clash of rival visions concerning its nature. The treatment of the visions which lost had profound implications for the victors.

Two individuals considered the problem of American national character in detail but in very different ways in this period: Michel-Guillaume Jean de Crèvecoeur (1735–1813), who wrote as J. Hector St. John; and Benjamin Franklin (1706–1790), who wrote as himself and under many pseudonyms. We take them as representative here, partly because their texts (as we shall see in a moment) have become central to later explanations of the evolution of American national character, but also because the contrast between those texts and the reality of their lives speaks eloquently to the contradictions embodied in that character from the beginning. Franklin, renowned as architect of the wartime alliance with France and benign presence at the Constitutional Convention, was, almost to the outbreak of war, a leading figure in the British imperial world. Crèvecoeur, the first to describe "the American, this new man," ended his life returned to France, the idyll of his prerevolutionary America shattered by the Revolution. These muddled personal identities conflict with their key works, Franklin's *Autobiography* (1791) and St. John's *Letters from an American Farmer* (1782)[3], widely recognised by historians as defining statements of Patriot American national character. That recognition is epitomised by the judgement of Leonard Labaree and his colleagues, the editors of the Franklin papers:

> The autobiography is also a uniquely American book. After a life like Franklin's had become possible and could be described matter-of-factly, the Declaration of Independence seems understandable and much less revolutionary.[4]

This contrast is further elucidated by an examination of their other important writings: Franklin's many political pamphlets and private letters and Crèvecoeur's *Sketches of Eighteenth-Century America* (1925) and his late, neglected *Journey into Northern Pennsylvania and the State of New York* (1801).[5]

This broader investigation of their writings reveals the confusions of becoming American and describing the American which lay behind those texts, now considered such ringing endorsements of the American. The contrasts between them can seem considerable. Their approaches to the question of an American character, whose existence they both, implicitly and explicitly, acknowledged, differ significantly. Crèvecoeur explored it, proceeding out from an imposed unity which struggled to accommodate contradictions he could not ignore. Franklin appeared untroubled by the contradictions his writings show; his concern is the smaller issue of the politics of the empire. His acknowledgements of an American character are broad statements. It is not that Franklin does not question, but his questioning was confined, where Crèvecoeur's was not. Yet, just as their most famous writings appear to contain similar ringing endorsements of the new nation, so their private experiences saw similar plights as both confronted the revolutionary choice between British imperial and independent American worlds.

Before turning to the detail of their writings and lives, two preliminary matters must be dealt with: first, the evolution of, and contradictions within, the Patriot movement which culminated in the Revolution; second, the entanglement of artistic endeavour with this political movement, and as an expressive outlet for wider visions of America and Americans, and the problems facing participants in that movement.

The Peace of Paris in 1763, ending the Seven Years War, changed the attitude of the British government to its American colonies. This is not a view simply imposed by historians. As Franklin's case will show, contemporaries were aware that recent events had altered the situation of the British Empire. Allowing for Franklin's desire to draw a stark then/now contrast in his examination before the Commons over the Stamp Act in 1766, the evidence there presented remains telling:

> What was the temper of the Americans towards Great-Britain before the year 1763?
> The best in the world. . . . They had not only a respect, but an affection for Great-Britain, for its laws, its customs and manners, and even a fondness for its fashions, that greatly increased the commerce. Natives of Britain were always treated with particular regard; to be an Old-England man was, of itself, a character of some respect; and gave a kind of rank among us.[6]

Franklin then baldly stated that all in 1766 was changed. The Revolution which destroyed the triumphant empire of 1763 is usually attributed to the political debate which followed the Peace. This had two important dimensions: the policies of successive British administrations prompting multiple disagreements, and thus allowing debates about the location of power and the system of government to become a relevant occupation; and the actual detail of those debates. We encounter both in the particular context of Franklin's contribution to them. We do not encounter them in Crèvecoeur's writings.

The Patriot side became the dominant version of American national character, to be forcibly expressed in key documents such as Thomas Paine's *Common Sense* and The Declaration of Independence. The debate which produced those documents was the framework in which Crèvecoeur and Franklin reflected on the same issue, even if their writings do not always overtly acknowledge the fact. That framework needs some brief introduction.

The evolving Patriot vision of America was not uniquely American. As historians such as Bailyn and Wood demonstrated,[7] the Patriots drew, for their evolving theories of the colonial–mother country relationship, on a variety of Old World sources. Bailyn listed these debts under these headings: the heritage of classical antiquity; the writings of Enlightenment rationalism; the English common law tradition; the political and social theories of New England Puritanism, and the early eighteenth-century British oppositional theorists. Almost all of these were British or

European inheritances, and this Old World dependency was enhanced by the interpretation placed on those elements. For the Patriots focused, as the English oppositional writers had done, on a failure of Britain to live up to its unique constitutional arrangement. This precipitated a grave threat to liberty which the Patriots saw manifested in the attitude of the British government to the colonies. This has led to the suggestion that the Patriots were, in fact, more English than the English, that, rather than creating some unique new nation, they were simply looking to recreate a lost England in the New World.

Yet, even as the Patriots advanced this English heritage, they were also claiming a paradoxical uniqueness. Turning on its head the long standing claim that the colonists were, in certain ways, inferior, a claim which endured well into the nineteenth century, Patriots argued that they were somehow purer and better than their English brethren, grown decadent, weak, and unable to maintain their great constitution. Thus, Bailyn suggested:

> The changes that had overtaken their provincial societies, they [the Americans] saw, had been good; elements not of deviance and retrogression but of betterment and progress; not a lapse into primitivism, but an elevation to a higher plane of political and social life than had ever been reached before.[8]

Cultural life was here included, for the Patriots a key dimension of the America that they hoped to fashion. Certain Patriots, particularly aspiring artists, argued that the political transformation would fuel a cultural transformation, with America leading the rest of the world in both. Again, this drew on classical sources, in particular the idea of *translatio studii*, that civilisation moved inexorably from east to west, and America was thus destined to be the next stage for high artistic achievement. This was an idea developed by Bishop George Berkeley (1684–1753) in his poem entitled "Verses on the Prospect of planting Arts and Learning in America" (1726). Berkeley also argued that only one nation could be artistically great at any one time, an idea which fitted neatly with the developing Patriot claim to political uniqueness. Berkeley's themes were encapsulated in American terms by Hugh Henry Brackenridge and Philip Freneau in their epic poem of 1771, *The Rising Glory of America*.[9] Also that year, Franklin, writing to the artist Charles Wilson Peale, saw a similar destiny for the arts in America, albeit a transplanted European one:

> The Arts have always travelled Westward, and there is no doubt of their flourishing hereafter on our side the Atlantic, as the Number of Wealthy Inhabitants shall increase, who may be able and willing to reward them, since from several Instances it appears that our People are not deficient in Genius.[10]

Crèvecoeur, in his famous "Letter III—What is an American?" raised the same idea:

> Americans are the western pilgrims who are carrying along with them that great mass of arts, sciences, vigour, and industry which began long since in the East; they will finish the great circle.[11]

The connection between political and cultural excellence was expressed by Jeremy Belknap, historian and novelist, in 1780:

> Why may not *a Republic of Letters* be realised in America as well as a Republican Government? Why may there not be a Congress of Philosophy as well as of Statesmen? . . . I am so far an enthusiast in the cause of America as to wish she may shine Mistress of the Sciences as well as the Asylum of Liberty.[12]

American cultural activity was deliberately, perhaps unavoidably, entangled in the developing political narrative. This was particularly so with literature. The Revolution was effectively written into reality, not only through key documents such as *Common Sense* and the Declaration of Independence, but through the multitude of political pamphlets, sermons, and newspaper articles engaged in the debates of the years after 1763.[13] More, this situation endured after 1776. As Wood noted, "every aspect of American life . . . became politicized."[14] His specific reference was to the political turmoil of the 1790s, but the statement applied equally well to the decades before and after. Many of the key works of literature explored here were affected by this trend.

Literature, like politics, was also divided between American uniqueness and European influence. American writers grappled with the need to capture America and Americans while also striving for a place within the European cultural community, leading to further complex conflicts of literary forms and content.

The financial problems of aspiring writers were equally formidable, although this is an area of considerable disputation. Put simply, American writers throughout this period, with the partial exception of Cooper, found it impossible to live on their writing. They also complained frequently that the reading public ignored them. This study is not directly concerned with audience response but the problem possesses intriguing dimensions. For the general consensus is that literacy rates were high by the end of the eighteenth century. Evidence for this is both anecdotal and statistical. John Adams, in 1765, commented that:

> A native of America who cannot read and write is as rare an appearance, as a Jacobite or a Roman Catholic, i.e. as rare as a Comet or an Earthquake.[15]

Franklin implied a similarly literate population when writing to David Hume in 1760 of his pleasure that the audience for English writers would be increased by the expanding American population.[16] Statistical evidence irons out obvious regional differences, to arrive in one case at a figure of 70–75% literacy among White males.[17] In New England, the rate may have been as high as 90%, in back country Pennsylvania, perhaps 65%. Now, these figures are deceptive because the American population was much smaller than the British population, thus the market for potential authors in America was more limited than in the mother country. This was compounded by a publishing industry which was in its infancy, the lack of a sound transportation network, and the perennial swamping of the market by cheap pirated reprints of English works due to the lack of an international copyright law.

Despite these difficulties, American writers went on writing and publishing. Given their frequent complaints about its reception, this raises a further question about the nature of their audience. Did it, in fact, want the cultural emancipation that leading writers dreamed of and, if not, does this say something about the commitment or lack of it, of the mass of Americans both to the Revolution and the new Republic? These are not questions which this thesis can directly hope to answer, but their existence must be borne in mind.

A CONFUSION OF IDENTITIES

Where Crèvecoeur asked the direct question, Franklin obscured it. *The Autobiography* does address the question of American character, presenting Franklin as the model American, but without Crèvecoeur's clarity. More, it ended the story in July, 1757, with Franklin's arrival in London as Pennsylvania agent.[18] This model is clearly tied to the Revolution and political settlement which followed, as Labaree and his colleagues recognised, but Franklin successfully obscured the confusions attendant on that connection. His political pamphlets, shorter newspaper pieces, and private correspondence shed additional light but are complicated by Franklin's perennial adoption of different personas and by a lack of serious engagement with the question. Franklin's concern was with the political relationships of the empire, in which American character was implied, but never wholly explored. The editors of the Franklin papers recognised that the central act of Revolution was the transformation of individual Patriots from Englishmen to Americans, and that Franklin "provides only tantalising glimpses" of that transformation.[19]

The key writings then, are those connected to Franklin's political career (we do not address his personal relationships or scientific interests). That political career, in itself, illustrated the confused state of the Anglo-American relationship in the years after 1760, and that year possessed an especial significance because of the publication of his pamphlet, "The Interest of Great Britain Considered, With Regard to her Colonies, and the Acquisitions of Canada and Guadaloupe" (hereafter referred to as the Canada Pamphlet). Franklin had already raised problematic aspects of the mother-country/colony relationship in a newspaper piece of the previous year, often termed "Defence of the Americans." That piece is particularly notable for early evidence of Franklin's confusions of identity, and for a determined assertion of the colonists as "English," but the Canada Pamphlet is the more extended treatment at this period.[20]

Franklin had been in London since 1757, serving as colonial agent for the Pennsylvania Assembly. Since the mid-1750s, the Assembly had been feuding with the colony's proprietors, the Penns. This feud anticipated issues taken up by the wider struggle between the colonies and the British government. The warning signs were already visible, if the consequences were obscure. The specific issue was the nature of Pennsylvania's taxation system and whether the proprietors' lands should be taxed. The broader question concerned ultimate authority, and whether it lay with the governor, appointed by the proprietors, or the Assembly.[21] Franklin, between whom and the proprietors existed a state of mutual loathing, was in the thick of these disputes, disputes of systems not character. His immediate scheme was to petition the king to make Pennsylvania a royal colony, thus ousting the proprietors entirely. The Assembly adopted this scheme in 1764, but it was overtaken by the subsequent disputes between the colonies and their mother country.

But, by 1760, Franklin had a new concern. Britain's victory in the Seven Years War led him to detailed consideration of the future of the British Empire, and the colonies place in that empire. His views on this subject, published in the Canada Pamphlet that year, formed part of a general pamphlet debate precipitated by recent military events and encompassing some sixty-five pamphlets. The central question was which territories, Canada (supported by Franklin) or Guadaloupe, should be acquired at the approaching peace negotiations. But broader questions soon arose regarding the possible effect both of such acquisitions on the American colonies and on their relationship with the mother country. Franklin's contribution, written under the guise of an anonymous Englishman, was his most extended and direct consideration of the questions of colonial character and imperial relationships. It demonstrates that already in 1760, he possessed the seeds of the reputation which he would later describe, in 1768 as the consequence of his many printed reflections on the subject,

> I do not find I have gained any point in either country, except that of rendering myself suspected by my impartiality; in England of being too much an American, and in America of being too much an Englishman.[22]

Revealingly, given that the first British Empire was at its height, the Canada Pamphlet of 1760 saw these two identities playing off against each other, a representation of Franklin's underlying confusion. It is not that the pamphlet anticipates independence, for it is clear from other aspects of Franklin's life and writings at this time that he was genuinely myopic about the possibility. Yet, despite this myopia, the issue was haunting him even then. Thus, his dismissals of it are perfectly genuine but the extent to which, simultaneously, he anticipated what would, in fact, happen is a striking indication of his personal confusion.

Franklin initially justified the retention of Canada to avoid renewed threats to colonial security. The likelihood of further wars if this was not done is a fairly obvious point, but Franklin built on this with some fairly disparaging comments directed at both the putative strength and the character of his American countrymen. First, he stressed, at length, their vulnerability, in contrast to the position of Britain:

> Here we are separated by the best and clearest of boundaries, the ocean, and we have people in or near every part of our territory. . . . In America it is quite otherwise. A vast wilderness thinly or scarce at all peopled, conceals with ease the march of troops and workmen.[23]

Then, he lumped all frontier inhabitants, both French and English colonists, together in a highly unflattering description, which obviously explains why those on the British side of any line can hardly be expected, adequately, to defend the vast wilderness already described,

> The people that inhabit the frontiers, are generally the refuse of both nations, often of the worst morals and the least discretion, remote from the eye, the prudence, and the restraint of government.[24]

Wars, in which Britain must be involved, will inevitably result; therefore, it is entirely in British interests to claim Canada as the spoils of victory. Thus far, this is a well-argued appeal to a British audience. But Franklin then dealt with the suggestion that the future wars, if Canada were not retained, could be avoided, or their evils mitigated, by a series of defensive frontier forts. In disposing of this idea, relative merits began to become flipped. Franklin now questioned whether the British administration could always be relied upon for military aid, while taking care to stress the high quality of the present administration:

> Happy as we now are, under the best of kings, and in the prospect of a succession promising every felicity a nation was ever bless'd with: happy too in the wisdom and vigour of every part of the administration, particularly that part whose peculiar province is the British plantations . . . we cannot, we ought not to promise ourselves the uninterrupted continuance of these blessings.[25]

Franklin now dealt with the question raised by those opposing the acquisition of Canada, of whether that acquisition would hasten American independence. He does so to dismiss it, but yet recognised America's capacities for growth:

> I think this increase [in population] continuing, would probably in a century more, make the number of British subjects on that side the water more numerous than they now are on this.[26]

But Franklin saw this population as decisively British:

> The inhabitants . . . are, in common with the other subjects of Great Britain, anxious for the glory of her crown, the extent of her power and commerce, the welfare and future repose of the whole British people. They . . . have been actuated with a truly British *spirit*.[27]

Franklin turned swiftly to the economic relationship, arguing in detail that the expanding colonies would simply provide an expanding market for the goods produced by the mother country. But the question of independence persisted, to which Franklin responded first by reiterating the colonial contribution to the mother country:

> The mother [political body] being of full stature, is in a few years equal'd by a growing daughter: but in the case of a mother country and her colonies, it is quite different. The growth of the children tends to encrease [sic] the growth of the mother, and so the difference and superiority is longer preserv'd.[28]

Next, he again attacked the colonial character:

> Those we now have, are not only under different governors, but have different forms of government, different laws, different interests, and some of them different religious persuasions and different manners. Their jealousy of each other is so great that however necessary an union of the colonies has long been for their common defence and security against their enemies, and how sensible soever each colony has been of that necessity, yet they have never been able to effect such an union among themselves, nor even to agree in requesting the mother country to establish it for them.[29]

There is a notable comparison here with Crèvecoeur, who accepted the need for the mother country to hold the disparate colonies together, but did not see the same pervasive "British spirit." For Franklin, in 1768, inevitable colonial growth did not imply the growth of a specifically American character. Yet, Franklin concluded by outlining, with astonishing prescience, precisely how independence could occur:

When I say such a union is impossible, I mean without the most grevious tyranny and oppression. People who have property in a country which they may lose, and priviledges which they may endanger; are generally dispos'd to be quiet; and even to bear much rather than hazard all. While the government is mild and just, and important civil and religious rights are secure, such subjects will be dutiful and obedient. The waves do not rise, but when the winds blow. What such an administration as the Duke of Alva's in the Netherlands, might produce, I know not; but this I think I have a right to deem impossible.[30]

Franklin's faith in the empire was almost certainly genuine at this period, as witnessed by his conviction that the solution to Pennsylvania's governmental problems was to replace the proprietors with the king, and his complete failure to anticipate the strength of American reactions to the Stamp Act. Yet his assessment, perhaps unwittingly, displayed the alternative possibility. It was striking evidence of the confusions of the American question.

These confusions are amplified in Franklin's letters of this period. A crucial subtext is the divergence between British and colonial viewpoints, and Franklin's denial of that divergence. The Canada Pamphlet and "Defence of the Americans" explicitly challenged British perceptions of that divergent possibility. A letter to David Hume from September, 1760 displayed the same concern:

> I am not a little pleas'd to hear of your Change of Sentiments in some particulars relating to America; because I think it of Importance to our general Welfare that the People of this Nation should have right Notions of us, and I know no one that has it more in his Power to rectify their Notions, than Mr Hume.[31]

Here Franklin also addressed the theme of colonial growth, again stressing its benefit within an imperial context:

> I assure you, it often gives me Pleasure to reflect how greatly the *Audience* (if I may so term it) of a good English Writer will in another Century or two be encreas'd, by the Increase of English People in our Colonies.[32]

This theme of colonial growth, and the colonies and their inhabitants as English or British, are really the only things Franklin consistently has to say about American\colonial character.[33] We see the former in this letter to Lord Kames, from February, 1767, and repeated elsewhere:

> America, an immense Territory, favor'd by Nature with all Advantages of Climate, Soil, great navigable Rivers and Lakes, &c. must become a great Country, populous and mighty; and will in less time than is generally conceiv'd be able to shake off any Shackles that may be impos'd on her . . .[34]

The latter often surfaces in pamphlets, thus, in 1766 he lamented:

> The Welch you [the English] have always despeised [*sic*] for submitting to your government: But why despeise your own English, who conquered and settled Ireland for you; who conquered and settled America for you?[35]

Similarly, in a 1768 pamphlet, he claimed:

> The Americans are our brethren. Let us not begrudge them the enjoyment of the rights, liberties and privileges that belong to them as Englishmen.[36]

Personal discussions of America in his correspondence are similarly limited, reiterating these themes, with an attitude depending on his geographical location and his political position vis-à-vis the two nations at that particular moment. There was no system to it, and discussion was never as extended as in the Canada Pamphlet. Franklin oscillated in these years, demonstrating his divided self, his need for both Old and New Worlds, his sense that imperial America might yet work. Writing to Mary Stevenson, after his return to America in 1762, he complained:

> Of all the enviable Things England has, I envy it most its People. Why should that petty Island, which compar'd to America is but like a stepping Stone in a Brook . . . why . . . should [it] enjoy in almost every Neighbourhood, more sensible, virtuous and elegant Minds, than we can collect in ranging 100 Leagues of our vast Forests. But, 'tis said, the Arts delight to travel Westward. You have effectually defended us in this glorious War, and in time you will improve us.[37]

We also see here the cultural question. At that time, he wrote also to William Strahan, in one letter insisting:

> I feel here like a thing out of its place. How then can I any longer be happy in England? You have great powers of persuasion, and might easily prevail on me to do any thing; but not any longer to do nothing. I must go home.[38]

Preparing to board the boat, his view altered:

> I cannot, I assure you, quit even this disagreeable Place without Regret, as it carries me still further from those I love, and from the Opportunities of hearing of their Welfare.[39]

In 1772, as he felt his ability to influence events slipping, he wrote to his son in a similar vein:

> I grow homesick. . . . I see here no Disposition in Parliament to meddle further in Colony Affairs for the present. . . . I have indeed so many good kind Friends here, that I could spend the Remainder of my Life among them with great Pleasure, if it were not for my American Connections, and the indelible Affection I retain for that dear Country, from which I have so long been in a state of Exile.[40]

The moment renewed influence appeared possible, Franklin reversed himself. Following Lord Hillsborough's resignation from the position of Secretary of State for the Colonies later in the year, he wrote far more cheerfully to his son, almost revelling in his reputation in England:

> [I have] a character of so much weight that it has protected me when some in power would have done me injury. . . . The k[ing]. too has lately been heard to speak of me with great regard.[41]

This time, when he spoke of homesickness, it began to sound more like a claim of rote than something genuinely felt,

> a violent longing for home sometimes seizes me, which I can no otherwise subdue but by promising myself a return next spring or next fall, and so forth.[42]

A letter to Samuel du Pont de Nemours from October, 1770, when a departure for America appeared likely, again illustrates his divided nature (with the third factor of his identification with France and, more broadly, Europe, which became increasingly significant towards the end of his life):

> Would to God I could take with me Messrs. Dupont, Dubourg, and some other French Friends with their good ladies! I might then, by mixing them with my Friends at Philadelphia, form a little happy society that would prevent my ever wishing again to visit Europe.[43]

In one pamphlet alone, dating from 1765, did Franklin consider the specifically American national character more deeply. But, what begins as New England, becomes all the colonies:

> The first settlers of New England particularly, were English gentlemen of fortune, who, being Puritans, left this country with their families and followers, in times of persecution, for the sake of enjoying, though in a wilderness, the blessings of civil and religious liberty; of which they retain to this day, as high a sense as any Briton whatsoever; and possess as much virtue, humanity, civility, and let me add *"loyalty to their Prince"*, as is to be found among the like people in any part of the world; and the other colonies merit and maintain the same character.[44]

At one level, this is a familiar Patriot argument, tracing the present character of the colonists somewhat questionably back to the early arrivals, conveniently forgetting the rather less glorious history of the Chesapeake landings. Yet, it is riddled with contradictions. There is the determined characterisation of the colonists as English, the confused comparison with an unidentified "like people." Since Britain and its constitution are to be set apart, it is difficult to know to whom Franklin was referring. Above all, there is the claim to a colonial unity. This may have been true at the time of the Stamp Act unrest, although ambivalences existed even then. It may simply be part of Franklin's claim that the colonists should receive equal treatment. But it was such statements as these which paved the way for crucial divisions to be obscured.

There are, then, national characters apparent in Franklin's writings, but they are not the central concern. They feed into Franklin's more substantial concerns about the political infrastructure of empire, and the letters and pamphlets solely devoted to the intricacies of that debate are far more numerous. There is also a personal dimension to the debate in a quite different way to Crèvecoeur. As will be seen, Crèvecoeur used his experience to extrapolate a story for the wider polity. Franklin's various complaints are often petulant, his laments concern his personal political influence, or the absence of particular friends. Franklin responded to America and Americans according to the moment, taking up the question when necessary, otherwise ignoring it, and untroubled by the lack of a thorough conception of that nation. He recognised the reality, as in this letter to Joseph Galloway of 1770, but the deeper meanings did not concern him:

> I am perfectly of the same Sentiments with you, that the old Harmony will never be restor'd between the two Countries, till some Constitution is agreed upon and establish'd, ascertaining the relative Rights and Duties of each.[45]

Thus, there is an accidental quality to Franklin's journey from Englishman to American. Franklin, unlike Crèvecoeur, or Irving's Rip van Winkle, did not scream, unless he were howling behind his mask during Wedderburn's Cockpit assault of 1774.

Given these factors, Franklin's achievement in becoming a Patriot, and masking his earlier complicities, was remarkable. It hinted at that cold-bloodedness noted by Lawrence and Edwards.[46] That act only saved the individual Franklin; his greater achievement was to retrospectively save Franklin as model Patriot American when, in reality, he was often anything but.

The tool employed was *The Autobiography*, left unfinished in 1771. The problems of intention and audience raised by the private papers and pamphlets seem multiplied. The work was written in four different sections. Part One was directly addressed to his son William, then the Royal

Governor of New Jersey, and was composed in the summer of 1771. In 1784, he wrote Part Two, mostly taken up with the art of virtue. Only in 1788 did he return to the direct narrative, bringing it down, in Part Three, to his arrival in London in 1757. Sometime in 1789–90 he worked on the brief Part Four, discussing his negotiations with the proprietors. Publication compounded this problematic composition. Franklin's intentions at his death are unclear. His papers were bequeathed to his incompetent grandson, William Temple Franklin, who took until 1818 to publish an edition lacking Part Four. The most popular earlier edition, published in 1793, contained only Part One, with a continuation of Franklin's life drawn from a biography by Henry Stuber. Only in 1868 was the full text, including Part Four, published in an edition by John Bigelow, and only in 1949 was an edition published, edited by Max Ferrand, which is accepted as an accurate rendering of Franklin's intended text.[47]

All this stemmed from Franklin's actions, or lack of them at his death, when the third evolution of his thought regarding the work had occurred. The book possessed two different audiences, and by the time Franklin was writing the final parts, was bedevilled by the conflict between the history Franklin sought to claim, and the reality a continuation of the story would compel him to recount.

Franklin began the book in 1771, confusing two audiences in his mind. Part One was begun as an apparent letter to his son William, the Royal Governor of New Jersey, but the audience rapidly broadened to "my posterity."[48] If a genuine attempt to advise William, and given his age and position this seems unlikely, it would flounder on the Revolution, over which they parted ways. Correspondence shows them on good terms through 1773, but already in 1771 William was reassuring friends that he did not share his father's politics.[49] But, in 1771, that broader posterity was equally unclear. Part One could do little more than tell the story of Franklin's early life with clear moral lessons, and trust to time to establish who was being created.

Thus, we see the young man starting out with nothing, the struggle to establish himself in business, and the first embroilments in politics, all with their moral lessons attached. A significant example here, given subsequent developments, was Franklin's experience in 1724 of Governor William Keith of Pennsylvania who offered to set him up in business:

> Had it been known that I depended on the Governor, probably some Friend that knew him better would have advis'd me not to rely on him, as I afterwards heard it as his known Character to be liberal of Promises which he never meant to keep.[50]

This episode anticipates many subsequent events. Franklin does nothing to debunk the high praise that the Governor has heaped upon him in proposing this arrangement, and his personal naivety is admitted to in such a way as to be almost endearing:

Yet unsolicited as he was by me, how could I think his generous Offers insincere? I believ'd him one of the best Men in the World.[51]

The story emphasises the importance of raising yourself by your own capacities, with particular reference to the importance of learning. The implication of this tale is that its product, the model Franklin, naturally deserves the parade of people who pass across the stage in the latter sections of Part One, heaping respect upon him.

Franklin's description of his situation upon his return to America from London in 1726 illustrates this clearly. He resumed a position in a Philadelphia printing business where, despite one or two bad apples,

> with the rest I began to live very agreeably; for they all respected me, the more as they found Keimer [his employer] incapable of instructing them, and that from me they learnt something daily.[52]

Here is the model in action, and, as is perennially the case in the work, Franklin's good offices soon brought their reward. Keimer fired him, but a fellow employee, Meredith, turned out to have a father who "had a high Opinion of" Franklin[53] and promptly offered to establish them in their own printing business in New Jersey. Alongside this success, Keimer's dependency on Franklin forces his employ in a job for the New Jersey government, through which Franklin was able to cultivate a number of influential friends. Unsurprisingly, we have a bout of praise from one of these:

> I forsee, that you will soon work this Man out of his Business & make a Fortune in it in Philadelphia.[54]

And a bout of respecting,

> These Friends were afterwards of great Use to me, as I occasionally was to some of them.—They all continued their Regard for me as long as they lived.[55]

All this is by now being framed by broader models of behaviour, formed on the return voyage of 1726:

> Perhaps the most important part of that Journal [of the voyage] is the *Plan* to be found in it which I formed at Sea, for regulating my future Conduct in Life. It is the more remarkable, as being form'd when I was so young, and yet being pretty faithfully adhered to quite thro' to old Age.[56]

This plan has strong similarities to that which Franklin would advance in detail in Part Two of *The Autobiography*. Having essentially formed the man, Part One broke off in 1730, as Franklin was drawn back into current politics. Resuming the work in 1784, he argued that the two sections were written with different motives. He supported this claim with two letters, from Abel James and from Benjamin Vaughan, which discuss the importance of Franklin's continuing the *Autobiography*.[57] Abel James, responding to Part One, emphasized the importance of Franklin's example to the youth of America:

> I know of no Character living nor many of them put together, who has so much in his Power as Thyself to promote a greater spirit of Industry & early Attention to Business, Frugality and Temperance with the early American Youth.[58]

Vaughan's letter, although expressing similar sentiments, was considerably more detailed. He listed four reasons why Franklin should continue the work: to forestall anyone else writing it; because it will "present a table of the internal circumstances of your country;" because "All that has happened to you is also connected with the detail of the manners and situation of a *rising* people;" and because Franklin's life will be vital in the "forming of future great men and improving the features of private character."[59] Vaughan clarified the meaning of Part One. The story of Franklin's youth was the demonstration of how Patriot America had developed. Franklin was, himself, the answer to Crèvecoeur's question. Vaughan spelled out that it was the Revolution which gave the story relevance:

> The immense revolution of the present period, will necessarily turn our attention towards the author of it; and when virtuous principles have been pretended in it, it will be highly important to shew [sic] that such have really influenced; and, as your own character will be the principle one to receive a scrutiny, it is proper, (even for its effects upon your vast and rising country, as well as upon England and upon Europe), that it should stand respectable and eternal.[60]

Clearly there is an element of self-advertisement here, with Franklin in advance wishing to emphasise the relevance of his testimony. That testimony could hardly put him on a higher pedestal. If Vaughan's letter, regardless of Franklin's intentions in publishing it, was any indication of Franklin's reputation in this period, John Adams' fury at his fame is not to be wondered at, especially if he recognised the manufactured element. It is also notable that the example is both for America and beyond, Franklin as the beacon for all mankind. But, instead of continuing the story from 1730, Franklin, after discussion of the establishment of the Library Company, presented instead his Art of Virtue, a project discussed in his letters as early as 1760, and hinted at during Part One.[61] Vaughan's letter prepared for this diversion, arguing that the reformation of private character required both Franklin's life story and his treatise on the Art of Virtue. The definite moral message of Part One supported this asserted relationship. But the positioning was also an artistic rewriting of history. Franklin bridged the gap between the end of Part One and the letters which open Part Two with the following statement:

> Thus far was written with the Intention express'd in the Beginning and therefore contains several little family Anecdotes of no Importance to others. What follows was written many Years after in compliance with the Advice contain'd in these Letters, and accordingly intended for the Publick. The Affairs of the Revolution occasion'd the Interruption.[62]

The letters in question made explicit connection between the two parts. But they also removed the need for the very thing they seemed to request, which Franklin here delicately alluded to. The Revolution had transformed the meaning of Franklin's experience, but a narrative of that transformation would have presented a muddled story, inappropriate for advising the rising generation. Here appears the third factor, the problem of describing his whole life, which affected Parts Three and Four.

Before turning to that, the moral example Franklin did present, in lieu of continuing the narrative itself, must be addressed. Franklin introduced the project thus:

> It was about this time that I conceiv'd the bold and arduous Project of arriving at moral Perfection.[63]

This is a fairly sweeping plan and obviously fitted well with the rising glory theme of American identity into which Franklin now saw *The Autobiography* slotting. There was, in the creation of the country, something of a quest for perfection. It is, in its scope, an interesting contrast to the early 1726 plan, of which only an outline now survives, expressing a more limited hope that, "henceforth, I may live in all respects like a rational creature."[64]

This perhaps excessive scheme was well born out by the list of thirteen virtues which followed. Number thirteen, "HUMILITY—Imitate Jesus and Socrates,"[65] is especially striking. The suggestion that moral perfection is attainable is somewhat unsettling, and perhaps explains why many have found the work difficult to stomach.[66] Franklin proceeded, as in Part One, to show himself at fault, in order to be able to show himself triumphant. Thus he admitted in introducing the table:

> I soon found I had undertaken a Task of more Difficulty than I had imagined: While my Care was employ'd in guarding against one Fault, I was often surpriz'd by another.[67]

But here Franklin's fallibility is more troubling. He first acknowledged one particular failure:

> This Article [Order] therefore cost me so much painful Attention & my Faults in it vex'd me so much, and I made so little Progress in Amendment, & had such frequent Relapses, that I was almost ready to give up the Attempt, and content my self with a faulty Character in that respect.

He defended this with a story of a man who wanted the whole of an axe to shine like the edge, but this required so much labour that the man decided the speckled axe was preferable. Franklin appeared to accept that his project may not in the end be entirely practical:

> For something that pretended to be Reason was every now and then suggesting to me, that such extream [*sic*] Nicety as I exacted of my self might be a kind of Foppery in Morals, which if it were known would make me ridiculous; that a perfect Character might be attended with the Inconvenience of being envied and hated; and that a benevolent Man should allow a few Faults in himself, to keep his Friends in Countenance.[68]

Franklin then reiterated his inability to master the virtue of order, making clear that this "pretended Reason" is to be condoned. This might seem to imply a softening, a recognition that mankind is not perfectible and that it is the attempt which counts. Franklin's next remarks support this analysis:

> Tho' I never arrived at the Perfection I had been so ambitious of obtaining yet I was by the Endeavour made a better and a happier Man than I otherwise should have been, if I had not attempted it.[69]

Arguably, Order is hardly the most critical virtue. Yet, this approach, allowing for the picking and choosing of virtues, seems to risk serious misuse in the hands of a less scrupulous adherent to the Art of Virtue than its creator. Nor does it end here. For Franklin now returned to the list of Virtues to explain that number thirteen, humility, was a late addition. He allows a friend to criticize him here:

> A . . . Friend . . . inform'd me that I was generally thought proud; that my Pride show'd itself frequently in Conversation; that I was not content with being in the Right when discussing any Point, but was overbearing & rather insolent.[70]

But this friend is sharply repaid. For Franklin's response, having conceded the small point of adding Humility to the list, is to blow the whole exercise to pieces:

> I cannot boast of much Success in acquiring the *Reality* of this Virtue; but I had a good deal with regard to the *Appearance* of it.

Not only are blemishes inevitable, but one may act deceptively in the cultivation even of those areas where one presumes to have expunged them. Franklin went on to declare that it was precisely to this illusion of humility "that I had early so much Weight with my Fellow Citizens . . . and so much Influence in public Councils when I became a Member."[71] And this is to be the model for the rising generation.

Part Two ends, then, on a note both of forthright reassurance, making failure to attain perfectibility acceptable, and profound subversion, making the faking of virtue as acceptable as its actual attainment if the ends, in this case proper influence in public affairs, are good. Even Franklin's apparently most serious failures have excellent effects. We suddenly seem a long way from the model that the letters which open Part Two seem to request, and the table of virtues to provide. We are also left with a mystery, as to what precisely Franklin's intentions here were. In personal terms, it seems possible that this is another Franklin preemptive strike. He sought to get in with a self-criticism and justification in advance of the historians. But the inclusion of the Vaughan letter at the start of Part Two signals a wider justification. The audience has shifted at this point from a personal posterity to a national posterity, signalled by that letter's reference to the rising generation. It is, therefore, probable that Franklin is, in fact, crafting a justification and instruction for the entire nation. It is, then, sufficient to adopt the appearance of virtues on a national scale just as much as a personal scale if the ends are good. Any blemishes that may be found in Franklin's conduct, and thus any blemishes in the nation he embodied, are entirely for the good of the nation.

Having made this justification, there is no sense in continuing the narrative. Embarking on Part Three, Franklin hinted at the problem:

> To shorten the work as well as for other reasons, I omit all facts and transactions, that may not have a tendency to benefit the young reader, by showing him from my example, and my success in emerging from poverty, and acquiring some degree of wealth, power and reputation, the advantages of certain modes of conduct which I observed, and of avoiding the errors which were prejudicial to me.[72]

Since the story was left off in 1730, Franklin could proceed for a space without undue difficulty. The familiar method is duly resumed. We observe the now more rapid rise of Franklin through his business and scientific successes, and various services to the community. Two events stand out: first Franklin's struggle with the large dominant Quaker community of Pennsylvania over state defence; second his account of the Albany Plan of Union in 1754.

The Quaker dispute first showed Franklin's influence at work, both in obvious terms at a public meeting where a pamphlet by Franklin meets "not the least Objection,"[73] and more self-deprecatingly:

> the Philadelphia Regiment . . . chose me for their Colonel; but conceiving myself unfit, I declin'd the Station, & recommended Mr Lawrence . . . who was accordingly appointed.[74]

But the broader comments are more troubling. Having described his success with a new defence Association, born out of the pamphlet already described, he hammers away at Quaker disingenuousness, noting that "the Defence of the Country was not disagreeable to any of them, provided they were not requir'd to assist in it."[75]

To support this argument, he cited numerous evasive votes for defence funds in the Assembly:

> The common Mode at last was to grant Money under the Phrase of its being *for the King's use*, and never to enquire how it was applied.[76]
>
> The double standard is notable here, because it was shown as perfectly acceptable to evade principles if the cause was a good Franklinian one. Franklin criticised the Quakers for not behaving as he did in Part Two:
>
> [They suffered] these Embarrasments . . . from having establish'd & published it as one of their Principles, that no kind of War was lawful, and which being once published, they could not afterwards, however they might change their minds, easily get rid of.[77]

Principle, like certain virtues, should be abandoned the moment it becomes inconvenient. Yet, the Quakers have actually behaved exactly as Franklin did in changing their tactics under the appearance of maintaining their virtue. The difference, of course, is that they failed to maintain appearances, as Franklin concluded:

> To avoid this kind of Embarrassment the Quakers have of late Years been gradually declining the public Service in the Assembly & in the Magistracy. Chusing [*sic*] rather to quit their Power than their Principle.[78]

Virtue, or the appearance of virtue without power, is thus mocked, with rather worrying connotations for the rising generation.

The section on the Albany Plan of 1754 raises a different problem. Apart from the occasional glancing reference, discussion on politics in the latter half of Part Three and the brief Part Four is concerned with the struggle for control of Pennsylvania between proprietors and assembly. Here, Franklin briefly revisited the lost Empire, reflecting thus on the failed Plan of Union:

I am still of Opinion it would have been happy for both Sides the Water if it had been adopted. The Colonies so united would have been sufficiently strong to have defended themselves; there would then have been no need of Troops from England; of course the subsequent Pretence for Taxing America, and the bloody Contest it occasioned, would have been avoided.[79]

One might be deceived into detecting a wistfulness here for that which was lost, except that Franklin's conclusion is dismissive:

But such Mistakes are not new; History is full of the Errors of States and Princes. . . . The best public Measures are therefore seldom *adopted from previous Wisdom*, but *forc'd by the Occasion*.[80]

There is a familiar detachment to this. Franklin wanted to make himself the model Patriot American, but this attitude sets him apart from his fellow revolutionaries. He had lacked the passion that actuated Crèvecoeur's visions, and fuelled Paine's fury. He could not see the transformation in the same way as they had done. Worse, to describe the truth of it would have displayed an unhelpful muddle. It is thus entirely appropriate that Part Four peters out. The appropriate, necessary narrative is already written. Franklin may not have consciously decided to leave the work unfinished, but he did persistently postpone its continuation. He must have known, as did Jefferson in devising his tombstone, that the public would remember the lessons he wanted them to remember.[81] There was no need to muddy the waters. But muddy was exactly what the Revolution was, and the decisions of men like Franklin and Jefferson to evade that bore a high price, as the experience of Crèvecoeur, and those who followed him, testified.

THE OTHER AMERICANS

Your suspicion that sundry others, besides Govr Bernard had written hither their Opinions and Counsels, encouraging the late Measures, to the Prejudice of our Country . . . is I apprehend but too well founded. You call them *traitorous* Individuals whence I collect, that you suppose them of our own country. There was among the twelve Apostles one Traitor who betrayed with a kiss. It should be no Wonder therefore if among so many Thousand true Patriots as New England contains there should be found even Twelve Judases, ready to betray their Country for a few paltry pieces of Silver. Their *Ends* as well as their *Views* ought to be similar.[82]

Shall I discard all my ancient principles, shall I renounce that name, that nation which I held once so respectable? I feel the powerful attraction; the sentiments they inspired grew with my earliest knowledge and were grafted upon the first rudiments of my education. On the other hand, shall I arm myself against that country where I first drew breath, against the playmates of my youth, my bosom friends, my acquaintance? . . . Must I be called a parricide, a traitor, a villain, lose the esteem of all those I love to preserve my own, be shunned like a rattlesnake, or be pointed at like a bear?[83]

Franklin's *Autobiography* excluded the true nature of his transformation from Englishman to American, effectively denying that the English Franklin ever really existed. We have explored this rewriting of his past both in personal terms, and in terms of the nation he was seeking to create, but it has a further implication. All Americans of English birth or descent had, at some point, to make that transition from Englishman to American, or to decide that they would not make it. And some Americans without English antecedents saw themselves as making the same choice, Crèvecoeur being the most famous. The second part of Franklin's *Autobiography*, the Patriot claims of Paine and Jefferson which preceded it, all attempted to claim that the only true Americans were those who made the transition. But the Revolution, in fact, destroyed an earlier vision of America, whose proponents considered themselves as American as the Patriots. Crèvecoeur is a key literary witness of this group, because he crafted an American character more thoroughly than anybody else in the years before the Revolution and because that character was appropriated into the Patriot myth. As Albert Stone put it, in a recent edition of *Letters From an American Farmer* (1986):

American literature, as the voice of our national consciousness, begins in 1782 with the first publication in England of *Letters*.[84]

Crèvecoeur's *Letters* were such a voice, but Crèvecoeur could not follow his own anticipations. In a slightly different context, Manning recognised that Crèvecoeur's *Letters* were both a "celebration of America, and its tragedy."[85] Both mattered.

This exploration of Crèvecoeur focuses on his version of American national character, presented primarily in *Letters From an American Farmer* (1782), but it also considers the contrast between this vision and what actually happened, and the implications of this for that vision, which seemed to express so clearly to Americans who they were. As Jeffrey H. Richards put it, we explore the contradiction in Crèvecoeur's work which meant that:

The man who gave Americans for many generations the picture of themselves they most wanted to see—the tolerant, prosperous, land-holding, peaceable and domestic people outlined in Letter III—also

America, within the Empire.

gave them in "Landscapes" the image of its opposite, a nightmare of popular cruelty and personal despair.[86]

Before turning directly to Crèvecoeur, a few words about the Loyalists are necessary. We noted the argument that the Revolution was not sufficiently revolutionary because it excluded women, African Americans, and Native Americans. It also did not immediately grant power to poorer White men in many areas. Remarkably, such lists of the excluded usually omit the obvious group, the Loyalists. Palmer highlighted their importance, statistically comparing the French and American Revolutions and suggesting that a far greater number of people, given the relative difference in population size, were exiled by the latter, most never to return.[87] The case of Crèvecoeur, although not a fully-fledged Loyalist,[88] showed that his British American counterparts were not simply placemen, servants of the Crown who had no conception of America. Many possessed a vision of America within the British Empire often similar to that which Franklin once possessed and which they were not prepared to abandon. It is this vision which the Declaration denied.

Crèvecoeur, like Franklin, complicates study by adopting various names and personal histories. He was born into the petty Normandy nobility on 31 January, 1735, and his full baptismal name was Michel-Guillaume Jean de Crèvecoeur. After an early quarrel with his father, he lived with some maiden ladies in England before ending up in Canada on the eve of the Seven Years War and enlisting in the French militia.[89] After a period of apparent good service in that body, he resigned his regular army commission in 1759, under circumstances that remain mysterious. Having left the army, he rapidly refashioned his identity. En route to New York, he began to call himself J. Hector St. John. This was probably no more than a prudent measure in the light of the continuing war, but it became the identity he retained throughout his time in the British colonies, and through which he addressed his audience in *Letters*, giving it significance.

The following years were divided between extensive travelling throughout the British and French colonies, and periodic land surveying. Gradually, he sought deeper integration into British American society. In 1765, he became a naturalised citizen of the colony of New York. In 1769, he settled on a farm in Orange County, which he named Pine Hill, and married Mehitable Tippet, a member of a prominent Dutchess County family (who would flee to Nova Scotia in 1779). The wedding again symbolised Crèvecoeur's confused identity, since he signed his full French name in the documentation. When he left the farm in 1778, Crèvecoeur had three children. This farming life formed the key basis for Crèvecoeur's most famous work, *Letters From an American Farmer*. Considering this time frame, it is the more remarkable that the *Letters* give so little indication of the era's political disputes.

The production and publication of *Letters*, and its companion volume, the *Sketches*, is, like *The Autobiography*, complex. Exact dates of composition are nonexistent, but it is generally assumed that most were composed after his establishment at Pine Hill. It is also uncertain whether Crèvecoeur decided on their organisation. When he fled America in 1778, under circumstances we shall return to, he probably brought with him all the manuscripts which eventually comprised the two volumes, but a slim possibility exists that it was Crèvecoeur's publisher in London who decided on their organisation. The first volume also promised, in the advertisement, that a second volume would shortly be forthcoming.[90] These issues are here simply noted; they will be discussed in more detail in the context of the textual analysis.

Crèvecoeur further confused matters by adopting different authorial identities. As J. Hector St. John, he published the first two London editions (1782, 1783) and the various Irish reprints of the same period of the *Letters*.[91] When he rewrote *Letters* for French publication in 1784 and 1787, his authorial designation was altered to St. John de Creve Coeur.[92] This designation was applied to the new editions published in the early 1900s. The first and only American edition (until 1904) was published by Mathew Carey in 1793 in Philadelphia.[93] It appears to be a reprint of the first London edition, thus styling its author as J. Hector St. John and omitting the note from the second London edition stating that the author had accepted public employment in New York.[94] It, therefore, seems likely that the American reader, in particular, could have remained ignorant of the fact that the American Farmer and Crèvecoeur the consul were one and the same. In France, the new editions made the identification clear. What the British or Irish reader may have thought about the matter is more difficult to say.[95]

This authorial confusion was exacerbated by Crèvecoeur's adoption, within *Letters*, of the persona of the Farmer.[96] These shifting personas show the confused state of national characters. In contrast to Franklin, Crèvecoeur found it impossible to exclude the tragic realities of that confusion.

In addition to these confusions, *Letters*, like Franklin's *Autobiography*, is curiously structured. "Letters I and II" explain the work's motivation and describe Crèvecoeur's alter ego, the American Farmer and his imaginary European correspondent, to whom the Letters are supposedly addressed. "Letter III" moves on to consider the whole "race" of Americans. Next are five letters giving a detailed account of Nantucket Island, and the work concludes with the ominous sequence of the visit to Charleston, the duelling snakes, and the final letter, which faces the outbreak of the Revolution. That catastrophe is briefly, and somewhat bizarrely, postponed by "Letter XI," describing a visit to the botanist, John Bartram (1699–1777), a friend of Franklin's. At first sight, this seems a somewhat confused arrangement of issues, and argues for external arrangement of the material. In fact, links between the letters are considerable, and show early on the conflict that

Crèvecoeur sought to suppress between his dream and the reality. These are so intertwined that Crèvecoeur frequently contradicted himself from page to page, even from line to line. This sense of contradictions may actually be the most profound illustration of the atmosphere of pre-Revolutionary America, but it is precisely this sense of contradiction which is most obscured by the focusing on the celebratory aspects of the work.

"Letters I and II" set up the idealised Crèvecoeur as Farmer James, the simple tiller of the soil, whose European correspondent "is the first enlightened European I had ever the pleasure of being acquainted with."[97] This persona is strengthened by Crèvecoeur's inability to proceed in an orderly way; ideas are repeated, contradicted, and muddled together, although in a manner that bizarrely strengthens Crèvecoeur's argument. Against this is set the fluency, demonstrated in the *Letters*, which questions the Farmer's claim that writing is a novelty to him. This character, both personal and national, is not something as simply codified as Franklin's political constructs. Nor is it simply a fictional creation, as has been suggested. Farmer James is a literary representation of Crèvecoeur as he strove to transform himself from his adoption of the name J. Hector St. John. The imagined and the real are mingled in the literary creation and in the society described.

Upon the partial fiction of James, Crèvecoeur built a fictional past where his land and farm were bequeathed to him by an equally simple farmer father. In miniature in "Letter II," Crèvecoeur presented glimpses of the idealised world he would apply to the whole country in "Letter III," notably, in view of what was to come, in this passage:

> Where is that station which can confer a more substantial system of felicity than that of an American farmer possessing freedom of action, freedom of thoughts, ruled by a mode of government which requires but little from us?[98]

There is some support here for Franklin's often expressed view that if only the British returned to the pre-Stamp Act status quo, all would be well. From this, Crèvecoeur proceeded to more personal matters, describing his family and farming life in harmony with nature. He appears an excellent example of another of Franklin's ideas, that agriculture was the most appropriate form of employment.[99] Crèvecoeur also stressed this point as a lure to Europeans:

> No wonder we should thus cherish its [land] possession; no wonder that so many Europeans who have never been able to say that such portion of land was theirs cross the Atlantic to realise that happiness.[100]

But, even at this early stage, a contradiction creeps in. For, although "Letter II" stressed the wonders of the American life, and its appeal to the Old World, it began with sentences which, if only platitudes at this stage, had potentially worrying implications. Crèvecoeur contemplated advantages which English farmers possessed over Americans, and commented:

> Good and evil, I see, are to be found in all societies, and it is in vain to seek for any spot where those ingredients are not mixed.[101]

Thus, at the outset, Crèvecoeur acknowledged that his quest, which was precisely to evade any recognition of evil in his idyllic world, was doomed. Here we see the American problem: is the country going to break this cycle, is it going to prove the possessor of a new character beyond such possibility of failings?

Having set himself up as a typical individual American, Crèvecoeur applied this nationally, in the famous "Letter III." This document is remarkable because, beneath statements as sweeping as "we are the most perfect society now existing in the world,"[102] Crèvecoeur exposed the confusions of his society. It is unclear whether the colonists are of European or British extraction. At first, Crèvecoeur put his picture into the mouth of an Englishman, in phrases echoed in Franklin's writings:

> This is the work of my countrymen, who, when convulsed by factions, afflicted by a variety of miseries and wants, restless and impatient, took refuge here. They brought along with them their national genius, to which they principally owe what liberty they enjoy and what substance they possess.

This might be the Franklin of the early 1760s speaking, giving utterance to the idea that the New World is only a more perfect England. But Crèvecoeur also acknowledged the larger European dimension, noting "[he] traces in their works the embryos of all the arts, sciences, and ingenuity which flourish in Europe."[103]

A more detailed description follows, of a land without aristocracy, of a land where, "the rich and poor are not so far removed from each other as they are in Europe," and the conclusive evidence for the "most perfect society:"

> Here man is free as he ought to be, nor is this pleasing equality so transitory as many others are.[104]

All this seems to foreshadow Paine and Jefferson, supporting Jefferson's claim that the Declaration "was intended to be an expression of the American mind."[105]

Also congruent with that document is the importance in "Letter III" of unity. Crèvecoeur reiterated several times that, although the focus seems to be on individual acts, in a society where "each man works for himself," something broader is being constructed from this. Crèvecoeur built this through repeated reference to a group identity:

"We are a people. . . . We are all animated. . . . We have no princes. . . ."[106]

This act of creative union mirrors that of The Declaration of Independence, and contrasts with the more individual version constructed by Franklin, although he utilised a similarly representational idea. Crèvecoeur next acknowledged the confusion of races in the New World, although he still asserted that they had been moulded into one:

> They are a mixture of English, Scotch, Irish, French, Dutch, Germans, and Swedes. From this promiscuous breed, that race now called Americans have arisen.

Again contradiction follows:

> The eastern provinces [New England] must indeed be excepted as being the unmixed descendents of Englishmen.

Crèvecoeur's way out is reminiscent of Candide:

> I am no wisher and think it much better as it has happened.[107]

All must be for the best in this "most perfect society," to accept that it might have been better otherwise is to undermine that claim of perfection. Yet, that acknowledgement of difference does undermine the attempted unity which the reiteration of "we" has built up through the preceding paragraphs. As with much of Franklin's writings, it is not a case of being judgemental, of slamming Crèvecoeur for contradictions which were probably unconscious but of recognising the existence of those contradictions.

The argument now reaches its climax. Crèvecoeur reiterated the transformative effect of the New World, emphasising again the newness of everything, and that:

> Everything has tended to regenerate them . . . in Europe they were as so many useless plants, wanting vegetative mould and refreshing showers; they withered, and were mowed down by want, hunger, and war; but now, by the power of transplantation, like all other plants they have taken root and flourished!

Nature and political organisation are here of equal importance. Contradicting his earlier dismissal of aristocrats and kings, a king now becomes vital:

> It [the government] is derived from the original genius and strong desire of the people ratified and confirmed by the crown.

Clearly something is needed to hold the disparate colonists together, yet Crèvecoeur is simultaneously arguing that the colonists are not disparate at all, and the text now repeats this contradiction at greater length. Crèvecoeur now asked, as if he had not just spent several pages answering it, his famous, oft-quoted question:

> What, then, is the American, this new man?[108]

This springboard prompts some of the book's most passionate rhetoric, providing fulsome sketches of the "rising glory" vision of American character. Crèvecoeur emphasised its newness in two ringing passages, as if mere repetition could make it true:

> An American leav[es] behind him all his ancient prejudices and manners, receives new ones from the new mode of life he has embraced, the new government he obeys, and the new rank he holds.
>
>   The American is a new man, who acts upon new principles; he must therefore entertain new ideas and form new opinions.[109]

The word "rank" clearly contradicts the assertions of equality. More, the whole has an air of assertion about it, akin to some of Franklin's utterances on the subject. The new attributes are, presumably, the absence of king and aristocracy, the equality created by the wide availability of land, the forging of these various nationalities into a new people, yet, in each case, Crèvecoeur's text contests its own claims.

The second part of the recapitulation follows. Crèvecoeur, as at the start of "Letter III," surveyed his country. But where before his analysis aimed at unity, now he acknowledged distinct regional differences. Here, for the first time, some really dubious people creep in and intriguingly, as in Franklin's Canada Pamphlet, they live on the frontier. The frontiersmen, Crèvecoeur explained, "were driven there by misfortunes, necessity of beginnings, desire of acquiring large tracts of land, idleness, frequent want of economy, antient [sic] debts."

Nor do they seem to improve once there. Despite the opportunities of the frontier, "men appear to be no better than carniverous [sic] animals of a superior rank."[110]

Now, for all their extolling of the merits of the agricultural life, Franklin never farmed, and Crèvecoeur had a variety of other careers from the military to the diplomatic. There may be something of the inverted snob here. But, whether this is so or not, it does not remove from either of them the fundamental contradiction that these descriptions create. They do not square with Crèvecoeur's earlier claims for the superiority of the new American.

Crèvecoeur attempted to redeem these men, issuing the personal example of his father and a regional example, that of the area in which he was then farming. But his father is, here, a literary fake, since Crèvecoeur senior never came to the New World and the length of time this seems to have taken undermines Crèvecoeur's earlier ecstatic claims for rejuvenation, which imply an almost overnight effect. Now, not only can it take "forty years," but not everyone seems to merit it, "[this area of the country] is now purged, a general decency of manners prevails throughout, and such has been the fate of our best countries." Crèvecoeur's ultimate response is to claim, "In all societies there are off-casts."

But America is not supposed to be like all societies. Crèvecoeur, himself, earlier stressed that it was a new world with new men, who act upon new principles. Any hint of off-cuts flagrantly contradicts that ideal. Crèvecoeur's acknowledgement of variety now seems to run away with him. For, having fragmented the Americans into model farmers and frontiersmen, he fragmented them into the various colonies:

Whoever traverses the continent must easily observe these strong differences which will grow more evident in time.

All this serves to make the necessity of the crown clear. There is simply nothing else to hold these disparate people together, though Crèvecoeur in his confusion proceeded to clutch at straws, declaring:

Their only points of unity will be religion and language.[111]

What religion, and what language, he does not, indeed cannot, explain, since to do so would illustrate the fallacy of his own argument. And "Letter III" has one final, revealing, sting in the tail, considering Crèvecoeur's eventual fate. In another repetition, Crèvecoeur again attempted to explain that critical transformation by which the European becomes American, although here the American is still to be a citizen of the British Empire. His detailed description followed another new arrival as he enjoys the hospitality of the established community and is promptly hired, so that "he finds himself with his equal, placed at the substantial table of the farmer."

Soon, his transformation begins:

He begins to feel the effects of a sort of resurrection; hitherto he had not lived, but simply vegetated; he now feels himself a man because he is treated as such.

Yet, this transformation is not assured, only occurring, "if he behaves with propriety, and is faithful." The possibility of failure exists. The implications are troubling. Apparently, only by following this path can transformation be achieved. "He begins" by so doing "to forget his former solitude and dependence; his heart involuntarily swells and glows; this first swell inspires him with those new thoughts which constitute an American."[112] Soon he is forming schemes to raise himself in the world, schemes with more than faint Franklinian overtones, whereby "he . . . spends two or three years, in which time he acquires knowledge, the use of tools, the modes of working the lands, felling trees. . . .Critically, it is only at the completion of this transformation that he is become an American:

From nothing to start into being from a servant to the rank of a master; from being the slave of some despotic prince, to become a free man, invested with lands to which every municipal blessing is annexed. . . . It is in consequence of that change that he becomes an American."[113]

In place of the assertions that open "Letter III," this model plan details exactly how one might become an American. But this plan has two serious implications. First, that there is only one way to become American. Second, there exists, even in America, the possibility of failure. This, more than anything else, excuses the frontiersmen. They, it now appears, simply lacked the qualities necessary to achieve the status of Americans. In this version of Crèvecoeur's dream, there may not be "room for everybody in America."[114]

"Letter III" thus built a collision between the realities and Crèvecoeur's dreams with the author perhaps not entirely conscious of the contradictions. Temporarily he surmounted them, partly by the force of his language, and partly through the example of Andrew the Hebridean as a second model American, in addition to the Farmer. Andrew's life story forms the second half of Letter III; he may have been based on a real immigrant but we cannot be sure. The use of a non-Englishman as exemplar serves to cement Crèvecoeur's emphasis on the broad range of ethnicities who may be remade into Americans. This is followed by "Letters IV–VIII," which in their descriptions of Nantucket provide a geographical model colony to accompany the model individuals:[115]

It seems to have been inhabited merely to prove what mankind can do when happily governed![116]

These are the most tranquil parts of the book, although the comments on the Amer-Indians raise issues which foreshadow the catastrophe of "Letter XII." The impossibility of perfection is acknowledged again, as in "Letter II," in this case in connection with the opium habit which Nantucket's female population have adopted, much to Crèvecoeur's surprise, given the quality of life. Here, Crèvecoeur was accepting:

where is the society perfectly free from error or folly?[117]

The challenge to his idealised America becomes really problematic with "Letter IX"'s famous description of Charles Town, South Carolina, with slavery only the most obvious problem. This letter becomes a counterpoint to the idyll of "Letter III," as Crèvecoeur touched on various aspects of southern slave-owning society and the consequences of that society for the wider world.

He described the dominant classes of White society, with its planters, merchants, and lawyers, where "nothing can exceed their wealth, their power, and their influence,"[118] a picture disturbingly at variance with the earlier emphasis on the equality of American society. Crèvecoeur first analysed the threat to poorer Whites, "who, while contending perhaps for their right to a few hundred acres, have lost by the mazes of the law their whole patrimony."[119] Only then did Crèvecoeur raise the question of slavery, and in a manner which strikes equally at the character of the owners:

> The chosen race eat, drink, and live happy, while the unfortunate one grubs up the ground, raises indigo, or husks the rice, exposed to a sun full as scorching as their native one, without the support of good food, without the cordials of any cheering liquor.

Crèvecoeur goes on to denounce the external consequence of the system through the slave trade. Earlier he advocated the New World as beacon for the Old, here the relationship is far more pernicious:

> Wars, murders, and devastations are committed in some harmless, peaceable African neighbourhood where dwelt innocent people.[120]

Crèvecoeur also highlighted another effect of the system, a theme familiar to later antislavery writings, the corrupting effect on religion, describing the response to an anti-slavery clergyman:

> Sir . . . we pay you a genteel salary to read to us the prayers of the liturgy and to explain to us such parts of the Gospel as the rule of the church directs, but we do not want you to teach us what we are to do with our blacks.[121]

Crèvecoeur sensed the self-perpetuating nature of the system, commenting that the only hope of alleviating the situation rested with the planters, whose entire upbringing prejudiced them against such an act. Crèvecoeur did acknowledge northern ownership of slaves, and tried to claim that they led better lives than their southern brethren, but this has an air of attempted self-convincement. Remarkably, Crèvecoeur partially acknowledges Black equality:

> There are a thousand proofs existing of their gratitude and fidelity: those hearts in which such dispositions can grow are then like ours; they are susceptible of every generous sentiment, of every useful motive of action.[122]

This is in keeping with "Letter III," except that the system part of the "most perfect society" denies its realisation.

"Letter IX" is most famous for its concluding image:

> I perceived a Negro, suspended in the cage and left there to expire! . . .
> The birds had already picked out his eyes. . . . His body seemed covered
> with a multitude of wounds. . . . The living spectre, though deprived of
> his eyes, could still distinctly hear, and . . . begged me to give him some
> water to allay his thirst.[123]

But it is Crèvecoeur's perceptions of the wider implications of the system
which are of greater significance. For he saw that the tragedy of slavery was
not confined to the personal fates of the slaves, but embraced the owners,
and the ripple effect upon America and the wider world. More, in gro-
tesque reversal of "Letter III," which emphasised the difference between
Old and New Worlds, "Letter IX" describes the defence of slavery in terms
of precedent:

> We are told . . . that slavery cannot be so repugnant to human nature
> as we at first imagine because it has been practised in all ages and in
> all nations.

As a logical consequence, instead of America being an escape from Old
World history, as "Letter III" implied, it becomes a helpless prisoner of it:

> The history of the earth! Doth it present anything but crimes of the
> most heinous nature, committed from one end of the world to the
> other? We observe avarice, rapine and murder, equally prevailing in
> all parts.[124]

The American is no longer a new man. It is in this context that knowledge of date of composition is most missed. For the Letter, in addition to
overturning the philosophy of "Letter III," in its wider reflections effectively
anticipated the calamity of "Letter XII," the account of the Revolution. For
this disastrous history is predicated on a certain view of mankind:

> Men, like the elements, are always at war; the weakest yield to the most
> potent; force, subtlety, and malice, always triumph over unguarded
> honesty and simplicity.[125]

This race produces a particular disaster:

> Hence the most unjust war, if supported by the greatest force, always
> succeeds.[126]

Regrettably, we do not know if this was written after the Revolution began
or whether Crèvecoeur was anticipating, with astonishing prescience, the
fate he was to suffer in the coming war. Either way, the letter ought to have
warned the Patriots:

What little political felicity is to be met with here and there has cost oceans of blood to purchase, as if good was never to be the portion of unhappy man. Republics, kingdoms, monarchies, founded either on fraud or successful violence, increase by pursuing the steps of the same policy until they are destroyed in their turn, either by the influence of their own crimes or by more successful but equally criminal enemies.[127]

The stage is set for the catastrophe (to Crèvecoeur) of the Revolution, but the book postpones this disaster, first with a disquisition on snakes, then by introducing yet another narrator, this time a Russian (probably fictional), describing a visit to John Bartram, the botanist, a real person. The description of this visit in the penultimate "Letter XI" provides an echo of the world of "Letter III." Pennsylvania now becomes the example which corroborates the sweeping optimism of that letter, with Bartram embodying the progress of the arts and sciences in America.[128] Again too, future glory is anticipated, in similar terms of growth to those Franklin espoused:

> . . . the foundation of thy civil polity must lead thee in a few years to a degree of population and power which Europe little thinks of!

There is the same insistence on liberty, this time expressed through Bartram, though it rings somewhat hollow considering the text of "Letter IX":

> . . . tyranny can never take a strong hold in this country; the land is too widely distributed; it is poverty in Europe that makes slaves.[129]

The letter concludes with an episode of tranquility, a moving description of a Quaker Meeting for Worship. All this makes "Letter XII"'s opening, despairing declaration of intent the more shocking:

> I wish for a change of place; the hour is come at last that I must fly from my house and abandon my farm!

For all the ambiguities of the text to this point, so deep a transformation is difficult to anticipate. With this semifictional exploration of his Revolutionary experience, Crèvecoeur blasted apart the idyllic atmosphere that the earlier letters mostly cultivated. Although the possibility of physical escape exists, the mental weight is permanent:

> I never can leave behind me the remembrance of the dreadful scenes to which I have been witness; therefore, never can I be happy![130]

The problem is further explored in *Journey*. Society, in competition with individual progress before, is now central:

What is man when no longer connected with society, or when he finds himself surrounded by a convulsed and half-dissolved one?[131]

Crèvecoeur's escape plan cements this, whereby it is insufficient to succeed in isolation. Before escape, Crèvecoeur must account for his situation. This account is confused concerning both physical threats and disputed issues. The letter opens with a description of that threat that ought, given the preoccupation of the letter, to refer to the Patriots but has distinct overtones of an Indian threat, problematical given Crèvecoeur's escape plan.[132] The revolutionary dispute forces a denial of the earlier letters:

> I lived on . . . without ever having studied on what the security of my life and the foundation of my prosperity were established.[133]

Given those letters, this appears highly disingenuous. But there is a deeper truth here. There was, in the earlier letters, a genuine inability to comprehend the realities, giving a curious parallel with Franklin in his refusal to explore American character in detail. But Crèvecoeur's conclusions are more problematic. These are partly an aspect of the simplistic Farmer James, too simple to comprehend such things:

> Much has been said and written on both sides, but who has a judgement capacious and clear enough to decide?

But they also undermine the principles of both sides:

> Most men reason from passions.[134]

Here, positions are forged from convenience, not principle, in certain ways a more military application of Franklin's pamphleteering style. Real debate has failed:

> As a citizen of a smaller society, I find that any kind of opposition to its now prevailing sentiments immediately begets hatred.

This is tied to a broader attack on the nature of mankind:

> How easily do men pass from loving to hating and cursing each other![135]

And the conflict increasingly resembles an Old World war:

> It is for the sake of the great leaders on both sides that so much blood must be spilt; that of the people is counted as nothing.[136]

In war, in this New World as in the Old, it is the masses, particularly the farmers with whom Crèvecoeur tried to identify himself, who suffer. Further, in a key reversal, the Old World becomes a sanctuary:

> Securely placed as you are, you can have no idea of our agitations.

The contrast with the state of the New World and the idylls of "Letter III" is clear:

> . . . pity the lot of those whom you once called your friends, who were once surrounded with plenty, ease and perfect security . . . [137]

What the earlier evidence made clear to the reader, but obscure to Farmer James, is now clear to all. Old and New Worlds end up precisely the same; Americans are as capable of evil as Europeans. There is no brave new world:

> The innocent class are always the victims of the few; they are in all countries and at all times the inferior agents on which the popular phantom is erected.[138]

His illusions apparently shattered, Crèvecoeur, "a lover of peace,"[139] is left with an impossible choice where his position as the archetype for this new man, the American, has collapsed:

> Both extremes appear equally dangerous to a person of so little weight and consequence as I am, whose energy and example are of no avail.[140]

The position of the Loyalists was severe enough, but Crèvecoeur, seeing the same human flaws in all is, in attempting neutrality, even worse off, between the fearful anticipatory spectre of two parties:

> What can an insignificant man do in the midst of these jarring contradictory parties, equally hostile to persons situated as I am?

There is no rising generation of Patriots aided by Providence here. Rather all are controlled by a darker power:

> Our fate, the fate of thousands, is necessarily involved in the dark wheel of fortune.

The rightness of either cause will be decided by whoever is victorious, and the only course may be for all men to act without principle, "as chance, timidity, or self-preservation directs."[141] Farmer James does not follow this course, Crèvecoeur's conduct was more dubious.

And even now, even after this horror, this chain of consequences has not yet reached its terrible conclusion. Life, at least thus far, may still be preserved, although motives and characters be foresworn. Crèvecoeur's problem is an inability to be of this ilk. Life in such a manner is intolerable to him, and this brings him to the ultimate link in the chain. The terrible question escapes:

> What, then, is life, I ask myself; is it a gracious gift? No, it is too bitter; a gift is something valuable conferred, but life appears to be a mere accident, and of the worst kind: we are born to be victims of diseases and passions, or mischances and death; better not to be than to be miserable.[142]

The idyllic picture of "Letter III" could not be further away. But this was not the end of the story, merely the nadir of Crèvecoeur's despair. Now, he presented an escape attempt for the preservation of his American dream.

We noted the claiming of Crèvecoeur as a reluctant Loyalist. Given his circumstances at the time of publication (1782), this would have been the logical position to take. The Revolution had destroyed his ideal, even his very identity; he had every reason to rail against it. But, his strategy is much more complex, involving a dual exit route, one way for the Farmer, recounted in "Letter XII," one way for Crèvecoeur himself, both resulting from his refusal to accept the death that his conclusions demanded.

Farmer James fled into that ambivalent frontier wilderness, determining to live among the Indians. Trying to discern the author's reasons for this literary choice is problematic. Earlier references within the *Letters* to the Native Indians are few[143] and do not anticipate such a sanctuary; in fact, quite the opposite. The longest discussion, part of "Letter IV"'s Description of Nantucket Island, concerns the decline of the local Indians. This results from two tribes fighting a long and debilitating war over fishing rights, which war Crèvecoeur condemned out of hand:

> So prevailing is the disposition of man to quarrel, and to shed blood; so prone is he to divisions and parties; that even the ancient natives of this little spot were separated into two communities, inveterately waging war against each other, like the more powerful tribes of the continent.[144]

Again the stain may spread beyond the Indians, although Crèvecoeur carefully distinguished the White islanders from this on the grounds of their Quaker faith:

> They [the Indians] have been treated by these people [the Nantucket Quakers] as brethren; the peculiar genius of their sect inspiring them with the same moderation which was exhibited at Pennsylvania.[145]

The similar descriptions, applied to Indians in "Letter IV" and Whites in "Letter XII," give little clue to Crèvecoeur's motives in sending the Farmer among the Indians. A possible answer is that the device derives from Crèvecoeur's continued belief in himself as an American, evidenced in his later life and writings. Thus, through this flight, Crèvecoeur attempted to sustain in literature what he could not sustain in life. Even this is won with considerable struggle. Crèvecoeur recalled, uneasily, cases from the Seven Years War, not mentioned at all thus far, of children kidnapped by the Indians who showed no desire to return. Again, he is almost trapped between that danger and the threatening "education of the times."[146] A flight to the Indians, the necessary celebration of them, has a kudos which a retreat to the Old World would not possess, fitting into the literary tradition of celebrating the noble savage.[147]

> There must be in their social bond something singularly captivating, and far superior to anything to be boasted of among us; for thousands of Europeans are Indians, and we have no examples of even one of these aborigines having from choice become Europeans!

But deep prejudices remain, "the strongest prejudices would make me abhor any alliance with them in blood."[148] It cannot be bright confident morning again:

> I do not expect to enjoy, in the village of—, an uninterrupted happiness; it cannot be our lot let us live where we will; I am not founding my prosperity on golden dreams.[149]

Crèvecoeur still looked back to his lost ideal:

> Permit, I beseech thee, O Father of nature, that . . . we may be restored to our ancient tranquillity and enabled to fill it with successive generations that will constantly thank thee for the ample subsistence thou hast given them.[150]

The flight is not finally performed, although it remains the anticipated next act, and the letter concludes with a prayer that that act, and the family's fate more generally, be blessed. In the text, Crèvecoeur sustained the illusion. It was a necessary act, given the hold the dream still had upon him, but it also had to cover the disturbing reality.

For Crèvecoeur actually fled, in 1779. with his eldest son, surviving a dangerous journey to New York, under suspicion from both sides, culminating in imprisonment and serious illness there for several months before he could finally sail for Europe in 1780. There he arranged for publication of the *Letters*, established his eldest son's position in French society, and gradually raised himself to view within it, a move which eventually enabled his return to America as a French diplomat, a key symbol of that belief in his American nature. But, by the time he returned, his wife was dead and his remaining children recovered only by chance, an abandonment which, whatever his psychological torments, leaves a stain upon his character.

Crèvecoeur's real flight, if morally rather more dubious than the Farmer's proposed escape, actually performed the same function. It enabled Crèvecoeur to sustain his dream of American possibility. His other writings corroborate this thesis. The first group, some eventually collected as *Sketches of Eighteenth Century America*, were of the same vintage as *Letters*, and repeat some topics. They confronted the Revolution in far stronger terms, particularly regarding the treatment of the Loyalists. They are the key source for the claim that Crèvecoeur was a Loyalist.[151] This claim is weakened by two factors: Crèvecoeur's decision not to publish these essays, including the only clearly pro-Loyalist one, and his renewed attempt to celebrate the American character in the *Journey*. These pieces, with the possible exception of "Landscapes," really show the chaos of identities unleashed by the Revolution.

The essays' nonpublication is unsurprising, given the extent to which they revisit and expand on themes from *Letters* without a significant alteration of tone. The ninth essay, "The Wyoming Massacre," revisited the possibility of an Indian sanctuary, rather more broadmindedly:

> The daughters of these frontier people will necessarily marry among the young men of the nation in which they have taken refuge, they have now no other choice. At a certain age, Nature points out the necessity of union; she cares very little about colour.[152]

It is just possible here that Crèvecoeur was aware of contemporary uneasiness about interracial relationships.

The seventh essay, "The Man of Sorrows," essentially another version of "Letter XII," commented more brutally on the Revolution:

> Men in a state of civil war are no longer the same. . . . The most unjust thoughts, the most tyrannical actions, the most perverse measures, which would have covered them before with infamy or would have made them dread the omnipotence of heaven, are no longer called by these ancient names; the sophistry of each party calls them policy, justice, self-defence.[153]

The gentleman farmer, a likely repeat of Farmer James, laments the impossibility of lying by, despite his keeping his opinions to himself.[154] His fate, contrasted with James's, is more brutal, as the Patriots attempt to hang him, though he escapes for trial, where he is acquitted. This hints at possible partiality on Crèvecoeur's part, yet is balanced by the "impartial trial" and the man's acquittal. The ultimate fate, the loss of the idealised life, is also the same:

No government, no set of men can ever make him amends for the injury he has received.[155]

The eleventh essay, "The American Belisarius," repeated a similar story but added a new piece of confusion:

I am persuaded that there are several members in Congress and in every province who . . . would shed tears over the ashes of this ruin; but these men at a great distance direct the revolution of the new orb. It is the inferior satellites who crush, who dispel, and make such a havoc in the paths which it is to follow.[156]

Where, in "Letter XII," Crèvecoeur made the many victims of the few, he now seems to attempt exoneration of at least some in authority. Crèvecoeur was questing for points of reconciliation. The parallel with the argument that the king would eventually put right the failings of his ministers is also intriguing.

The final piece in *Sketches* is more problematical, not an essay at all but a play in six tableaux, entitled "Landscapes." The six scenes take place across one day. The setting is not specified, but given the Quaker presence and events it may be presumed to be rural Pennsylvania shortly after the formal outbreak of the Revolution, with a set of characters to represent the various perspectives. The major characters are the patriots, Deacon Beatus and his wife, Eltha; the local patriot commander Colonel Templeton; and two travelling observers (a Russian, Iwan, who may spring from the Russian who visits Bartram in Letter IX; the name is the same) and Ecclestone, specifically described as "an American gentleman."[157]

Here, balanced argument is replaced by indisputable condemnation of the Patriots for their treatment of the Loyalists. Earlier sanctuaries are removed. That of the law:

They [the Tory prisoners] can expect nothing from the law; it extends its benefits but to the favourers of the new cause.[158]

That of beneficent leaders, when the Patriot Deacon retorts:

I am, you know, but the voice of the people; 'tis they that govern us.[159]

Either the evil leaders are manipulating the mob or the mob has become a fearful monster. The Fourth Tableau supports the latter argument. Several Quakers attempt to reduce fines levelled upon Loyalists, but are rebuffed since the Patriot commander, Colonel Templeton, cannot control the situation:

Quakers—"Can't we appease thy people without so much plunder? It gives them an example of rapine."

Col.—"That is not the case. The people must be indulged."[160]

The fourth tableau also returned to the European comparison, in a dialogue between two travelling observers, Iwan, a Russian, and Ecclestone, an American. Ecclestone makes the familiar case against the Patriots:

'Tis cursed hard to see . . . this fellow, his wife, and the junta dispose of all the social happiness of a country; commit the greatest barbarities, accumulate injustice upon injustice . . . yet go and worship with an easy conscience.

But Iwan points out that people have always acted in this way, again skewering the claim that Americans are different. Iwan's conclusion is critical:

Talking about it only serves to make matters worse.[161]

This is the final aspect of Crèvecoeur's choice. "Letter XII" maintained a precarious neutrality. "Landscapes" was not published. Crèvecoeur permitted the version of history Ecclestone feared and Franklin tried to craft:

When the accounts of this mighty revolution arrive in Europe, nothing will appear there but the splendid effects. The insignificant cause will be overlooked; the low arts, this progressive succession of infatuations, which have pervaded the whole continent, will be unknown. The brave, the warlike Americans will be blazoned out as the examples of the world, as the veteran sons of the most rational liberty.[162]

Crèvecoeur's reasons for this may be inferred from what he did publish. Clearly the remaining essays did not contain sufficient fresh material for a complete second volume. Further, Crèvecoeur went to considerable lengths, in the torturous narrative of "Letter XII," and by his flight to Europe, to avoid the revolutionary choice. When *Letters* was published, there was every argument against such ambivalence. *Letters* as published gave Crèvecoeur entry into French literary society. Further assisted by a report on the cultivation of potatoes in Normandy, he gained the attention of the minister of marine, the Marshal de Castries, who controlled colonial appointments. The Marshal commissioned a broader report on America, the reception of which enabled Crèvecoeur to gain the appointment of French consul to New York, New Jersey, and Connecticut, which he retained between 1783 and 1790.[163]

During this period, he seems to have continued to use literature to refashion his American dreams, through two French language editions of *Letters* published in 1784 and 1787. These are not available in English translation, but appear to have varied substantially from the original, as Crèvecoeur attempted to frame the post-Revolutionary settlement in a positive way, a concern central to his final work, *Journey into Upper Pennsylvania and the State of New York* (1801). The fragility of this attempt is underlined by his acceptance of the halfway position of consul, when he might have returned to his Pennsylvania farm. Yet another individual history in *Journey* corroborates this, the colonist in question reflected on the mirage of America:

> For I know too well . . . the fatigues and disgusts of a new settlement to dare expose myself to one at my age; those back-breaking clearings are neither the Elysian Fields nor the groves of Thessalie, as they are sometimes pictured by a newly arrived European, who judges according to what he has seen and what he knows.[164]

Crèvecoeur's final book is a remarkable extended study of America, but during his lifetime it was published only in French and German. A full English translation only appeared in 1964, and is now out of print. But Crèvecoeur intended a circulation as wide as *Letters*. He attempted in the book a new answer to his own famous question. The attempt was compromised from the outset, but the fact of it and its neglect by readers and historians are significant.

The complexities of the text cannot have helped. The book is divided into three volumes, coupled to extensive footnotes providing substantial details on everything from Indian tribes, to wildlife, to the constitutional arrangements and population of the various states visited. Some material was certainly lifted from other sources.[165] All America is here in its chaos of possibilities.

The book deserves a more thorough consideration. We focus on key themes, Crèvecoeur's personal confusions of identity; the textual conflict between optimism and despair; his discussion of the Indian question and his discussion of the post-Revolutionary settlement.

Crèvecoeur attempted to bind his jumbled book together through one central journey, that of the unidentified narrator and his European companion, Mr. Herman. Virtually everyone they meet presents written narratives of their lives to them, which are duly interpolated into the overall journey. The unidentified narrator creates further confusion by claiming to be at a further remove; the second unidentified narrator recovered the manuscript of the first from a shipwreck, the first identifying himself thus:

> in some chapters designated himself only as an adopted member of the Oneida tribe, and in others only by four initials which I have indicated at the close of the dedication letter. (S[t].J[ohn].D[e].C[rèvecoeur].)[166]

These techniques of distancing are evidence of Crèvecoeur's confused identity. The Farmer, the ruined Crèvecoeur of 1780, and the consul of 1783, are all present in the text. The collapse of the collective voice corroborates this. In *Letters*, Crèvecoeur freely employed a collective "we." Here there is only a cacophony of individuals:

> I have a fine collection. . . . I devised a little system. . . . I am even more astonished.[167]

The idyll of "Letter III" and the despair of "Letter XII" both reappear, helplessly entangled. Thus, one of the representative farmers recounts his frontier life:

> Satisfied with our lot, we lead an active life, hardworking, it is true, but one that is peaceful and moderate, which the agitations of business and trade can no longer envenom. In a few years this clumsy-looking shelter will become a snug and charming dwelling, and this region a rich and cultivated land.[168]

There is glory here, but glory not yet fully achieved, and the same settler ends up admitting a wilful blindness:

> Hope . . . hides from him carefully any harshness, permitting him to see in the distance only fertile fields, lush meadows, and blooming orchards, ease and independence.[169]

This conflict is also visible in the treatment of the new political settlement. By dedicating the book to the late Washington, and celebrating the remarkable transformation achieved by the Revolution in the Preface, Crèvecoeur attempted to make himself a Patriot after the event, though even here the bloody price lurks.[170] He gave the same farmer an appropriate paean to the new settlement:

> If ever your talents and the esteem of the public open to you the doors of representation in the government, never forget that union makes for strength in United States; that the grandeur and the prosperity of this new empire are founded only on this unity. All the laws destined to cement it will obtain your vote and your support, as well as the ones whose aim will be the encouragement of clearing land and the perfection of farming methods. That is the national character, the guarantee of religion and virtue which has brought us rapidly from the weakness of infancy to the vigour of adolescence.[171]

But elsewhere the despair raged, concerning the press:

> The cries of a crowd of malcontents, sedition mongers . . . the lying or sophistic declamations of anonymous writers . . . can all that be considered the voice of the American people.[172]

political parties:

> What courage, what firmness will you [a Congressman] need then to obey the inspiration of your conscience and resist the pressure of political parties, this scourge of countries where freedom reigns.[173]

and the underlying tendencies of humanity:

> It will be clearly demonstrated that, in the new as well as the old world, man is not made to taste for long the benefits of liberty; a regime which indeed demands virtues and sacrifices incompatible with the passions and imperfections of human nature.[174]

The Indian question also displays Crèvecoeur's conflicted identity. The opening chapter presents an interview between the narrator and an Indian official named Colonel Crawgen. Crawgen laid out the standard White interpretation, anticipating the rapid destruction of the tribes from alcohol and disease.[175] He lamented their baffling refusal to accept White ways:

> What . . . makes them prefer the roaming and precarious life of the woods to the more secure and settled life of farming?[176]

He ascribed it to their inferiority:

> All this proves that their intelligence is less susceptible to perfectibility than ours and that the races are inferior to those of Europe and of Asia.

In counterpoint, Crèvecoeur, the alleged adopted Indian battered Crawgen's claims, beginning to imply the existence of common human traits, irrespective of race:

> These hordes [the Virginia Indian tribes] were in a continual state of tension or resistance, a state which in Europe as well as here seems to be natural to man. If these tribes had had historiographers, the pages of their history would have presented in miniature the same scenes as those of the great Asiatic and European nations.[177]

This is expanded when he and Mr. Herman attend an Indian council. The Indians give their perception of the interracial relationship. Some of the philosophy is recognisable Crèvecoeur:

> There are good and bad among us, just as there are among them.[178]

But the central paean is more forceful than anything yet seen:

> In living like the White man, we will cease to be what we are: children of God, who made us hunters and warriors. We shall think, we shall act like them; and like them, we shall become liars, cheats, parasites, slaves to the soil which we cultivate, enchained by laws governed by papers and by the writings of lies.[179]

It is profoundly difficult to take Cooper's Indians seriously, marching nobly and savagely to their doom in the face of such earlier statements.

The final Indian voice is most complex of all. Introduced during a visit to Niagara Falls, this Indian has successfully adapted to agriculture, speaking of it in terms highly reminiscent of the Farmer, and in language which seems rather un-Indian.[180] Given the nature of the text, it is a strong possibility that this Indian represents a Crèvecoeur who did flee to the Indians during the Revolution. This Indian is an outcast, whose wisdom goes unheeded:

> For my part, as one of the old people, I wanted to speak forth, to plea, to urge, to restrain these blind young people; but they flung afar my advice as well as that of their own chiefs.[181]

This Indian is then echoed by Crèvecoeur (as narrator) in a late outburst. Musing on the improvements seen in America, he wonders if they will ever be transplanted to France which becomes, in an ultimate admission of failure, his native land once more. He anticipates the *Journey*, declaring his intention to describe all he has seen:

> Like a little bee which, fleeing its hive at dawn, returns only toward dusk, bringing the most precious findings, on my return after an absence of so many years I shall dare speak of what I have seen . . . unknown though I am. My too feeble voice will not be heard, I fear; but what does that matter?

To Crèvecoeur it does matter. This is the basis for the *Journey*, and, even here, he cannot resist one more riff on the future. Insisting, "I do not despair," he attempted the optimistic vision once again. What follows is, instead, a series of ominous, unanswered questions:

> Moreover, are we not nearing the end of the eighteenth century? Does not everything announce that the next century will bring in its wake one of the most memorable and one of the greatest epochs, designed to bring to birth ideas and inventions until now unknown, unforeseen, as well as everything which is good and useful that human ingenuity and industry can produce?[182]

Crèvecoeur kept returning to American examples because he wanted desperately to believe. He wanted to wipe away the horror of the Revolution, or at least to prove that what had been born from it made that sacrifice worthwhile. But it proved impossible. *Journey* failed to recapture the optimism of *Letters*. Crèvecoeur himself, for all his dreams of an Indian sanctuary, returned to France, and further ill luck. The French Revolution forced him into a Normandy exile. Passage back to America was denied.

The French government refused him a state pension. His son Otto, also a diplomat, was briefly imprisoned and, in 1806, Crèvecoeur suffered the worst of blows when his son Ally died. Although the advent of Napoleon may have eased his domestic situation, the lost American ideal still held his mind, fuelling the *Journey*. Mournful letters to his sons still dreamed of a life amongst the Indians, the escape he was never strong enough to attempt. He had become like the aged Indian at Niagara Falls, who lamented:

> What remains of me belongs only to the past, and this past is no more than the imprint of memories remote but still bitter. That is all I have gained for living this long.[183]

His death in 1813 passed virtually unnoticed; his books had already passed out of print.

Franklin, typically, had been luckier, dying with the *Autobiography* conveniently (un)finished in 1790. He had escaped the political turmoil of the 1790s. He enshrined the obscured part of his life. There was no need to write of the Revolution, since everybody knew his vital role, as John Adams irritably anticipated.

Crèvecoeur and Franklin represented an experience obscured by the rising glory paeans of the Revolutionary era. They experienced a world in which hearts and minds were supposedly transformed, and they knew only too well that that transformation had deeply divided their people. Both sensed the obscuring of those divisions, although in Franklin's case one suspects without much concern. Fresh divisions about the character and direction of the new republic rapidly emerged, but there remained no space or desire to remember the Revolutionary divisions.

Franklin is representative because he acquiesced in the movement to obscure, promoting a republic the character of which he had never entirely gotten to grips with. Crèvecoeur is representative because he made the most vivid exploration of that character, but believed that perfection had been achieved prior to the Revolution. He wrote about issues which were to obsess coming American writers: the Indian question, the character of the frontier, the inequalities of society, the contradictions between the dream and the reality. Recognising the multiplicity of the New World, of the American, he attempted the fashioning of a union in advance of the Patriot cause, recognising, despite himself, the illusory nature of his ideas. He was thus uniquely placed to recognise the new, Patriot, union's central illusion, that very claim of unity. He possessed an authority on this point that the Loyalists and Patriots who did write histories lacked. For, despite the agonies he suffered in the Revolution, he clung on to his dream of the new man the American. Few made so sustained an attempt to comprehend and come to terms with the Revolution. If the Patriots had really believed in their own rhetoric, they ought to have acknowledged him as an equal. Crèvecoeur understood that simply readmitting Loyalists and Neutrals within the new order, as Hamilton and others advocated, was insufficient. It was a fundamental question of recognising their right to that rebellion, of acknowledging the validity of their views. Instead, Loyalists who remained had to suppress their Loyalist past. In times of Revolution, the contradiction was a natural one. Perhaps it was even forgivable. But the sweeping of one division under the carpet left open the possibility of the sweeping aside of another. In an ideal nation as forcefully articulated as the new America, that had profound implications for the future.

2   Hugh Henry Brackenridge and the Dogma of Balance

I see, I see
Freedom's established reign; cities and men,
Numerous as sands upon the ocean shore,
And empires rising where the sun descends![1]

People must hope so much when they tear streets up and fight at barricades. But, whoever wins, the streets are laid again and the trams start running again. One hopes too much of destroying things. If revolutions do not fail, they fail you.[2]

On September 23, 1783, with the agreement of the Treaty of Paris, the American Patriots secured on paper the independence for which they contended. But that apparent victory reopened a problem obscured by the struggles for war and peace. The Patriots were confronted afresh by the question of what, precisely, independence meant.

We now examine the particular response of one writer, Hugh Henry Brackenridge, to this. First, we must establish the state of the nation within which he operated.

The question of independence, in 1783 just as in 1776, had two key dimensions. The first was a political and structural one: how was the country going to be governed? The second remained difficult to define but, in essence, was the broader question of which Americans were going to govern and what would indicate that they had achieved a rising glory for their nation, which many had anticipated in the years preceding the Revolution. Independence needed to mean something beyond a mere paper acknowledgement from Great Britain, or, indeed, acceptance of a framework for government.[3] Further, it is important to recognise the persistence of the British threat, a fact which lent vehemence to the different American perspectives on these questions.

The questions of 1783 were not new, but the manner of addressing them marked a sea change. Previously attention centred on the conduct of the war; the actual structures to build the new nation received little attention, as witnessed by the length of time it took to get the Articles of Confederation approved by the states.[4] As to the character of the people who were to operate those structures, there was a tendency, as we have seen, to assume glory. Now, the governmental structures took centre stage. The forging of the new Constitution in 1787 did achieve a remarkable thing. It got nearly everybody, with the exception of the exiled Loyalists, inside the same tent. As it turned out, this extended to keeping them inside that tent even in the face of bitter debates. What it did not resolve was the disparate nature of the many Americans thus encaged. Rather, it perpetuated the Revolutionary illusion.

Thus, in the famous preamble to the Constitution, essentially a more practical consolidation of the ideals of the Revolutionary War, the fiction of unity was remanufactured:

> We the people of the United States, in order to form a more perfect Union, establish Justice, insure domestic Tranquility, provide for the common defence, promote the general Welfare, and secure the Blessings of Liberty to ourselves and our Posterity, do ordain and establish this Constitution for the United States of America.[5]

The Constitution's key advocates pursued a similar line. Thus, John Jay, in the second Federalist Paper asserted:

> I have as often taken notice that Providence has been pleased to give this one connected country to one united people—a people descended from the same ancestors, speaking the same language, professing the same religion, attached to the same principles of government, very similar in their manners and customs, and who, by their joint counsels, arms, and efforts, fighting side by side throughout a long and bloody war, have nobly established general liberty and independence.[6]

Similarly, in his first Inaugural Address, Washington argued that God:

> has been pleased to favor the American people with opportunities for deliberating in perfect tranquillity, and dispositions for deciding with unparalleled unanimity on a form of government for the security of their union and the advancement of their happiness.[7]

Such proclamations partially stemmed from that fear of the continued British threat already mentioned, but with unfortunate consequences. This fictitious unity not only airbrushed Loyalists, Anti-Federalists, and dissentients at the Convention from the polity (in Washington's case practically labelling them as having acted contrary to God), but also denied the possibility that further factions might emerge.

Elsewhere, *The Federalist Papers* did face this fragility. Madison's famous Tenth Federalist, although optimistic as to the prospects of controlling factions in a large republic, as against any other form of government, did not pretend that factions could be abolished.[8] Madison's Americans here are depressingly like any other people, for having listed at length the causes of faction, he remarked grimly, "The causes of faction cannot be removed."[9] As with individuals, so with regions. In the final paper, Hamilton emphasised the folly of renegotiating the Constitution, since it would be impossible to get representatives of the "thirteen distinct States" to agree a second time. Again a contradiction, since those thirteen States were elsewhere proclaimed as having been united into something called America.

As in the period leading up to the Revolution, this is not to denounce these expressions of unity. They were necessary to hold the new nation together, especially given the continuance of foreign threats, and they expressed a very important hope. They could also be seen, on one level, as a faintly curious exercise in self-deception about the nature of politics—that is, for factions, proto-parties, parties, whatever one wishes to call them, not to have developed would have been far more remarkable, especially in a society with few, if any, of the traditional ties of nationhood to create a sense of unity. But this was a real polity, and the deception had serious consequences. For it laid the foundations, under the new Constitution and despite those flashes of recognition in documents like the Tenth Federalist, for a state of denial as troubling as that which excluded Loyalists and neutrals during the Revolution. Thus, when factions did develop in the 1790s, each claimed to be the true Americans, and were thus prevented from recognising their opponents as equally American. The situation possessed a distinct whiff of the Revolutionary divide. It had similar consequences for those who were thereby threatened with exclusion from the polity, as in the case of the Loyalists and neutrals. It left the same stains.

We use Hugh Henry Brackenridge to explore this argument because, in the central experience of his life, he was trapped by this inability to recognise the possible existence of other definitions of American character. In the Whiskey Rebellion of 1794, he sought to mediate between competing factions, each claiming authority as Americans. Like Crèvecoeur, he found that there was no middle path.

Brackenridge frequently complained of neglect at the hands of his contemporaries, suggesting thereby that John Quincy Adams was unusual in both noting and celebrating Brackenridge's epic, *Modern Chivalry*: "It will last beyond the period fixed by the ancient statutes for the canonisation of poets, a full century."[10]

The epic, Brackenridge's best known work, was published in seven instalments between 1792 and 1815.[11] It traced the apparently endless adventures of the aristocratic Farrago and his Irish servant Teague (symbol of the lowest elements of White society), wherein Farrago struggles to keep his servant in the subservient position to which he believes he belongs, and Teague persists in disastrous breakouts from it. The book is essential to an understanding of Brackenridge, but it should not be read in isolation.

Brackenridge's complaints at his contemporary neglect were accompanied by worries about his posthumous reputation. In 1806, he anticipated:

> But I do not flatter myself that my memory will survive me long. It is sufficient; at least, it is the utmost that I can expect, that it can survive a few years.[12]

Historians duly followed his lead. Since Claude M. Newlin's pioneering biography, only one monograph has been published.[13] Aspects of Brackenridge have been taken up by more recent scholars, including Cathy N. Davidson, Robert Lawson-Peebles, Christopher Looby, and, most effectively, Joseph J. Ellis, but these are chapters in longer studies whose length cannot encompass the breadth of Brackenridge's career.[14] It is that breadth of experience, coupled with the interconnection of his political and literary pursuits which make Brackenridge of such importance.

For Brackenridge did two things unique among imaginative writers of this period. He used writing to reflect on all the major events of the period, from the Revolution to the War of 1812. By contrast, Crèvecoeur left America in the 1780s; Franklin died in 1790, while Irving and his contemporaries only started writing after the Revolution. Brackenridge's unique literary record deserves to stand beside those of political figures such as Thomas Jefferson and John Adams. Unlike those whose writings were often private letters, Brackenridge used his writing to engage in constant public dialogue. Nor was that dialogue performed from the comfortable seclusion of an ivory tower. Brackenridge was active on the ground in all the key events he chronicled.

That direct connection had a crucial effect. In Brackenridge, it is possible to trace the slow development of a Patriot's disillusionment. From early, extremely patriotic poetry, Brackenridge became progressively more unhappy with the state of America.

Brackenridge will be explored in three sections. First, his committed involvement with the Patriot side in the American Revolution, and his first attempts, intimately connected with this, to foster an educated, American reading public through his magazine, *The United States Magazine*. Second, his political activity in the years surrounding the Whiskey Rebellion, and his key realisations brought on by his involvement in that rebellion. Finally, his continued pursuit of concerns forged during the earlier part of his life, both as a state judge, and through his writing in the later sections of his epic fiction, *Modern Chivalry*.

ORIGINS

Hugh Henry Brackenridge was born at Campbeltown, Scotland, in 1748, and came over with his family to America in 1753. Little is known about his childhood, although there are the customary stories about an early obsession with books, which, while possibly apocryphal, may be justly applied to his later life. The family settled in Western Pennsylvania, where Brackenridge remained almost his entire life, and which was clearly his spiritual home. He taught in a school for five years, between the ages of fifteen and twenty, before being admitted to Princeton, where he was a contemporary of James Madison.

At Princeton, Brackenridge formed a literary partnership with Philip Freneau (1752–1832), the epic poet, and subsequent member of the Connecticut Wits, long regarded as the preeminent literary figures of the period. The connection was subsequently revived through Brackenridge's short-lived periodical, *The United States Magazine* (1779), which regularly published Freneau's poems. Their first college collaboration was a satirical fantasy entitled *Father Bombo's Pilgrimage*, written in 1770 but, with the exception of a couple of excerpts, lost until the 1950s.[15] The book, written in alternate chapters by the two aspiring writers, concerns the hapless Bombo's pilgrimage from Princeton to Mecca, which he reaches all in a rush in the final chapter. The episodic style, and the helpless situation of Bombo despite his belief in his own learning, anticipate *Modern Chivalry*; in particular in "Book III:II" where Bombo, despite answering most of the questions incorrectly, is appointed a school-teacher, a definite hint of the permanently overpromoted Teague.[16] Also perhaps significant, in the light of what was to follow, is a scene on board ship in III:I, when Bombo muses on the appropriate course of action as the ship is assaulted by an Irish privateer:

> "Here I found myself in a miserable plight; for should I seem to act the Coward on the present occasion, my fate would be unavoidably fixed if the Frenchman gained the Victory, but if I fought gallantly I would be treated as a prisoner if the privateer conquer'd; I therefore resolved to steer a mean between both."[17]

Their more significant collaboration was the epic poem entitled *The Rising Glory of America*, written to mark their graduations in 1771 and often given as a prime example of the belief of Americans in the idea of *translatio studio*, although, in fact, the work is rather more complex than such analysis or its title suggests. This work has become the key symbol for the literature of the period in subsequent studies.[18] It seems to represent the Patriot vision of a rising America, of America as the new top nation, but the poem actually presents a much more confused world. It is the attempt to present the vision and the confusion that attends that attempt that make the poem a crucial source.

Before discussing the work itself, a textual problem must be noted. Two versions of the text exist. One, from 1772, is presumed to be that of the original address, upon which they collaborated. The other, from 1786, was revised by Freneau. The alterations visible are an intriguing further example of the kind of mental evolution going on in American minds at this period, in this case for Freneau, but lie outside our concerns here.[19]

A first oddity about the poem is that it devotes considerable space to the past, as a basis for the present rising glory, but this past, in fact, creates a worryingly murky world. The poem explores, in the kind of history of the world fashion which Irving would later satirise, the origins of the Indians, dismissed grimly as "a savage race of men."[20] The poem proposes various eastern origins for the Indians, its crucial point being that, wherever they came from, they have declined since their residence in America. To show the colonists as glorious, it is obviously necessary to demonstrate the Indians as inadequate. Yet, this analysis opens the possibility of the New World environment adversely effecting its inhabitants, although the poets do not confront this.

Instead, having established the decayed character of the native inhabitants, their rescuers sweep on stage:

> Now view the prospect chang'd . . .
> A new, a fair a fertile world arise . . . [21]

The poem now established a cogent myth behind the arrival of these colonists:

> By persecution wronged,
> And popish cruelty, our fathers came
> From Europe's shores to find this blest abode,
> Secure from tyranny and hateful man.[22]

Intriguingly, in celebrating the world thus created, the poem singled out William Penn and Pennsylvania. Now, this may have been Brackenridge's hand, as the native Pennsylvanian, although Freneau did not expunge the sentiments in 1786. Yet, if Brackenridge's hand, it anticipated views he would later express, concerning the necessity of Western Pennsylvania as a balance between the eastern and southern States. Henry Adams expressed a similar view about Pennsylvania in the *History*. Brackenridge's future views are further anticipated with the comparison of Penn to Solon, the Athenian lawgiver, a comparison he would employ again, much more personally, during the Whiskey Rebellion.[23]

The problem of the present of 1772 now begins to emerge. A sequence of virtuous figures are introduced, whom America will afterwards emulate. These are Braddock, Johnson,[24] Franklin, and Whitefield.[25] But all of these, with the possible exception of Franklin, are British. This is dramatically illustrated in the case of the moral drawn from Johnson's acts. He is celebrated for having tamed the Indians, here dismissed in particularly savage language:

> Unstable as the sea, wild as the winds,
> Cruel as death, and treacherous as hell . . . [26]

This has been done by peaceful means, in contrast to those used by the bloodthirsty Spaniards, and his countrymen are encouraged to emulate him, but they are also clearly labelled as members of the Empire:

> We boast no seats
> Of cruelty like Spain's unfeeling sons.
> The British Epithet is merciful:
> And we the sons of Britain learn like them.
> To conquer and to spare . . . [27]

The poem moves from this to a celebration of the various means by which the Americans make their livings, again in contrast to the Spaniards, who only sought easy riches in mineral form. Hard work is the order of the day here, either in agriculture or in commerce. Above all these however, and here the authors were certainly showing their bias, are science and the arts:

> Hither they've [the muses] wing'd their way, the last, the best
> Of countries where the arts shall rise and grow
> Luxuriant, graceful . . . [28]

Here, demonstrating the ambivalent position of the various imagined nationalities, Franklin is introduced as the rival to Newton, "Britannia's sage." More problematic is the fact that all this, glorious although it unquestionably is, is but a staging post. Ultimate fulfilment is yet to be attained and, when the poem turns to consider that final prospect, doubt creeps in:

> And hopes the day when Britain's sons shall spread
> Dominion to the north and south and west
> Far from th' Atlantic to Pacific shores?
> A glorious theme, but how shall mortals dare
> To pierce the mysteries of future days,
> And scenes unravel only known to fate[?]

This uneasiness is brushed aside but the vision presented hardly clarifies matters:

> I see, I see
> A thousand kingdoms rais'd, cities and men
> Num'rous as sand upon the ocean shore . . . [29]

The conflicted character of this prospect is further established by the claim that soon the New World will have its own "Alexanders, Pompeys, . . . kings."[30] Hardly appropriate revolutionary sentiment, or a prospect likely to ensure that "here fair freedom shall forever reign."[31] But the more serious problem, or perhaps an unwittingly prescient analysis, is this reference to a thousand kingdoms, for this hardly suggests a dominant British empire, or a United States of America. Though, in 1772, let us remember, it would have been quite surprising had they done so. The poem proceeds to a litany of European icons to be reproduced in America, St Petersburg in the North, a Babylon in the south and so forth.[32] But these images of achievement are to be constructed in a world where:

New states new empires and a line of kings,
High rais'd in glory, cities, palaces
Fair domes on each long bay, sea, shore of stream
Circling the hills now rear their lofty heads.[33]

Even if we accept that this is a purely American civilisation which is to be constructed, it is certainly not such a one as the Patriots would wish to be particularly associated with.

It is the end of the poem which raises the most serious questions. It continues in the anticipatory vein, but with a Biblical tone such that, by the end, it is unclear whether this glorious future is to be realised in America before the end of the world or if America is all that is to be left after the end of the world. More significantly, it is made perfectly plain that America cannot escape the march of time. It will endure all else:

Till all those glorious orbs of light on high
The rolling wonders that surround the ball,
Drop from their spheres extinguish'd and consum'd;
When final ruin with her fiery car
Rides o'er creation, and all nature's works
Are lost in chaos and the womb of night.[34]

Not only is the Rising Glory of America a vision yet to be fulfilled, it is also a vision whose fulfilment will be finite. More, in the present it is a vision still unevenly poised between a colonial past and an, as yet, uncertain future. The poem corroborated the concerns of Crèvecoeur and Franklin explored in Chapter 1, but it also anticipated the extent of Brackenridge and Freneau's subsequent journeys. Freneau would become a Jeffersonian hack, editing the principal Democratic–Republican newspaper, the *National Gazette*, to which Brackenridge occasionally contributed. But in this poem we glimpse the possibility that either one of them might have remained loyal to the first British Empire, as so many of their countrymen did. The poem is caught on the threshold of choosing whether or not to become a Patriot American. Brackenridge, it would turn out, recognised the burden of that decision more profoundly than his collaborator, though their divergence took time to emerge.

Brackenridge's next literary efforts consisted of two plays, *The Battle of Bunkers-Hill* (1775) and *The Death of General Montgomery* (1777), a second epic poem, *A Poem on Divine Revelation* (1774), a collection of highly political sermons, and his short-lived *United States Magazine* (1779). Besides writing, Brackenridge continued to teach, obtained his master's degree from Princeton in 1774 and, in 1776, became a Presbyterian chaplain in Washington's army.

The balance of these writings, in particular the plays and the sermons, was decisively patriotic, serving as forceful calls to arms. Although both plays are tales of blood, it is made perfectly plain that this blood is being spilt in a good cause. As the Preface to *Bunkers-Hill* proclaimed:

> The task—be ours with unremitted toil,
> To guard the rights of this dear purchased soil,
> From royal plunderers, greedy of our spoil,
> Who came resolved to murder and enslave,
> To shackle FREEMEN and to rob the brave.[35]

Brackenridge slightly tempered this with the partial humanising of Thomas Gage, Commander-in-Chief of the British Army, who is permitted to muse in troubled tones over the treatment of prisoners. Yet his ultimate use is as reinforcement of the Patriot cause through his acknowledgement of their passionate belief in it, and the way they overcome their lack of military training.

In their dominant propagandist tone, then, the plays are significant both for the locking away of the possibility of Brackenridge as British American hinted at in *The Rising Glory of America* and because they highlight the extent of the change to Brackenridge's later critique of such revolutionary excess. But the plays do anticipate that critique in one respect. They make no attempt to obscure the horrors resulting from violence. A glorious age may be born from this war, but the price will be a high one. Moreover, just as the potential of empire hovers over *The Rising Glory of America*, so here, the memory of that lost ideal lingers:

> Burst are those ties, alas! and scattered wild,
> That join'd the parent to the faithful child.[36]

This lends a piquancy to the denunciations of the British; they must be an utterly forsaken people, just as the Americans must be a chosen people, for if neither of these characterisations is true, then what is all this blood being spilt for? A similar sense of the dangerous possibilities behind revolutionary fervour also surfaced in the opening sermon from Brackenridge's collection,

The Bloody Vestiges of Tyranny. It condemned British conduct, comparing it to Cain's. But the characterisation began in a much broader frame, asking dangerous questions, extending Cain's legacy homeward, "What man is there among us who has not found in himself a sentiment of some revenge against a brother from some improper cause and principle?"[37]

Although he proceeded to draw stark distinctions between the almost angelic Americans and the almost devilish Brits, his earlier rhetorical question remained in his mind. Concluding, he emphasised, "Let fathers teach their sons the degenerate nature and the name of Englishmen."[38] Only by educating the next generation in the example of this misconduct, this failure of humanity, can America avoid going down the same path. Most presciently for his own fate, Brackenridge remarked:

> By this [enslavement] they have intended to prevent the growth of every art and science in this country; for without freedom, learning shall decay and no art can flourish.[39]

Thus, although Brackenridge was a forceful, convinced Patriot, the memory of what had gone before still lingered. Indeed, his fury against the British is reminiscent of the fury which drove Franklin: it was precisely the awareness of that which was lost which made the Revolution so painful. This recognition has a further consequence. Poems such as *The Rising Glory of America* are frequently criticised for their ludicrously overoptimistic vision of America's future. But that strained optimism makes far more sense when it is placed in this context. Because the Patriots were undertaking an act never before successfully completed, and sacrificing something many of them had deeply revered, they had to believe in the wonder of what they were creating. The expressions of certainty were so forceful precisely because they were so uncertain.

Brackenridge's observation of the war was crucial to his later writings. His writings of the time sensed the entangled nature of the arts and the new republic. Brackenridge consistently reiterated his belief that a key, perhaps the key, dimension of rising glory was an independent American culture. It was to put his belief into practice that he left the army in 1778. Returning to Philadelphia, he embarked on *The United States Magazine*, which lasted for six bimonthly issues, covering 1779. This has been praised by Frank Luther Mott as the greatest of the contemporary myriad of (mostly short-lived) magazines and periodicals.[40] *The United States Magazine* was supposed to be a literary counterpart to the military struggle which still continued. In his sermons, Brackenridge had already indicated his fear of a looming degeneracy of spirit among the Americans, even as they fought for their freedom. *The United States Magazine* aimed to combat this danger before it became serious. It is in these periodicals that Brackenridge's central concern, which informs all his writing and political activities, is first openly made clear. In the sermon, he attacked tyranny on the key point that it stifled learning. In the "Introduction" to the *United States Magazine*, he made clear that it was this ignorance which he saw as the great danger to the new society which was to emerge from military victory. He noted the key transformation which at least some Patriots hoped the Revolution would bring about, "the path to office and preferment, lies open to every individual."[41]

But, he insisted that each individual must properly prepare himself to take up that office:

> It becomes him [the humble farmer or artisan—whom Brackenridge cast as his intended audience] to obtain some knowledge of the history and principles of government, or at least to understand the policy and commerce of his own country.[42]

The magazine was intended both to educate the populace for their role in the new nation and to prove, by the success of that education, that the populace was worthy of the new nation being created by the acts of the armies. The country's fitness for independence would be further demonstrated by the successful reception of a magazine devoted to high class literary endeavour; the two entwined concerns examined in Chapter 1.

The contents of the magazine are striking. Most critics have focused on Brackenridge's second work of fiction, the serialised short story "The Cave of Vanhest," which, again, has some intriguing parallels with Crèvecoeur's *Letters*, here describing the narrator's encounter on the frontier with a family who have sought refuge there from the revolutionary turmoil. Of more interest, considering the magazine's aims, are the various political pieces, some clearly by Brackenridge, some lifted from other sources. Considering that Brackenridge is often accused of shifting political positions with monotonous regularity, there are indications here that already the preoccupations which fill the pages of *Modern Chivalry* were gnawing at him. A good example are the "Maxims for Republics," printed in the first issue, which distinguish "between power being *derived* from the people" (wholly proper in a republic), and "all power being *seated* in the bulk of the people" (likely to produce a tyranny just as much as dictatorship).[43]

Like the sermons and, in its own slighter manner, *The Rising Glory of America*, the *Magazine* conveys the confusion of mind that Brackenridge and others were suffering. Just as he proclaimed his own high hopes for the country, and his own endeavours, so he doubted those hopes. Regrettably for American letters, neither the financial situation of wartime Philadelphia nor the reading public was calculated to support such a magazine, and the final issue was published for November–December, 1779. In it, Brackenridge noted bitterly that many would doubtless be delighted at the silencing of the publication, particularly "the people who inhabit the region of stupidity, and cannot bear to have the tranquillity of their repose disturbed."[44]

For the first, but not the only, time in his career, Brackenridge declared that he was turning his back forever on public life and a literary career. Scowling, he set his shoulders to the Atlantic, and trudged off to begin a legal career in Pittsburgh, Western Pennsylvania, while the war rumbled on behind him.

COLLISIONS

> Let him be of the mind to fight from hill to hill, from vale to vale, and on every plain, until the enemy be driven back and forced to depart, until the tyrant shall give up his claim and be obliged to confess that true men, that Americans are not to be subdued.[45]

> A revolution did not suit me, nor any man else who had anything to lose, or was in a way of making something. . . . The repealing the law, by an exhibition of force, might be the only thing in view, with the people, at the moment; but I well knew they would not stop there. The opposing one law would lead to oppose another; they would finally oppose all, and demand a new modelling of the constitution; and there would be a revolution; or they would be suppressed. For my part, I had seen and heard enough of revolution, to have any wish to bear a part in one.[46]

We noted the transformation in the terms of the debate on American character crafted by the Constitution. In a moment, Brackenridge's personal involvement in that crafting will be examined. First, a little more must be said about the political situation which developed within the reestablished republic.

That situation was characterised by the reemergence of political parties. Federalists and Democratic–Republicans diverged initially over Hamilton's funding system and the power which seemed to be drifting into the hands of both the Secretary of the Treasury and his speculative followers. This breach was widened by the developing news of the French Revolution. These points of dispute are not the central issue.

For, as Hofstadter and others have noted, the country ideology which the Patriots espoused argued that parties were an evil, and their development something to be deeply feared.[47] But this belief existed alongside two other interpretations of the problem of parties. Monroe argued that because the American people, exceptionally, were basically homogenous in their class and interests, there was no need of parties in the new republic.[48] Madison, drawing on Hume, as we have seen, accepted the inevitability of parties and sought to control them.[49]

Madison is significant here because he showed an awareness of this paradox. He recognised both that parties were undesirable and that they were inevitable on account of human nature. He might also have recalled that the Revolution precisely demonstrated his fears. Yet Madison, as the 1790s progressed, would turn from this recognition, becoming the chief lieutenant of the Democratic Republican party which denied the legitimacy, the Americanness, of its opponents. This position, and its opposite, represented by Hamilton and the High Federalists, was partly predicated on the traditional denial of party legitimacy. The other side could not be legitimate because there wasn't supposed to be another side. Historians tend to give whichever side they subconsciously favour in the party dispute the benefit of the doubt on this claim, while criticising their rivals. The plain fact is that both sides were equally culpable.

Yet a third view did exist, espoused particularly by John Adams.[50] Adams, like Madison in his Federalist phase, accepted the inevitable existence of parties. He saw these parties as forming two blocks, one of aristocrats and one of the people. These divisions were inevitable, for as aspirants among the people rose, they would take on the habiliments of aristocracy and so perpetuate the division afresh. Adams' solution to the problem was the idea of a third force to balance the other two. This third force would be made up of disinterested men, a role which, as president, he would seek to play. This viewpoint is present in much of Brackenridge's career after the Revolution, and Brackenridge's fate mirrored Adams' since both discovered that virtually nobody else accepted the theory. The fact that these two politically active men attempted to put the theory into practice suggests that it deserves more serious consideration alongside the conventional narrative of the Hamilton\Jefferson battle than it has yet received.

Before turning to Brackenridge's experience, one other point must be made. That Brackenridge was as ambitious for his personal rising glory as for the nation's has been made clear. That Adams was ambitious was a criticism persistently hung about his neck. But Madison, Hamilton, Burr, and especially Jefferson were also ambitious. They covered that ambition with their specious theories; men such as Brackenridge and Adams had at least the grace of honesty, although they could be tempted, as Brackenridge was while serving in the state assembly in 1786–87.

Brackenridge's decision to abandon Philadelphia and attempt to make his fortune in the West placed him in a location peculiarly advantageous for observing these strains in the new nation's structures, which would surface first in the battles over a new Constitution and later over interpretations of that document. The decision revealed the complexities of his character, laying the groundwork for subsequent events. Partly, it was based on a financial calculation. His literary magazine had failed and, although he was now trained for the bar, competition among lawyers in Philadelphia was fierce. On the frontier he might enjoy a freer hand. His ambition to rise remained, and it is clear that he imagined that it would be easier to rise on the frontier, in legal, literary, and (though he did not openly express it) political terms. But this vision of the frontier proved to be seriously at odds with reality. Competition for legal business was equally fierce in Pittsburgh, and literary culture, in its infancy in Philadelphia, was in an even more embryonic state in the West. While Brackenridge would show uneasiness about the monied, aristocratic world of the East, he simultaneously wanted to develop literature to an eastern standard in the West.[51] His parting shot from the *Magazine* should also be borne in mind; for those inhabiting the region of stupidity existed in both worlds.

These complex motivations were demonstrated in his diverse activities in the West. Alongside his legal activities, he began a programme of cultural improvement, opening a bookstore; actively supporting the establishment of the first newspaper, the *Pittsburgh Gazette*, in 1786; and founding Pittsburgh Academy, which subsequently became a university. But he also turned his attention firmly towards politics, successfully gaining election to the state assembly in 1786, and subsequently becoming involved in the local battle over the new Constitution.[52]

Two significant collisions with the views of the majority of his constituents then occurred, significant in themselves and because a disconnection between Brackenridge's proclaimed loyalties and his actual behaviour would also emerge during the Whiskey Rebellion, with more serious consequences. While it is important to recognise Brackenridge's failings, these do not invalidate the significance of the principles of political action he strove to advance.

During the 1786 election, Brackenridge specifically promised to support a law to allow Western settlers to pay for their lands with state certificates of indebtedness. Concluding that these certificates were mostly falling into the hands of eastern speculators, he changed his mind and opposed the law. He was duly attacked by his Western rivals, led by William Findley:

> [He is] a gentleman who professes the greatest acquired abilities, and most shining imagination, [but who] makes a prey of the people's confidence, betrays their interests and trifles with his own solemn profession, he may expect the people to look upon him with indignation and treat him with contempt.[53]

This political feud dragged on until the Whiskey Rebellion in 1794. This particular collision shows the clearest contrast between the role Brackenridge desired to inhabit, and the one he actually performed. In one of his *Pittsburgh Gazette* responses, Brackenridge set out his ideal clearly:

> From this oath [of office] it must appear that a representative is not supposed to be a mere machine, like a clock wound up, to run for many hours in the same way; he is sent to hear from others, and to think for himself, as well as to vote . . . [54]

Supporting testimonials also appeared in the *Pittsburgh Gazette*, at least one of them from an Easterner:

I am well convinced that Mr Brackenridge went to Philadelphia divested of any party views, and meant to take that advantage of the parties as might best enable him to serve the country he represented.[55]

Yet it is clear that Brackenridge did vote against perceived Western interests in some cases, and the possibility that he hoped thereby to gain political preferment from the Eastern members of the Assembly cannot be ruled out, despite those hopes, if hopes they were, being disappointed. The insults he heaped upon Findley in the press, calling him "vermin," questioning the paternity of his children, and labelling him a drunk, challenge his claims to the character of a gentlemanly representative of nonpartisan judgement.[56]

The second collision is somewhat less murky. Again in contradiction to the dominant Western view and his fellow western representatives, Brackenridge staunchly defended the new Constitution. This exacerbated the mutual antagonism of the two sides, particularly for Brackenridge when he was rejected as a delegate to the state ratifying convention. In the assembly, both sides adopted dubious tactics—the Easterners exploiting their dominance to push for acceptance of the Convention and the resultant document, the Westerners going into hiding to ensure the Assembly lacked a quorum. As before, Brackenridge compounded his situation by responding in print against both Findley and the folly of the voters, introducing the character of Teague for the first time, who would become a central figure of *Modern Chivalry*:

> "What wonder then that this Teague Regan,
> Like Asteroth, or idol Dagan,
> Should here receive our reverence
> In spite of truth and common sense;
> Men in all ages are the same,
> And nature is herself to blame,
> Who has not given to all an eye,
> Of sapience and philosophy.[57]

It is worth noting here that the character who becomes representative of a much broader swathe of Americans started life as a nasty slur against a more successful political rival who specifically was not an Irish Catholic labourer. Although this whole episode exposes the fragility of Brackenridge's claims to a certain position in society, it must also be acknowledged that, in the struggle over ratification, the evidence for Brackenridge's "treachery" to Western interests is less clear-cut than in the former case.

These episodes anticipated several dimensions of Brackenridge's role in the Whiskey Rebellion. While there was the element of personal ambition, this was tied to a specific view about the mode of political action—one compromised over the debt issue, but much less so in the Rebellion. These were tied to a broader view about the educated taking a lead in public affairs, and being permitted to instruct the ignorant, with the written word as a crucial element. In these earlier episodes, reason clearly gave way to passion and insult on both sides, and Brackenridge's pretensions were noticeably weaker than in the case of the Rebellion or in *Modern Chivalry*, but the presence of the principle, however compromised, is significant. Finally, these episodes indicated the dangerous tendencies of a political climate which demanded a clear and sustained choice of sides, a position already at odds with Brackenridge's theory of the role of the individual politician, if not yet completely with his practice. And already in these skirmishes, Brackenridge was forced to a period of silence, recalling Crèvecoeur's journey into the silence of the frontier at the conclusion of *Letters*. As Brackenridge put it:

> Pride and good policy would not permit me to leave the country, until I had conquered the prejudice; I knew that to be practicable, by lying by until the popular fury should waste itself; it required time but I had patience. But it was necessary for me to be silent, and add nothing more to the popular odium.[58]

The Whiskey Rebellion would see many of these tendencies played out, but in a far tenser environment, and with far severer consequences both for Brackenridge and the principles he sought to champion.

That Rebellion was a dispute which broke out between the western provinces of Pennsylvania (and to a lesser extent the neighbouring provinces of Virginia), and the federal government in the early 1790s, over the excise tax on whiskey. This tax had been instituted by Alexander Hamilton as part of his program of federal finance which had to pay off the Revolutionary War debts, and aimed, by raising the revenue to do so, to tie the populace into the Union. Instead, in the case of the whiskey tax in Pennsylvania, the policy looked likely to drive men from the Union.[59]

The economic problem the farmers faced stemmed from their being on one side of the Alleghany mountains, while their markets were on the other. Grain transportation was thus expensive, and the cheapest method was to distill the grain into whiskey and transport it by water. The shortage of hard currency had also made whiskey a key unit of barter. Further, the tax fell unfairly on the smaller businessman because it was levelled on the capacity of the still rather than the volume of whiskey produced.

The situation was exacerbated by a combination of federal failings and a wrapping of the whole in language and ideas inherited from the Revolution. The federal failings arose from a national attitude to the West which mirrored the dismissive attitude of the state assembly. Alternative markets might have been accessed via the Mississippi, an issue pushed by Brackenridge during his term in the assembly, but the federals failed to secure this. Most of the farmers in the area rented their land from absentee landlords, including prominent federal office-holders. The nearest available free land lay in Ohio, but federal forces had recently been defeated by the Indians there.

Western underrepresentation in government provided an obvious explanation for these failures. Westerners could perceive that they lacked the political clout to ensure that their problems were taken seriously.

What gave these grievances their power was the use of the rhetoric of the American Revolution by the rebels, who claimed that the new systems of government were falling victim to precisely those evils which, when perpetrated by the British, resulted in Revolution. Making this connection led, in some minds, inexorably to the same logical conclusion which forced itself on the Continental Congress. Those opposed to the tax moved slowly to a call for secession from the new Union. That the idea of secession was opposed by many (and very probably the majority), that it would almost certainly have failed, and that the question was never put to military settlement, are all good points. But they do not remove the fact that the question was raised, nor that many, both in the government and among the rebels, took it seriously, Hugh Henry Brackenridge among them.

Brackenridge's nature was bound to embroil him in the dispute. He had written about, and participated in, every important political discussion since his arrival in the area and this was to be no exception. Indeed, he had already defended a group of men for attacking an excise office, which also called forth a *National Gazette* article from his pen urging that the federal authorities treat the matter gently, that they recognise the degree of mistrust of them present on the frontier. The federal government, unsurprisingly, took no notice.

A brief clarification of terms is here necessary. "Revolution" referred both to the memory of the American Revolution and, for Brackenridge, to the more recent example of the French Revolution. Brackenridge understood it to mean the overthrowing of the existing government and its replacement by some other form. "Rebellion" embraced the specific acts by which that government was going to be overthrown, whose total effect would be a revolution. "Secession" implied the breaking of the Union, as the patriots had broken the first British Empire between 1776 and 1783. The ownership and meaning of these terms was being contested by the various parties, and Brackenridge saw himself as holding a particular role in that contest because of his revolutionary experience. He was especially equipped to judge the correct application of these ideas.

Brackenridge's situation was complicated by two factors—first, his mere attempt to navigate between government and rebels at all, but second, because that attempt contained sufficient inconsistencies to exacerbate the suspicions of both sides, already raised by the mere attempt.

The principle he tried to apply was that of the dogma of balance, previously expressed through the mouth of Bombo, and by persistent reference to the ancient Greek legislator, Solon. Solon undertook various reforms of the Athenian political system, and his writings suggested that he saw himself as trying to achieve a compromise between the demands of rich and poor and finding himself despised by both—similarly did Brackenridge see himself striving for balance between the two sides in a more complex evolution of his stance as a state assemblyman. Once again, he was not wholly disinterested. In the Rebellion, he glimpsed an opportunity, by becoming a latter day Solon, to achieve the political status he believed he deserved, to find his rising glory. Yet it is too simple to see this as mere personal ambition; the republic depended on it. This was bound up with Brackenridge's revolutionary past. Because of that past, he conceived a particular right to guide people through this similar controversy. But that right was not merely an individual one but also concerned the character of the republic. For the sake of the republic, as much as for his own, such a role had to be possible. The old Revolutionary needed to be heeded.

He described his experiences in the Rebellion the following year in *Incidents of the Insurrection*. This book deserves far more consideration than it has yet received,[60] because of the significance of the failure it chronicled. Brackenridge was partly concerned with personal rehabilitation. The extent to which this turns the narrative into a questionable source is mitigated first because the manner of the attempt mitigates against that rehabilitation—that is, Brackenridge either fails or chose not to expunge his failings, and second, because the conflicts between how he wished to have acted and how he actually acted are the more revealing of the plight in which his political principles landed him, and the consequent flaws in the new republic. However, taking the potential bias independent of that, it is worth noting that the other major contemporary account, written by Brackenridge's long-term political rival, William Findley, despite neglecting Brackenridge in the bulk of the account substantially accepted the truth of *Incidents* towards the end of his book.

Turning then to *Incidents* itself: as with most of Brackenridge's writing, the book is bedevilled by a multitude of agendas and approaches. Partly, it attempts to tell the story of the Rebellion, primarily from Brackenridge's perspective. This gives it a curious flavour, almost creating a sort of relived history with Brackenridge as the central protagonist, perhaps the unrecognised hero. By describing the flow of events, without the benefit of hindsight, Brackenridge sought to make clear his motives at each point in the drama. Initially, Brackenridge claimed it as an attempt to rehabilitate his reputation:

> What I write is with a view to explain my own conduct, which has not been understood, it is possible I may not be able to remove the misconception of every one. I am aware how difficult it is to change opinions even with the best cause on my side.[61]

Yet, this end was pursued by a curious route. Indeed, the work has something of an element of memoir to it, "I regarded my memory for the sake of my family."[62]

More critically, it damns many leading locals, the federal government, and the people themselves. This approach, and the very fact of the work, convincingly illustrate the transformation that has occurred since his decision to stay silent after the Constitution debacle. Brackenridge still wished for a place in public life but he was determined this time to have it only on his own terms. The lesson was becoming more important than the outcome.

There is one final important point to be made before turning to the detail of the book. Brackenridge may have conceived himself as heroic, but he was not infallible. He is no more perfect in the story that he tells than any of those whom he describes. Yet the limitations which emerge make his experience the more compelling and important. *Incidents* described an American attempt to rise: the fact that that attempt was rejected gave a chilling warning about the type of risings which the new republic permitted.

The book itself begins with a headlong plunge into the confrontation, with rebels threatening to burn down the house of one of the excise inspectors.[63] Brackenridge sets out with others to try and restrain the mob, convinced that persuasion may prove efficacious. In this case, they arrive too late, and the violent tone of the mob leads them to retreat before they reach the arena of violence. Thus, Brackenridge's declaration of his willingness to incur popular disfavour by opposing the violence rings somewhat hollow. Since he subsequently abided by it, it is worth taking some note of the content. He emphasised that his performance of such a role would destroy his credit with the people. He acknowledged that it would go against his own ambition, since his name had just gone forward as an assembly candidate. Finally, he made a rhetorical judgement on the longer term consequences:

> It may be said, I would have obtained credit afterwards with the people themselves, for preventing what in cool reflection they would see would have been dangerous. With some I might have obtained credit, but with the far greater part, I would not.[64]

The violence that Brackenridge condemned rapidly breeds further violence. The mood is particularly inflamed when the rebels succeed in intercepting letters in the mail from local notables which are critical of their conduct. Brackenridge's comparison of the popular mood with past occasions is striking:

> I had seen the spirit which prevailed at the time of the Stamp Act, and at the commencement of the revolution from the government of Great Britain; but it was by no means so general, and so vigorous, amongst the common people, as the spirit which now existed in this country.

This is a fascinating statement on a number of levels. It presents the familiar connection between the present insurrection and the Patriot movement in the coming of the Revolution. But it also reminds the reader that not everybody supported that movement, any more than they support the present uprising. And, crucially, Brackenridge knew what he was talking about. He was a direct witness to the revolutionary events he refers to here, and, as we have seen, he was at least implicitly aware of the possibilities of the other side. And yet, despite his championing of the principle of revolution, first as a patriot and right up to the execution of Louis XVI, Brackenridge now changed sides, arguing grimly:

> The opposing one law, would lead to oppose another; they [the people] would finally oppose all, and demand a new modelling of the constitution; and there would be a revolution; or they would be suppressed.[65]

That feeling that the end must be immensely worthy to justify the bloodshed, occasionally visible in the early plays, is now centre stage. On this occasion, the end is not sufficiently worthy, but Brackenridge, recalling the bloody pictures of his revolutionary writings, implied that the price may always be too high, "For my part, I had seen and heard enough of revolution, to have any wish to bear a part in one."

In the face of this violence, Brackenridge reflected on the impossibility of the remaining option, "to lie by was impossible; no man would be suffered to remain neutral. I thought, therefore, of emigrating."[66]

Neutrality was no more possible in 1794 than it had been in 1776. The difference for Brackenridge, the fervent revolutionary, was that he now found himself in the position he essentially dismissed in the earlier revolution. And the problem was equally profound for, as Brackenridge recognised, what was at stake was also the same; it was the issue of what precisely it meant to be an American. If Brackenridge could not endure as a citizen of the republic, what did that imply for that republic?

At this point, Brackenridge's despair was still containable. He did not yet flee. Instead, remaining in Pittsburgh, he now embarked upon his self-posed challenge of mitigating the extremes of the mob, whose next move was to march on Pittsburgh, demanding the offending letter writers be handed over, or the town would be burned. Brackenridge deployed his greatest scorn here against those men who were intelligent enough to see the dangers but who stood idly by, or went along with the majority for fear of their fate if they did not:

> It was impossible to know the real sentiments of almost anyone amongst the multitude, how far they were there from necessity or of choice.

This was, and so Hamilton recognised it, the crux of the matter. If the rebels could truly claim to speak for the American people then their claims must be met, otherwise the very principles of the American Revolution were denied. Hamilton, naturally, denied that the rebels spoke for the people. Brackenridge straddled both positions. Seeing the strength of popular feeling, he argued that it was exacerbated by the fact that unscrupulous individuals in positions of power went along with, rather than seeking to restrain, the mob. It was precisely that restraining role which he sought to perform, a practical act of educating the masses to compare with the paper education attempted in the *United States Magazine*.

To a degree, he succeeded, although the ultimate unwillingness of the rebels actually to shed blood, demonstrated on several occasions in *Incidents*, and the clear fact that the federal government was not going to back down, may have assisted in this. But Brackenridge's victory, if such it was, came at a heavy price. For neither side appeared able to accept the possibility that conscience might force men to stand between the two. Thus, Brackenridge found himself persistently under suspicion from the more unruly elements of the rebels, to whom many of his fellow gentlemen were kowtowing, while, simultaneously, discovering a conviction on the part of the federal representatives that he was a rebel.

His predicament reached a climax when the federal militia eventually arrived in Pittsburgh. Rumours were flying that he was to be summarily executed by them, and attempts were made upon his life. His attempts to reason with the officers and to explain himself to the troops were rebuffed and he found himself practically under house arrest. Musing on this, Brackenridge again emphasised the central lesson of his experience:

> I reflected that people would always talk more than they would do; and that putting me to death would be more in the language, than in the intention of the mass. . . . But I reflected also, that this very strain of talking, though not originating from intention of act . . . yet might lead some inconsiderate and unprincipled men to perpetrate what they heard spoken of.[67]

Brackenridge's sense of the danger of demagoguery, of the potential for unwise speech to fuel uncontrollable passions, is striking. He followed it up with an astounding analysis of Hamilton's motivations. The funding system, let us remember, was designed to bind both the wealthier elements and the populace to the Union. Here it has almost split the Union apart, raising fundamental questions about the right to rebellion and the location of power. Brackenridge now argued that it was in Hamilton's interest to find the rebellion the work of a seditious few, to remove the potentially dangerous imputation that a popular movement had been crushed by a tyrannical government. Again, what is of paramount interest here, are not the questions of whether a revolution was really likely, or of whether it could have succeeded, but the view taken by contemporaries of these events, and the interpretations they made of them. Critical are two points. This rebellion is not supposed to be going on in the first place, but, if it must go on, it certainly should not be being dealt with in this manner. Brackenridge was an old Revolutionary. If even he was now threatened under the name of traitor, which he clearly was, it suggests that something had gone seriously wrong in the dream of a "more perfect Union."

Freshly disillusioned on the frontier, as he was in Pittsburgh, Brackenridge, awaiting anticipated arrest, reconsidered the example of Solon, from Plutarch's *Lives*:

> I meditated upon his [Solon's] laws, making it death for a citizen, in any civil tumult, not to take a part; for by taking a part, on one side or the other, the moderate citizens will be divided, and mixing with the violent, will correct the fury, on both sides, until an accomodation can be brought about.

This, Brackenridge argued, was the course he had been pursuing during the Insurrection. He regarded it as, at best, but a partial failure:

> I saw that the laws of Solon would apply chiefly to a small republic, where the moderate men were known to each other, and could explain themselves in the course of the negotiation.

This he now saw as the explanation for the Federal government having suspected him.[68] He also saw it as resistant to improvement. So, once again, Brackenridge declared his retreat from such public service:

> If the like scene should happen again, I will not conduct myself on the principle of Solon's law. Let people that are to be expelled, get out of the country the best way they can, and let the executives and insurgents settle their own negotiations; I will have nothing to do with them.[69]

We have travelled a considerable distance from the man who had negotiated with the mob outside Pittsburgh several months earlier at some risk to his life.

Before leaving the Rebellion, we may note the other version of his experiences, which Brackenridge told through the fictional medium of *Modern Chivalry*. In this case, the folly of the people extends to those in power, most notably the president, who appoints Teague (Farrago's Irish servant) to the post of an excise officer. Brackenridge follows this up, through Farrago, with an acerbic comment on Washington's (who is not directly named) appointments policy, in the name of encouraging Teague to conduct himself properly in his new office:

> The President of the United States . . . is said to have the virtue, or rather the excess of one, never to abandon the person whom he has once taken up; or at least to carry his attachment to an extreme of reluctance in that particular; whether owing to great slowness in conceiving

unfavourably of any one; or to pride of mind, in an unwillingness to have it thought that his judgement could be fallible.[70]

This is striking both for the critique of Washington, whose subordinates bear the brunt of criticism in *Incidents*, and for the broader moral it points up, that all are equally subject to the frailties of humanity, even so great a man as Washington.

The rebellion, then, follows much the same course as in *Incidents*: we see, again, the dangers of the mob as it threatens to set upon Teague, and the subsequent danger to the Captain when he tries to reason with them. This he does in a forthright manner, which is suggestive of the kind of line Brackenridge would have liked but did not dare to take in reality:

> Is it not a principle of that republican government which you have established, that the will of the majority shall govern; and has not the will of the majority of the United States enacted this law?[71]

Farrago also pursues a second course that Brackenridge had debated and rejected, fleeing from the scene after Teague's office is burnt down. In an intriguing coda, master and servant meet an émigré French aristrocrat who has retired into the wilderness. The link is again drawn between the two Revolutions, the émigré insisting:

> [He considered the Captain] in the light of an emigrant with himself, having been obliged to abscond, from sans culotte rage, and popular fervour, which, though not of the same height with that in France, yet was of the same nature, and different only in degree.[72]

Secluded in the wilderness, Farrago and the Frenchman proceed to a wide-ranging discussion of the Revolutions within their respective countries, a discussion in which, ultimately, they are pretty nearly in agreement since the question comes down to one simple point. No matter what means may be devised for a change in systems of government, and no matter how justified it may appear, violence will still result. The direct case in question is France, but the application may be extended to America, since the example, the excise rebellion, is playing itself out beyond their wilderness seclusion, even as they engage in their discussions:

> [For] reform once begun, it was found impossible to arrest it at a middle point. It may be resolved into a thousand causes but the great cause was the insatiable nature of the human mind, that will not be contented with what is moderate. For though there were doubtless a considerable portion of the nobility who were opposed to any diminution of their power and pageantry; yet . . . as great an evil existed in the wish of

extreme equality in others; or rather, a wish to bring all things to a perfect level, that from thence they might begin to ascend themselves.[73]

Brackenridge, having at the outset of both revolutions, revelled in the wonderful prospects before each country, was damning them. But he was also offering a way out. Obliquely, by publishing the example of his conduct, in a variety of media, he still sought to influence the public. Publication, in this sense, gave the lie to his *insistence* that he was washing his hands of the whole affair. It remained the best means of articulating his position: at one remove from the passions of public speaking which so often only played into the hands of the mob.

A period of temporary success seems to have resulted. Between this section of *Modern Chivalry*, dated 1797, and the next, dated 1804, a period of relative literary silence occurred, during which Brackenridge was an active, although again unsuccessful, candidate for the Democratic–Republican campaign in the state elections of 1798, for which participation Governor Thomas McKean of Pennsylvania elevated him to a state judgeship. He was also involved in the campaigns of 1800. His motivation for this renewed political involvement seems somewhat obscure. Perhaps he was moved by a respect for Albert Gallatin, a key Republican figure in the state, with whom he had cooperated during the Rebellion. Perhaps he genuinely now saw the Republicans as the best hope for putting his principles into practice, a further indication that his hopes for a rebirth of society were not yet completely dead. Perhaps he still yearned for political office, now a lost cause with the Federalists. It may well have been a combination of all these factors.[74]

What must not be forgotten is that, regardless of this period of literary silence and continued political activity, the experience of the Whiskey Rebellion could not be wholly erased. The memory of his failure remained with Brackenridge. Soon, a new extremism would make itself apparent to him, and the pen would start to sketch a new adventure for Farrago and Teague. But, although the land would be new, the lesson would be exactly, devastatingly, the same.

ENDURING

> . . . I do not conceive myself to be, what I will acknowledge, I was once disposed to think myself, a thing endued with faculties above the capacity of ordinary mortals. But had it not been that I had some idea of this kind, I would not have made the exertions that I have made.[75]

I feel myself disposed to bring this volume to a conclusion; not that I have said the thousandth part of what I have to say, but because I wish to ly [sic] by a while until I see what effect what I have said, may have upon the community. I do not mean as to any approbation of the work, for that is of little moment; but what reform it may work in morals, and manners of the people. It is for them I labour, though perhaps they may little thank me for it.[76]

Brackenridge's career after the Whiskey Rebellion continued to be marked by the twin, mutually informing, occupations of politics and literature. But these principles were now tempered by increasing despair concerning both his personal prospects and the effect on society his writings might be expected to have.

It is of key importance that Brackenridge was constant in his principles, even though this was sometimes obscured by his humour and his style. That these are more frequently stated in Part Two of *Modern Chivalry* (1804–1815) arose from the deeper experiences Brackenridge had received, but it was only a question of frequency. The principles were the same and at their heart was the dogma of balance. Accepting this, the confusion of *Modern Chivalry's* structure, the muddled narrative of *Incidents*, Brackenridge's oscillation between East and West, between Republican and Federalist, acquires a deeper logic. We have shown this dogma at work upon the small scale of the Whiskey Rebellion, but it also abides as a key note throughout *Modern Chivalry*, the work for which Brackenridge is best known. It is present from the outset, but obtains a deeper power and emotion, as Brackenridge's practical experiences began to infect the narrative, and his trust in the good qualities of the people to ebb away. *Modern Chivalry* is thus no mere burlesque on frontier life, but a series of variations on this vital political theme.[77] This analysis is informed by seeing the book in two halves, although the final section of Part One, dating from 1797 anticipated the mindset and altered approach which dominated Part Two. But these two halves are not concerned with different principles, rather, in Part One the principles are subordinated to the literary endeavour. In Part Two, this is reversed. After the Whiskey Rebellion, amusement was insufficient, it was now necessary to instruct.[78]

Brackenridge first began work on the book that would become *Modern Chivalry* in 1788–9. Then the work took the form of a poem, *The Modern Chevalier*, principally concerned with satirising William Findley's involvement in the ratification of the Constitution.[79] The poem anticipated the multiple narrators of the prose version. In this, both book and poem were falling into the tradition of Crèvecoeur's assumption of Farmer James, Franklin's various personae, and the multiple narrators of Irving's *Sketch Book*. So, here, we see in the Chevalier, Farrago, in Traddle, Teague, and in,

> this writer in Gazette
> He is a rascally marmozette[80]

the personage of Brackenridge himself. Important themes are also visible, notably the problem of those without the capacity for it entering politics, summed up in this unhappy rhyme:[81]

> The saying hits th' nail on th' head;
> "Let every cobler stick t' his trade,"[82]

But the poem takes care to make clear that it is not the trades of these "lower" people to which objection is made, but their apparent determination to step outside their stations. Also striking, as a more poetic summary of Brackenridge's motives than is often apparent in the prose text, is the Chevalier's description of his role:

> Am of the order, and a Knight
> Whose object is to set things right;
> Depress th' unworthy and raise up
> The preferable to the top,
> And injury and force restrain
> Of warriors sword, or writers pen,
> Distributing best services
> And keeping commonwealth in peace.[83]

The humorous tone of the poem persisted in the early instalments of *Modern Chivalry*. Here the focus is most clearly on the adventures of Captain Farrago and his Irish servant, Teague. These fall into two categories. Farrago plans the journey as an observation of the country, while Teague manages to embroil himself in every incident they come upon.[84] Throughout the book, these adventures are interspersed with the reflections of a narrator. In Part One, the narrator can seem merely another character. In Part Two, Brackenridge spoke much more directly through that narrator, as the focus moves to the broader theories, rather than Teague's specific adventures.

It is upon those adventures that Part One is focused, as Teague seeks any number of positions for which he is unsuited, from Congressman, to philosopher, to Indian chief. The first of these almost exactly replayed the debate of *The Modern Chevalier*, but expressed the central theme with important clarity. Both the narrator and Farrago decry, as Brackenridge did in the poem, the desire of unfit people to become statesmen, but the narrator also emphasises that there are equal fools among both rich and poor:

> Genius and virtue are independent of rank and fortune; and it is neither the opulent, nor the indigent, but the man of ability and integrity that ought to be called forth to serve his country.[85]

Madisonian principles are also advanced here, the narrator suggesting that it is out of the conjunction and opposition of these forces that the country is enabled to move forward. Crucially, here, the book still has faith in the capacities of the people, "The people are a sovereign, and greatly despotic; but, in the main, just."[86]

In these early sections, there is more humour than anger about Teague's behaviour; indeed, Farrago's main complaint about it seems to be that he is perennially threatened under the new system with the loss of his servant. But it turns out that this personal loss has profound implications and, again, illustrates Brackenridge's central point, clearly demonstrated in a striking exchange over slavery. Both the narrator and Farrago weigh in here with such complex reasoning that it is difficult to tell to which side the reader is expected to adhere. Teague has again slipped from his master's side and taken up acting, and Farrago decides to replace him with a slave. He is challenged by a Quaker who asks whether, considering his appearance of learning, he can reconcile slavery with his principles. Farrago retorts that all nature is governed by such a system:

> What right have you to invade the liberty of a playful young colt, more than of an African inhabitant?[87]

The Quaker asserts that "there is a difference . . . a negro is a human creature, and possesses all the natural rights of man."[88] Farrago's response is a profound blow to these principles:

> But what are the natural rights of man? Are they not finally resolvable, as in the inanimate world, into power on the one hand, and weakness on the other.[89]

If this were not sufficiently clear, Farrago then spells it out, "there should be master and servant, or in other words owner and slave."[90]

A disturbing dimension is thus added to the confrontations we have, up until now, often laughed at. And Farrago does not stop there. He complains that having a servant is problematical because the servant retains the right to retire from the position and to haggle over wages. It is much better, then, to have a slave. Now Farrago hits on his most crucial point, arguing that there is the capacity, nay, the desire for slavery in every man:

> Why is it, that even after the convulsion of a revolution in a government, in favour of liberty, there is a natural tendency to slavery; and it finally terminates in this point. The fact is, a state of liberty is an unnatural state.[91]

There is absurdity in the example that follows, that Caesar made a good leader but would have made a lousy valet and, of course, the Quaker is able to take the easy way out, sticking to his denunciation of what we would today regard as Farrago's racism. But it leaves aside the broader, equally worrying, question of the consequences of turning society topsy-turvy which Farrago and Teague's adventures have explored.

The narrator now weighs in with a series of arguments and mockeries. He denounces the churches, among whom only the Quakers have declared against slavery:

> The assemblies or synods of the Presbyterian church, or conventions of the Episcopal, in America, have said nothing on this subject. Is an omission of this kind reconcilable with the idea, that it is a natural evil, or a moral wrong.[92]

Then he comments that those involved in the slave trade must be ruined if it is immediately abolished, just as criminals must be ruined if forced to desist instantly from their criminality. Therefore:

> I have always thought a defect in the criminal codes of most nations, not giving licence to the perpetrators of offences, to proceed, for a limited time . . . until they get their hands out of use to these pursuits, and in use to others.[93]

But all this tends to a quite astonishing conclusion. In this case, and contrary to his general principles, one must have either total subjugation or total abolition, in order to be morally right. For, any gradual response is simply condoning a moral failing on one side or the other. Now, this might appear to make a mockery of Brackenridge's consistency, but the reasoning is not so simple. Rather, Brackenridge again shows that any position may tend to folly, that there may be as much foolishness in a compromise as in an extreme. In this instance, it almost seems that the world is simply mad and there is nothing that can be done about it.[94] Yet there is a further possibility that before slavery, there is simply no solution, that it is so complex a problem that even Brackenridge's brand of humour cannot laugh it away.

Significantly, in addressing slavery and a number of other issues, Brackenridge's work placed itself in a continuum, begun with Crèvecoeur and followed through in the work of Irving and his contemporaries. Thus, the vexed question of appearance and reality is again present, most obviously in the question of whether Teague, as an Irishman, really does accurately reflect his character:

> I shall say nothing of the character of this man, because the very name imparts what he was.[95]

But the fact of Teague's presentation in various assumed roles is more serious. When he is canvassed for the role of Indian chief, the network of fraud encompasses everybody. The government is too ill informed to penetrate such fraud, yet the fraudster is equally guilty, although he blithely points out,

It is a very common thing for men to speculate now a-days. If you will not, another will.[96]

Thus, the fearful doctrine of the slavery discussion is anticipated, and Farrago remarks, almost rhetorically, "Is it possible that such deception can be practiced in a new country."[97]

Yet Farrago proceeds to make such a deception entirely practicable, for although he condemns the deception privately, he refuses to denounce it in public.

More serious still are the larger conclusions implied by these episodes but less regularly spelled out. Thus, after yet another attempt by Teague to gain preferment, the narrator draws the broader moral, ladling on his favourite classical allusions, "for mankind in all ages have had the same propensity to magnify what was small, and elevate the low."[98]

Again, this is to recall Crèvecoeur's gloomy discovery that Americans suffer from the same flaws as any other people, a position diametrically opposed to the rhetoric of the rising glory with which Brackenridge's career had begun.

The early sections of *Modern Chivalry* provide further evidence of the unease that had already seeped into Brackenridge's soul, clearly datable to the imbroglio over the Constitution. As we have seen, the Whiskey Rebellion significantly deepened those concerns. It is the shadow of that experience, coupled with Brackenridge's disenchantments over the Jeffersonian ascendancy, which give the greater weight to Part Two of the work, a disenchantment which is concerned with far more than the fate of the judicial system. Part Two, in fact, becomes a miniature history of the republic, in which Brackenridge refounds America and tells the story all over again. This attempt to encompass America anticipated Irving's *History*, although the latter improved upon Brackenridge's sprawling style. Brackenridge also evolved specific satires on the themes of economy and logocracy (there being a superfluity of talk in the new republic). These were themes Irving worked more successfully in *Salmagundi* and *A History of New York*. Given that they were contemporaries during this second period of composition, it is interesting to speculate on who was influencing whom.

The breadth of Brackenridge's focus means that there are notable aspects to virtually every chapter. We focus here on the opening, and two themes which are intertwined across the second and third volumes; the continuing adventures of Farrago and Teague, and Brackenridge's reflections on recent political history. These are given through the same narrational voice which accompanies the voyagers throughout, but this is now Brackenridge without the mask.

The opening of Part Two does suggest a shift in the overt intentions of the book, although the mere fact of the narrator now openly expressing them does not remove their earlier presence. Now, it is baldly stated that, "I

mean this tale of a Captain travelling, but as a vehicle to my way of thinking on some subjects."[99]

The opening sections also emphasise, removing earlier confusion, that we
are not meant to take Farrago as a paragon anymore than Teague. For the
mess in which the village has gotten itself is a condemnation of his advice:

> Is this the satisfaction that I have, in returning amongst you after an
> absence of several years, to see man armed against man, and war waged
> not only in the very bosom of the republic, but in the village which I
> have instructed by many precepts?[100]

The detail of these principles was not always clearly stated, mirroring Farrago's confusion, but the work's central theme was and remained clear.
Here it is applied to a fresh case, a newspaper war:

> The people are divided, as will always be the case, if for no other cause,
> yet for the sake of division; because the pride of one man forbids him to
> think just as another does.[101]

This theme is, indeed. continually emphasised through the remainder
of the book, a fact which has formed the focus of much literary criticism.
But it is precisely this persistence, and the breadth of occasions upon which
Brackenridge turned it loose, which are so important. Again and again
he fires off remarks, sometimes in an almost throw-away manner, which
threatens to undermine the conventional picture of the new republic. Thus,
he readdressed the question of Teague's origins and asserted that he was
drawn from a Irish model for:

> The Americans have in fact, yet, no character; neither the clown, nor
> the gentleman. So that I could not take one from our own country;
> which I would much rather have done, as the scene lay here.[102]

This section also contains a discussion of celebrations on the Fourth of
July. Teague having been selected to give an oration, the captain muses on
the meaning of the day:

> The celebration of our national anniversary, will no doubt, be contin-
> ued while the union of these states exists. It may be continued by the
> parts probably after a dis-union; an event certain, and inevitable; but
> which, the wise and the good delight to contemplate as remote; and not
> likely to happen for innumerable ages.[103]

That a disaster will attend the republic if such men as Teague are allowed
to rise is nothing new in the narrative, but the sense of threat on all

fronts, this poisoning of even the national anniversary, is an especially striking example.

The interspersion of the two narratives actually began in Part Two Volume One, which described Brackenridge's attack on those who wished to dispense with the federal judiciary system. As a result of this and the broader folly to which it points, the Captain despaired of the village where he had, up to now, dispensed his wisdom. He, Teague, and a hodgepodge of followers set off into the West. Farrago takes his departure grimly:

> I will leave you for a while, and call off the bog-trotter to another ramble. Considering it as a banishment in fact, though not in name; and adopting the language of some under like circumstances, I will wish, *that the village may never have occasion to remember me or my observations*.[104]

After journeying through various settlements, including one where all learning is despised, which necessitates the gagging of the school teacher in their company, they arrive in country bordering on Indian settlements. America is now founded all over again, for here:

> Everyone that was in distress; and everyone that was discontented, gathered themselves unto him.[105]

The Captain is duly appointed governor, and the whole is described in glowing terms highly reminiscent of Crèvecoeur's new country:

> It has seemed to me that the streams run clearer in a new country than the old; they are certainly more abundant. . . . The emigrants coming also, from different quarters, and hitherto unknown to each other, do not bring with them latent or professed enmities: and the mind . . . is open wholly for new impressions.[106]

This is followed up by the crafting of a Constitution for the new settlement, with the various problems of governance revisited, this time through a satirical jibe at that famous phrase, "We the people:"

> Another question arose; was every man that wore a head, tag, rag, and bobtail, to assemble, and have a vote? . . ."We the people," admits of no exclusion. But are people to be admitted who have no understanding? Who can undertake to say of another that he wants sense?[107]

It is as if Brackenridge has gone back to the future. In this second part of the work, burdened by Brackenridge's experience of the history of the republic, there seems a desire to restate the importance of remembering how the country has got into the present situation. But this history has a crucial contemporary and future relevance for Brackenridge:

> But it is with a view to secure future times, that these things are handed down. For the cupidity of man still continuing the same, the like convulsions at no distant day will occur, and unless well-managed, will terminate in the overthrow of liberty.[108]

Yet, this brave reassertion of principle is mired in futility. It is as if, each time it is reexpressed in the hope of its being adopted, the author has to forget that he has already expressed the same principle numerous times, to no avail. The whole thing is clouded by a necessary, but frightening, amnesia. There must be a belief that the admonitions will have an effect, that a refounding of the republic is possible even though the very frequency of the assertion denies it.

This moral is, indeed, doubly pointed. For Brackenridge promptly showed the new settlement falling into the errors of the old. The various inhabitants, with Teague at their head, clamour for office. A weaver, who is not appointed, then starts clamouring for fresh amendments to the Constitution:

> A second chance he would have at all events, and it might be more favourable in the result; inasmuch as the very bustle he was making in the affair of the new constitution, would bring him into great notice, and increase his popularity, there being now an indifferent mass of citizens who were dissentients from the same motives with himself, and might promise themselves something from the confusion of affairs.[109]

Not only does the bulk of the populace rapidly sign on to this scheme, but they do so with a grossly inflated idea of what a constitution can accomplish, imagining it can beget them harvests without the trouble of sowing seeds and other such inflated fantasies.[110]

This fable of the new settlement reaches its climax in a debate over whether the vote should be extended to animals. The issue of gradations of humanity, which we earlier saw explored in the context of slavery, is recalled. The example of the civilisation of the savages is advanced to support the argument. Brackenridge's tendency to racism is again evident, since he appears to side against the savages here, but again his sense of natural gradations of humanity is more important. The equal folly of the White man is demonstrated when the meeting catches sight of something in the trees and concludes them to be already civilised opposums. A young man, for it is in fact young men in the trees, falls out and tries to head off the idea:

> Yet it but struck the notion deeper into the heads of the vulgar, of having accession from the quadrupeds at the next census of free inhabitants; and a man with a strong voice in particular called out that it should be

so. A bull happening to roar, and a horse to neigh at the same time, it was called out that it was the voice of the people.[111]

Brackenridge then moved from the specific to the general. This, he argued, was an example of the way the public meeting operated. Opinion might be swayed by the clever positioning of your supporters, as fortuitously occurred in the previous example, thus there will seem to be a majority. Strikingly, the Captain is now condemned, as he threatens to operate as a typical politician, by going with the majority:

> I know no proof of discernment in a republic greater than to forsee which way the current is like to set, and to sail with it; or rather, if you can influence at all, to seize by the forelock, and by disposing a few frogs in a pond to roar, make it to be supposed that public opinion is in the direction you chuse [*sic*] to have it. . . . this is *the principle upon which the greater part of politicians act.*[112]

The Captain is rescued by the blind Chief Justice, who deploys the familiar argument that if the beasts are to be considered as equals they will have to be released from their burdensome duties.

The shadow of the Whiskey Rebellion also hangs over Brackenridge's accounts of this new settlement. This description of the influencing of a crowd recalls the various such scenes in *Incidents*. Similarly, in discussing the state of Ireland with some recent immigrants, Farrago gloomily commented:

> For of what avail is disjointed opposition; partial insurrections, which like the struggles of beasts of burden, serve but the more to intangle, and furnish a reason, or at least a pretence for weightier chains, and stronger gearing for the future?[113]

While the fictional protagonists are reliving all these old problems, Brackenridge, through the vehicle of the narrator, is effectively presenting episodes in the recent history of the republic, shot through with the same habitual moral:

> The great moral of this book is the evil of men seeking office for which they are not qualified.[114]

These sections come closest to a clear exploration of Brackenridge's principles in action. They also show most clearly his connections with the beliefs of Adams. There is an obvious statement of this connection, where the moral noted is expanded:

> But there is another evil, as I have said the detraction from even the good qualities of those in power, and the denying credit even to the prudent acts of an administration.[115]

The explanation for this makes the shadow of Adams distinct:

> [This is] because every man covets distinction, and is ambitious of power; and where the government is by representation, all cannot have office at the same time.[116]

But Brackenridge does not confine himself to statements of principle. Instead, he produces concrete examples from contemporary politics. Towards the end of the work, Governor Farrago finally rounds on his critics and reaffirms his refusal to bend to their every will with a remarkable comparison:

> Do you take me for a *Jefferson*? . . . I would ill deserve your confidence if I made your whims my guide; or regarded popularity obtained in such a way. It never came into my head that, because I had got the chair of government, there was a millennium about to come, when all men would do justice, and there would be no occasion for judges and lawyers; nations could be coerced by proclamations; and no war would ensue.[117]

Again, we see the same points of satire occurring to Brackenridge as occurred to Irving. More, there is a remarkable correlation between this characterisation of Jefferson, and Jefferson's own comments on his accession to power, which we observed at the outset of this study.

To hammer home the point, Brackenridge the narrator devotes the following chapter to a direct discussion of Jefferson's presidency. These two pages sum up, effectively, the complications of Brackenridge's approach. He acknowledged his fallibility, a type of acknowledgement which was not widespread among politicians of this, or any, period:

> I will acknowledge, that in some matters I *erred with him*: approving of an embargo, and not seeing until a late day, that the policy was ineffectual.[118]

He then defended his presuming to offer opinions on the matter:

> It is natural for a person to think what he would have done had he been in the situation of another, even though he never had the idea of being in that situation. But having an interest in common with others in the management of the helm, it becomes more essentially natural for one to think what ought to be done.[119]

This is to reiterate another key pillar of Brackenridge's policy. Just as the ignorant should not assume roles in public life for which they are unfit, so it is essential for the future of the republic that the educated should advise on the management of affairs and, that their advice should be heeded. The precept of contemporary example is every bit as vital, perhaps even more vital, than the precept of classical example to which Brackenridge equally often alluded. Brackenridge goes so far as to claim that he made certain of the criticisms, particularly with regard to the importance of a navy, (another point of connection with Adams), direct to Madison, an act not entirely unlikely, considering their common educational experience, Brackenridge's involvement in the 1799–1800 Democratic–Republican campaign, and his connections with Gallatin.

Only having deployed these caveats does Brackenridge proceed to discuss the actual failings. Here, as elsewhere, he strove for balance, revisiting the key points of collision in the preceding years. His analysis, therefore, is not a simple condemnation of Jefferson but a judicious weighing, criticising his domestic, but praising his foreign, policy. It is as if Brackenridge is again trying to show how political debate should operate in his country.

Yet he concludes the chapter by shying away from this, arguing that this section may be struck out in future editions "when the scenes have passed away to which it refers."[120] Perhaps Brackenridge recognised that such political reflections would come to damage his literary reputation.

It is in these last sections of the book that Brackenridge's breadth of experience attains its ultimate significance. His ability to consider the relative merits of the Adams and Jefferson administrations is important, and rare, but he draws a more striking connection between the Whiskey Rebellion and the Hartford Convention. The connection is significant because Brackenridge condemned both, although he was plainly more in sympathy with the underlying grievances of the Whiskey rebels. Both events demonstrated for him the fragility of the republic; that the same lessons applied in 1815 as in 1794. Jefferson's new dawn was, on this reading, an illusion. The eternal human frailties that Brackenridge had expended so much ink to depict were unchanged.

Modern Chivalry possessed a similar unity to Brackenridge's own life. Farrago and Teague endured precisely the confused, muddled series of events which bedevilled Brackenridge's own life. The fact of their confusion, of their repeating their errors, was an example in itself. Thus, rather than complain that the book is repetitive, we would do better to ask why this is so. It might be argued that Brackenridge, unable to stop writing but with nothing new to say, simply unthinkingly repeated himself. This is an insufficient argument. Crucially, Brackenridge saw the same errors repeating themselves, so he continued to admonish them in the same way.

His lessons mattered in a nation which, in 1815 as in 1776, was denouncing as un-American those who rejected the dominant path. But they also mattered because Brackenridge, although he continued to dream of the possibility of American perfection, recognised that that perfection was as yet unattained. Ultimately, he questioned whether it ever could be:

In human affairs, there is no reaching the perfect in the application of principle. All that can be done, is to come as near it as possible, by a just discernment of circumstances. What is done, may be blamed; but there might be more blame, had the contrary been done.[121]

This was not a viewpoint likely to prove popular with Jefferson and others as they continued to proclaim that all was for the best in the best of all possible Americas. Brackenridge, like the defeated Adams of 1800, told Americans truths they badly needed to heed. Like Adams, he discovered that few wanted to listen, or, if they were listening, it was accomplishing little. Both Brackenridge and Adams had been stalwart Patriots. Their exclusions demonstrated that there was a flaw in the Jeffersonian Ascendancy. It was left to Irving to fully expose it.

3   The Defining Moment
Washington Irving and
A History of New York

> We have called by different names brethren of the same principle. We are all Republicans, we are all Federalists.[1]

> How many very strenuous and hard working patriots are there, whose knowledge is bounded by the political vocabulary, and who, were they not thus arranged in parties would never know their own minds . . . so that by following their own common sense the community might fall into that unanimity, which has been clearly proved, by many excellent writers, to be fatal to the welfare of a republick.[2]

In 1801, Thomas Jefferson attained the Presidency, and in his inaugural address performed a third rhetorical refashioning of the American polity. He asserted that the country was not divided, effectively denying, as he did so, that his victory was the product of an extremely bitter election campaign, the contending political parties in which were bitterly divided within themselves. He also reiterated the old strain of rising glory:

> A rising nation, spread over a wide and fruitful land, traversing all the seas with the rich production of their industry . . . advancing to destinies beyond the reach of mortal eye . . . [3]

All that was wanting, he suggested, was the right party in control of government:

> With all these blessings, what more is necessary to make us a happy and a prosperous people? Still one thing more, fellow-citizens—a wise a frugal Government. . . . [4]

These two pronouncements recalled the two earlier creations, the Declaration of Independence in 1776, and the Constitution in 1787–8. The same sentiments were professed now, papering over the same problem. All Americans were not of the same principle in 1801, any more than in 1776 or 1787, and yet those who were not of Jefferson's principle still believed themselves to be Americans.

The existence of rival visions of America and Americans was denied on those earlier occasions. The Declaration of Independence simply ignored the possibility of an opposite view. *The Federalist Papers*, defending the proposed Constitution, made a virtue of the possibility, suggesting that from the collision of opposed positions, one correct one would emerge. Jefferson's Inaugural stated a more forceful position, among his convictions as to what principles would govern the country under his administration, "absolute acquiescence in the decisions of the majority, the vital principle of republics, from which is no appeal but to force, the vital principle and immediate parent of despotism."[5]

This was a startling reversal of Jefferson's position in the 1790s, when he often urged his acolytes, and in the case of the Virginia Resolutions, himself advocated, the opposing decisions, which were then certainly being taken by Congressional majorities.[6] Jefferson, of course, would have claimed the support of the majority of the people. Here, too, there are qualifications. Earlier in the address, as Smelser noted, Jefferson argued:

> All, too, will bear in mind this sacred principle, that though the will of the majority is in all cases to prevail, that will to be rightful must be reasonable; that the minority possess their equal rights, which equal law must protect, and to violate would be oppression.[7]

But there are two corollaries to this. First, it is meaningless if the later statement is to have any force. The minority lack the ultimate power of rebellion, a contradiction Jefferson did not address, a contradiction perhaps typical of the man capable of holding two opposed ideas in his head at once. Second, it is followed by the famous statements concerning the unity of the people. If everybody is really a republican, and everybody is really a federalist, there is no minority to be protected. The section which follows this, clarified the point further:

> If there be any among us who would wish to dissolve this Union or to change its republican form, let them stand undisturbed as monuments of the safety with which error of opinion may be tolerated where reason is left free to combat it.[8]

Jefferson was so little concerned with those in error because he believed, or affected to believe, that they really were a tiny, insignificant minority, the proverbial few bad apples. The people, Jefferson firmly told John Dickinson, were on his side:

> Our fellow citizens have been led hood-winked from their principles, by a most extraordinary combination of circumstances. But the band is removed, and they now see for themselves.[9]

This was only to reiterate what Jefferson appears to have believed for much of the preceding decade. The American people, that mythical, undefined body, had been on his side throughout the struggles of that decade. Now that he, their embodiment, was in power, there could be no meaningful differences. Thus, it would simply not be necessary to apply the gag rule upon his opponents because they were so few and so insignificant. They were not true Americans, and would wither away.

That is to put a positive interpretation on Jefferson's remarks. It is possible that, in fact, Jefferson was determined to exercise power exactly as he believed the Federalists had been doing during the previous decade, with perhaps slightly more allowance to his opponents to voice objections, if with the same prevention of their having any effect. Challenging his administration would, thus, be made just as unacceptable in theory (and more so in practise) as challenging the Federalist dominance had been.

There is one further point. Jefferson's view of his opponents as a monarchy-loving minority will not hold for the outgoing president, John Adams, as C. Bradley Thompson convincingly demonstrated.[10] Jefferson's refusal to recognise Adams' true character, and the tendency of historians to cloak this failure as genuine misunderstanding, when the evidence is at least as suggestive that Jefferson indulged in acts of wilful blindness, is an issue requiring further exploration.[11]

Whether Jefferson believed his own subtleties, and however he arrived at them, their effect was to make his behaviour remarkably similar to that of his predecessors. It was also arguable that the same necessity to proclaim American unity existed as on former occasions. The country seemed on the brink of flying apart. Prudence and belief demanded Jefferson's text. None of this negated the fact that the text denied the legitimacy of the other Americans. That denial was, in 1801 as in 1776, in defiance of Patriot principles.

In 1801, there was a further issue. The texts of those earlier occasions did propose new visions. Jefferson's Presidency left much of the Federalist system intact, and dismissed comparatively few Federalists from office. If this made Jefferson's conciliation genuine, it simultaneously invalidated his assertions in the 1790s that the Federalist system and its protagonists were un-American. Neither Jefferson nor his historians ought to have it both ways.

The contradictions of Jefferson's Inaugural Address demonstrated that, in 1801, as on those previous occasions, the nature of America and Americans remained a deeply divisive question. This chapter examines Washington Irving's exploration of those renewed divisions.

Irving's quality was, like Brackenridge's, partly a consequence of timing. He lived between two worlds. He began to write while the Revolutionary memory was still raw, the connection of names between Irving and the Revolution's great hero is a neat symbol of this. The Revolution bore as heavily upon him as on Brackenridge or Crèvecoeur. Irving managed to transcend this burden, where Brackenridge failed. But in that transcendence, there was also a sacrifice. Irving reconciled the burden of the past with the reality of the present, but this was only possibly by a personal isolation, a voluntary silence. He could not romance that past as Cooper was to do.

This chapter pursues this experience in three sections. First, it examines Irving's early satirical writings, the collaborative magazine *Salmagundi* and the *History of New York*. These contained Irving's detailed explorations of his country, and his attempts to educate his readers about that country. Second, it considers the decade of near silence between that work and *The Sketch Book*, and the centrality of Irving's relationship to his country to that creative blockage. Finally, it examines the resolution of that blockage in *The Sketch Book*. In that work, Irving came to terms with the contradictory America he explored in his earlier satires, but was able to do so only through his physical exile in Europe.

DEFINITIONS

> I find that the people of this country are strangely at a loss to determine the nature and proper character of their government.[12]

> We begin to suspect that many people read our numbers, merely for their amusement, without paying any attention to the serious truths conveyed in every page. . . . not that we wish to restrict our readers in the article of laughing . . . provided they profit at the same time, and do not mistake our object.[13]

Washington Irving was born on 3 April, 1783, in New York City, just five days before the ceasefire between the Americans and the British was announced.[14] To this is attributed his Christian name. He was the first major imaginative writer to live entirely in the post-Revolutionary world. Although he lacked direct experience, the Revolution and its settlement were as central to his early writing as they had been to Crèvecoeur and Brackenridge.

His family background may be the key factor. His parents arrived in New York City, from England, in 1763. William Irving, his father, is recorded as a staunch Patriot, but that distinction must have been difficult to sustain in New York during the war, since the city and the state were among the more pro-British parts of the country. Consequently, it was also one of the locations most affected by the exodus of Loyalists at the end of the war.

Irving was the youngest of eight children, and during his early life maintained close relations with his elder brothers, including collaborating with Peter on *Salmagundi*. The family's professional background was a curious mixture of commodity sales and auctioneering.[15] Irving, himself, would be sucked into this business, to his ultimate regret, during and immediately after the War of 1812. His early education was less complete than that of Brackenridge. He attended, first, a school run by an old soldier, Benjamin Romaine, for eight years; a seminary run by a Josiah A. Henderson for one year; and finally a school run by Jonathan Fiske, which Williams described as tailing "off into a superficial study of Latin and into furtive lessons in dancing."[16] Unlike two of his elder brothers, he never enrolled at Columbia College. Irving's education at these establishments was very circumscribed. Even in reading, their libraries were very limited, and Irving appears to have been keener on romances than anything especially learned. Two points seem clear, first, that Irving was not particularly attracted to educational learning for its own sake and, second, that he left school with no very clear idea concerning his next move. There are also indications that the indolence which troubled him later was already a factor.

Whenever the artistic bug bit him, Irving faced the same problems as Brackenridge and others. New York society still frowned on literary endeavours. Irving's family was also hostile. Compelled to some more promising career, Irving went into the law. Unlike Brackenridge, he was never genuinely committed to the profession. Instead, he pursued a variety of distractions, from travel, to writing, to falling in love with his teacher's daughter. The first two anticipated his future life; the love affair was to prove a tragedy.

Irving travelled to France and Italy, and his accounts anticipated key themes of *The Sketch Book*. The early fascination with the Old World is present:

Every thing is novel and interesting to me. The luxury gothic looking buildings. The ancient churches the manners of the people—it really appears like another world.[17]

So, too, is the homesickness for the familiar world left behind:

Those who have never been far from home, have no idea with what fondness the imagination dwells upon the little spot of earth where our family and friends are collected and from which we are far distant.[18]

At home, sandwiching this journey, his brother Peter, no more assiduous a doctor than Irving was a lawyer, gave him opportunities for writing. He was editor of the *Morning Chronicle*, a Burrite paper to which Irving contributed a series of sketches in 1802. Irving summed up his position at this time in a letter to Amos Eaton, a fellow legal student:

I feel in a curious situation, manager of a paper, with the principles of which mine do not accord, obliged to use strict attention *and* constant application—to be economic and almost parsimonious of my time— things to which I have never been accustomed. I have been used to wander over the fields of fancy *and* Belles Letters and occasionally to tread the graver paths of History *and* science—but as to the rugged *and* intricate mazes of Politics, I always avoided them.[19]

Although the *Letters of Jonathan Oldstyle Gent.* focused on fashion and the theatre, politics quickly became Irving's central theme. Unfortunately, Irving's personal opinions prior to his early masterpieces are obscure. The Burrite connection was dominant in the family. Peter started a second paper, *The Corrector*, in 1804 to support Burr's New York gubernatorial campaign. Irving contributed to that paper, but his own political position was already unclear. A marginal comment in the letter to Eaton noted:

> His brother is editor of the Chronicle Express—I now take that paper—it is democratic and Washinton [*sic*] is Federal.[20]

In reality, Irving's allegiances were rather more complex than this, as Burstein has recently shown.[21] However, the crucial point where issue needs to be taken is less with Irving's specific allegiances and more with Williams' view that he, Irving, "had no profound comprehension of the principles at stake" in the political debates.[22] Williams saw Irving as principally interested in the spectacle of politics and in poking gentle fun at its practitioners. But, while this is certainly true of Irving's comments on electioneering in New York in 1807 and of much of *Salmagundi*, as the *History* shows, it is far from the whole truth.

Alongside *Salmagundi*, Irving observed one other key political event, the treason trial of Aaron Burr in the summer of 1807. He was appointed as a junior counsel for Burr, with perhaps some hope that he might use his pen in Burr's defence. In practice, he did little with pen or legal argument, beyond recounting his observations in letters to friends in New York.

These descriptions of the trial have some similarity to *Salmagundi* in tone, with General James Wilkinson, the chief witness against Burr, getting much the worst of it:

> Wilkinson is now before the grand jury, and has such a mighty mass of *words* to deliver himself of, that he claims at least two days more to discharge the wondrous cargo.[23]

The descriptions of Burr are warm, his demeanour contrasted markedly with Wilkinson. Irving also scathingly attacks his imprisonment:

> The only reason given for immuring him in his abode of Thieves—Cut throats & incendiaries was that it would save the United States *a couple of hundred dollars* . . . & it would ensure the security of his person.[24]

The family connection was clearly a factor here,[25] as also the tendency to hero worship observed by Williams.[26] Yet there is also the glimmering of a concern, which became central to the *History*. Irving's judgement is less on the actual truth of Burr's case, but on the behaviour exhibited towards him:

> Whatever may be his innocence or guilt in respect to the charges alledged against him . . . his situation is such as should appeal eloquently to the feelings of every generous bosom—Sorry am I to say, the reverse has been the fact . . . It has almost been considered as culpable to evince towards him the least sympathy or support; and many a hollow hearted caitiff have I seen, who basked in the sunshine of his bounty, when in power, who now skulked from his side, and even mingled among the most clamorous of his enemies.[27]

This concern for fair treatment recurred in the two major works of this period, *Salmagundi* and *A History of New York*. The 1807–8 series *Salmagundi or the Whim-Whams and Opinions of Lancelot Langstaff, Esq. & Others*, published as a magazine, clearly indicated the direction Irving was moving.[28] Since its publication, it has not received much critical attention. This may partly be the result of its fragmentary make-up, twenty editions published roughly every fortnight, usually containing three essays each. There is also the problem that it is a collaborative effort though, when reprinted, it usually appears under Irving's by-line alone.[29] In fact, it was a combined production of Washington Irving, his eldest brother William Irving, and James Kirke Paulding (1778–1860) whose sister was married to William. Paulding continued with satire thereafter, striking out at the British–American relationship in *The History of John Bull and Brother Jonathan* (1812) and life on the frontier in *Koningsmarke* (1823) among others.[30] William Irving is thought to have been involved in the early stages of planning for *A History of New York*. Given this trio of authors, there remains, unsurprisingly, a good proportion of the pieces whose authorship cannot be conclusively determined. This problem is not an insuperable barrier. Certain key essays which bear on the *History*, including several of the Mustapha letters, have been unanimously ascribed to Irving. Further, some years after publication, Paulding explained that most of the texts, no matter who had first written them, were edited and rewritten by one or other of the other two.[31] Sentiments expressed in essays ascribed to the other two also reappear in Irving's later writings, suggesting a high degree of mutual influence. In essence, it was a genuine collaborative effort. In keeping with this, and the magazine style of the day, the various essays were published under a variety of pseudonyms. These included Lancelot Longstaff, the editor; Anthony Evergreen, a theatre critic; William Wizard, a general critic; and Musapha an exiled Tripolitan slave-driver. A suitably dreadful epic poet, Pindar Cockloft, was also on hand. With the exception of Cockloft, all of whose contributions are ascribed to William Irving, the other soubriquets switch between the authors. This use of pseudonyms, repeated in the *History* also recalls Crèvecoeur's multiple personas.

The work combined lighthearted satire on contemporary society, with some fairly serious political criticisms. The authors also confront, head on, the various castigations of the literary endeavour current at the time. Thus, at the very outset, they address the problem that criticisms of society are frowned upon.[32] The authors found a new angle. Instead of insisting on their truthfulness, they went out of their way to emphasise their unreliability. They began with a wide-ranging definition of their targets:

> Our intention is simply to instruct the young, reform the old, correct the town and castigate the age; this is an arduous task and therefore we undertake it with confidence.[33]

but speedily cut the ground out from beneath their feet, "We write for no other earthly purpose but to please ourselves."[34] This device of pretending innocence to cover often trenchant criticisms was one of the major achievements of *Salmagundi*. They also made a virtue of the supposed idleness of the profession:

> [This] will be published whenever we have sufficient matter to constitute a number. . . . This will best suit our negligent habits, and leave us that full liberty and independence which is the joy and pride of our souls.[35]

The book, like *Modern Chivalry*, opens all targets to attack, even if the stage is ostensibly confined to New York society. It embraces an effective mix of light, frothy, social, and artistic satire, alongside the more biting political comment. This perception may reverse the contemporary reaction, when the objects of the social satire were more easily discerned and the effect possibly more biting. Either way, it is the mixture of subjects which makes the work so effective.

"Salmagundi II" illustrates this brilliantly.[36] This edition contained one of the lightest, frothiest pieces in the whole work, recounting a recent concert. Mr. Evergreen complained that "all modern music is but the dregs and drains of the ancient" before illustrating his immense knowledge on the subject, by claiming that "the scotch bag-pipe is the only instrument that rivals the ancient lyre, and I am surprised it should be almost the only one excluded from our concerts."[37] The man clearly needed Anna Russell's comedic discourse on that instrument. Around this musical mockery are built two striking comments on the present, and possible future, public response to "Salmagundi I."

In the opening "From the Elbow-Chair," Langstaff describes hearing the work read in a bookstore. One respondent is most uneasy about it:

> He hoped it did not mean anything against the Government—that no lurking treason was couched in all this talk. These were dangerous

times—times of plot and conspiracy,—he did not at all like those stars after mr. [*sic*] Jefferson's name, they had an air of concealment.

Another of the group takes up the challenge, defending the authors by suggesting that the stars merely stood for Mr. Jefferson's red breeches (intended to show his equality with the people and a favourite object of satire at the writers' hands), but this does not satisfy the gentlemen:

> The old man shook his head . . . gave a mysterious lord Burleigh nod, said he hoped it might be so; but he was by no means satisfied with this attack upon the president's breeches, as "thereby *hangs a tale*."[38]

Now, this could simply imply that the authors saw the red breeches as indicative of the whole tenet of Jefferson policies, against which they devote so many pages. It may refer to the frequent equation, often by High Federalists, of Jefferson with the devil. Since the Shakespearean original is said to imply a bawdy joke, it seems just possible that there may be some barbed reference lurking here to Jefferson's alleged liaisons with slave-girls.[39]

The authors defuse the situation by turning to music, but their sober side reemerges in the concluding "Advertisment." They note that one only has to describe an odd person, however fictional, and the entire population of the place is up in arms in mistaken self-recognition. Again, there is a sting in the tail, as the authors mockingly refuse to engage in any fighting resulting from their satires:

> It is not in our hearts to hurt the feelings of one single mortal, by holding him up to public ridicule, and if it were, we lay it down as one of our indisputable facts, that no man can be made ridiculous but by his own folly.[40]

This echoes, or possibly anticipates since we cannot be certain which came first, Brackenridge's assertion noted in the last chapter. Although the authors here quickly slip back into mockery, noting that it would be very inconvenient to fight since they might be killed and thus deprive the public of the benefits of their wit, this does not invalidate the earlier point.

Other links to past and future writings are also present. The struggle between France and Britain has mutated into a struggle between rival fashions.[41] There are hints at the importance of a romanticised past, a central theme of Irving's European writings of the early 1820s. More, Paulding, in "A Retrospect" in "Salmagundi No.XIII," anticipated a key theme of *The Sketch Book*. Reflecting on the response to the numbers thus far, he expressed the hope that:

> If . . . we have . . . brushed away one tear of dejection, and called forth a smile in its place . . . we shall feel almost as much joy and rejoicing as

a slang-whanger does when he . . . sacrifices one more illustrious victim on the altar of *party animosity*.[42]

The crucial texts of *Salmagundi*, from our point of view, are the Mustapha letters, the first of which appears in "Salmagundi No. III." These have proved of least interest to most critics, who see in them pale imitations of Goldsmith's *Citizen of the World* letters.[43] These letters deploy the satire of the American political system brought to more complex fruition in Irving's *History*. The famous, specific satire of Jefferson is only a facet of something much broader. This broader satire was a fresh recognition of the centrality of the political system to the question of American character. The Salmagundians, like Brackenridge, recognised the flaws and illusions of that system. The Mustapha letters also demonstrate the strange coherency of *Salmagundi*. All three authors contributed to the series, and the letters depend upon each other to build their message.

Mustapha's credibility is ostensibly undermined by his very character. As the principal slave-driver to the Bashaw of Tripoli, he is stigmatised as a complete outcast in republican America. It is mockingly implied that he cannot possibly comprehend what he is witnessing. Mustapha's incomprehension is frequently damning, partly because of the image that it implies America is projecting to the world and, partly because of the points of comparison drawn with that other world. Mustapha's incomprehension also recalls the struggles of the American writer to explain America, witnessed by Brackenridge, Crèvecoeur, and now Irving. The sixth Mustapha letter voices a familiar helplessness:

> Every new research encreases [*sic*] the perplexities in which I am involved, and I am more than ever at a loss where to place them in the scale of my estimation.

His contemplation of retreat recalled Crèvecoeur, and anticipated Irving,

> The philosopher . . . almost wishes he could quietly retrace his wandering steps, steal back into the path of honest ignorance, and jog on once more in contented indifference.[44]

The first letter mingled the social and political. Mustapha lamented the absence of his twenty-three wives, finding Americans' lack of wives unremarkable, given that American women possess tongues. Then, as the new arrivals proceed to their lodgings, an old shoe is thrown at Mustapha. The interpreter explains:

> that this was the customary manner in which great men were honoured in this country; and that the more distinguished they were, the more they were subjected to the attacks and peltings of the mob.[45]

There are, again, echoes of Brackenridge, and the world in which anybody with intelligence is frowned upon. Mustapha also introduces the *bashaw*, or president, Jefferson, who has fallen out of favour "by wearing red britches," before seizing on the heart of the American ideal. We have seen the sense of American superiority undermined in Crèvecoeur's comparisons with the Indians and Brackenridge's comments on the faults of the mob. The Salmagundi crew summarize the same argument with devastating simplicity:

> The people of the United States have assured me that they themselves are the most enlightened nation under the sun; but thou knowest that the barbarians of the desert . . . make precisely the same boast.[46]

The second letter, in "Salmagundi No. V," introduced the satire of ECONOMY. This, Mustapha explained, "is a kind of national starvation, an experiment how many comforts and necessaries the body politic can be deprived of before it perishes."[47] A military review is described, including a great many speeches, introducing a second key point of satire, "The battle was carried on intirely [*sic*] by *words*, according to the universal custom of this country."[48] The parade is on a considerable scale but, as a tailor explains to Mustapha, it has no military purpose whatsoever, "their rulers had decided that wars were very useless and expensive, and ill-befitting an economic philosophic nation."[49]

The show of military presence is, it seems, only for appearance. Mustapha ironically compares this "great scale" with the much larger bodies of men reviewed in Tripoli, a comparison the more scathing given that the Barbary states succeeded in forcing large amounts of tribute out of the United States over a number of years.[50]

It is with the third letter that the satire really becomes pungent. Mustapha now turned his attention directly to the system of government. The descriptions recall Brackenridge but are even more on the nose. Three types of governmental system are proposed: aristocracy, democracy, and mobocracy, and the third, claims Mustapha, comes nearest the truth of America. It is a mobocracy, in which a particular type has the most power:

> A man . . . who talks good sense in his native tongue, is held in tolerable estimation in this country; but a fool, who clothes his feeble ideas in a foreign or antique garb, is bowed down to, as a literary prodigy.[51]

This recalls an implied theme in *Modern Chivalry* where Farrago, for all his learning, can be as foolish as Teague. It also suggests that education can be misused, that the fool need only employ a few choice phrases to sway the mind of the mob.

The nation claims to be "one of the most *pacific* in the known world," but, according to Mustapha, is "engaged in the most complicated knot of civil wars that ever infested any poor unhappy country." But these are not wars of the sword, instead anticipated in Wilkinson's "mighty mass of words," and the battle fought entirely by "words," these are the wars of a LOGOCRACY. Just as a man with the slightest antique word at his command can sway the mob, so any man with the simple "gift of the gab" can take a leading role in the battle.

But the spoken duel is not the key element of this war. We noted the way in which America was written into existence through documents such as *Common Sense* and the Declaration,[52] a point which Mustapha recognised:

> Every offensive or defensive measure is enforced by *wordy battle*, and *paper war*; he who has the longest tongue, or readiest quill, is sure to gain the victory . . . will . . . put men, women, and children, to the point of the—pen.[53]

The letter recalls the endless justifications flowing from politicians' pens in the period. The circular letters of congressmen to their constituents, the justifications of Brackenridge or Findley for their part in the Whiskey Rebellion, Monroe's account of his mission in Paris all contribute to this war.[54] And, as Mustapha unsurprisingly recognised, the chief knights of this war, like "those, who, in former ages, swore eternal enmity to the followers of our divine prophet" are the editors or SLANG-WHANGERS. The echo of *Modern Chivalry* is unmistakeable. The knight is no longer the travelling Farrago, who has at least the grace to go out into the world in order to try and right its wrongs, but an editor sitting in his ink-stained office presuming to right the wrongs of a country and, indeed, a world which he has never seen.

Jefferson is now reintroduced. Mustapha described the ongoing war between this *bashaw* and the "higher classes" over his refusal to believe Biblical truths, and expressed astonishment at the abuse to which such a high official was subjected. Strikingly, and accurately if the Hartford Convention is considered, he described the conflict as a "civil war." Here it is a civil war not simply between elites, Jefferson, the High Federalists, and their personal slang-whangers, but one encompassing "every little town and village." Congress illustrates this, whose deliberations precisely mirror the chaos outside:

> For thou must know, that the members of this assembly do not meet together to find out wisdom in the multitude of counsellors, but to wrangle, call each other hard names and hear *themselves talk*.[55]

This jibe against the character of Congressional deliberations first surfaced in Crèvecoeur, was elevated in Brackenridge, and was now redeployed by Irving. If the system is the key to American character, then something is very seriously wrong. This letter introduces a gendered note, remarking that these Congressmen, so adept at talking and doing nothing "in a time of great peril and momentous event" might just as well be replaced by old women whose garrulity eminently qualifies them for such a role.

Up to now, there is a distinct lightness of tone to Mustapha's observations. But here something wistful, some deeper note of reflection begins to creep in. The echo of Brackenridge reaches a new level with a metaphor based on Quixote's windmill. The words are vanished:

> Words are but breath—breath is but air; and air in motion is nothing but wind.

The prospect of a consequently decaying country, a theme which becomes the centre of the *History*, is suggested:

> This vast empire . . . may be compared to nothing more nor less than a mighty windmill, and the orators, and the chatterers, and the slang-whangers, are the breezes that put it in motion; unluckily . . . they are apt to blow in different ways, and their blasts counteracting each other—the mill is perplexed, the wheels stand still, the grist is un-ground, and the miller and his family starved.[56]

This extreme image of the republic is in exact contradiction to the vision of rising glory. The country is totally disunited, and there is no progress at all, in fact the reverse. This is actually more devastating than anything in Brackenridge. For, in *Modern Chivalry*, the windmill never stopped turning. Teague's and Farrago's travels were endless. There is still some, even if deeply flawed, momentum. In Mustapha's vision, America has absolutely stopped. Here, the letter swerves from this fearful vision back to specificity, with a renewed attack on Jefferson's particular brand of "ventosity." In the *History* it proved impossible to swerve.

The final paragraph of the letter touched on yet another facet of the rising glory idea, again in no very pleasant terms. This is the collision between the competing American desires for uniqueness and for a place in the field of nations. The letter's conclusion suggests that this is achieved, but it is hardly the kind of achievement the Americans desired:

> The infidel nations have each a separate characteristic trait . . . the spaniards . . . may be said to *sleep* upon every affair of importance—the Italians to *fiddle* upon everything—the French to *dance* upon every thing—the Germans to *smoke* upon every thing—the British island-ers to *eat* upon every thing,—and the *windy* subjects of the American logocracy to *talk* upon every thing.[57]

Mustapha's arguments may retain a lightness of tone, but this is not all fool.

The fourth Mustapha letter, in "Salmagundi IX," returned more completely to the lighter tone, and the satire of Economy.[58] The inability of Congress to decide on the expenditure of even small sums of money without extensive debate is discussed, although even here there is a sting when Mustapha is told that the reason for this is that Congressmen are paid by the day. Thus large sums of money can be wasted trying to save the pennies.[59]

With the fifth letter, from "Salmagundi XI," the satire again branches out afresh, as Mustapha, in this case determined by all the available authorities to be Irving, turned his attention to perhaps the key event in American public life:

> I have beheld the whole city, nay the whole state, given up to the tongue and pen, to the puffers, the bawlers, the babblers and the *slang-whang-ers*. I have beheld the community convulsed with a civil war (or *civil talk*) . . . I have seen . . . that awful despot, the *people*, in a moment of unlimited power, wielding newspapers in one hand, and with the other scattering mud and filth about . . . I have seen liberty, I have seen equality, I have seen fraternity—I have seen that great political puppet-show—AN ELECTION.[60]

The election is the main battle in the unending war, and the spoils are clearly delineated, "OFFICE AND IMMORTALITY." The whole male populace is involved, and again the criticism recalls Brackenridge, "Every man . . . disinterestedly neglects his business, to devote himself to his country."[61]

These cobblers should, of course, stick to their lasts. Instead, they devote themselves to oratory, to the delight of Mustapha's local informant:

> An election . . . is a nursery or hot-bed of genius in a logocracy—and I look with enthusiasm on a troop of this liliputian partisans, as so many chatterers, and orators, and puffers, and slang-whangers in embryo, who will one day, take an important part in the quarrels, and wordy wars of their country.[62]

The endless capacity of the thing is again clear. This windmill may go round and round until judgement day, yet without the country enjoying any progress. Irving's skill here is to condense Brackenridge's vision into clarity. So he has Mustapha put his finger on precisely the consequence of this that Brackenridge continually, but less effectively, came upon. A "number of ragged, dirty looking persons" are pointed out to him. It is explained that "these are the representatives of the sovereign people who are the source of all power and authority in this nation," about to select their officials,[63] with the familiar consequence:

> A man, who possesses superior talents, and that honest pride which ever accompanies this possession, will always be sacrificed to some creeping insect who will prostitute himself to familiarity with the

lowest of mankind, and like the idolatrous Egyptian, worship the wallowing tenants of filth and mire.[64]

Once again, these barbs are surrounded by material in a lighter tone, depicting the various participants swigging from beer barrels, and a rather curious potential episode of bribery. But the bite is lurking to resurface in the final paragraphs. A hand bill is handed to Mustapha, written by the "ghost of Washington." Mustapha is appalled:

> Insulted hero . . . is it thus thy name is profaned, thy memory disgraced, thy spirit drawn down from heaven to administer to the brutal violence of party rage![65]

The character of Mustapha must be unaware of the savage irony at the heart of this. Mustapha, as a visitor, is presumed to know Washington as the Revolutionary hero, the first president. But, as Irving would have expected his audience to remember, Washington was also the author of a Farewell Address containing the eloquent plea for the extinction of faction. His name so clearly carries weight, but nobody wants to remember what he actually said. More, there is the strange confluence of Irving's and Washington's names, and the fact that Irving would spend his last literary energies on his mammoth biography of his namesake.

This is a sharp blow, but the power of *Salmagundi* is to leave no pauses. Where Brackenridge laboriously repeated himself, Irving's attacks tumble over themselves. In Washington's case, the nation's future was perennially at stake, that resonance is also diluted by overuse:

> For such is the *sandy* foundation of our government, that there never happens an election of an alderman, or a collector, or even a constable, but we are in imminent danger of losing our liberties, and becoming a province of France, or tributary to the British islands.

The overall consequence of this again recalled Brackenridge, recalled the people broken free from restraint. Mustapha began with the specific:

> It seemed as all the restraints of decency, and all the bands of law had been broken and given place to the wide ravages of licentious brutality. These, thought I, are the orgies of liberty, these are the manifestations of the spirit of independence, these are the symbols of man's sovereignty![66]

The subject of the Tripolitanian despot saw an equal despotism before him, "with what a fatal and inexorable despotism do empty names and ideal phantoms exercise their dominion over the human mind!"

The hinted principle of the end of the third letter is, here, unavoidable:

> The experience of ages has demonstrated, that in all nations, barbarous or enlightened, the mass of the people, the *mob*, must be slaves, or they will be tyrants."[67]

Tyrants, that is, until some ambitious figure, pledging first fidelity to their will, will subsequently become their master, although this tyranny is equally finite. The shadow of the French Revolution and the reign of Bonaparte, which latter Irving observed at first hand, is plain. But Irving's transplantation of it to American soil is intriguing. Brackenridge possessed first hand experience of the comparison, Irving did not, yet this text goes to the heart of the question. This letter also echoes that to Mary Fairlie of 2 May, 1807, yet the latter is far more playful in tone. It is perhaps a mark of genius to be able to build on such an experience the possible extremes to which it may run. That it is genius and not fancy may be supported by the experience of Brackenridge. Further, in the first of the series of essays spoofing travellers in America, in "Salmagundi No. IV: 'The Stranger in New Jersey,'" a "fine old blade," is noted in a tavern who "tells bloody long stories about last war—people, of course, all do the same."[68] It is possible there is an aural tradition here, that Irving, growing up in the early years of the republic was hearing stories not only about that last Revolutionary War but about the political controversies of the republic.

The sixth Mustapha Letter, ascribed to William Irving, expanding upon the points already examined, anticipates another theme for Irving's *History*, in this case the tyranny of this system of talk. Mustapha explained that the populace find sufficient matter to keep the endless talk going, owing to the inexhaustible subject of "POLITICKS." This appears to mean endless dispute about individual's characters. The example given emphasised the still-present relevance of that revolutionary past:

> Two of my fellow lodgers . . . were magnanimously employed in condemning a luckless wight to infamy, because he chose to wear a *red coat*, and to entertain certain erroneous opinions some thirty years ago.[69]

The lodgers justified this "by alledging that they were only engaged in *politicks*, and exerting that liberty of speech, and freedom of discussion, which was the glory and safeguard of their national independence."[70] We are back to the question of whether there should be any restraints to these beliefs with, of course, the argument that, without restraint, a revolution is bound to occur. The consequence is actually more severe than this. For the whole point about this world of logocracy is that it is not real debate, but empty ventosity. Americans are, in the view of these letters, arguing about the wrong things.

This letter also directly restated the Brackenridge thesis. It recalled the language of the Declaration, "one would suppose that being all *free* and *equal*, they would harmonize as brothers." It then reiterated that inequality was unavoidable:

> There will always be an inequality among mankind, so long as a portion of it is enlightened and industrious, and the rest idle and ignorant.[71]

This persistent claim of inequality deserves more recognition than is generally accorded it. Since tacit acceptance is given to the exclusion of slaves, Native Americans, and women from the political settlements that gave the key character to the new nation, it seems odd that there should be a reluctance to acknowledge an inequality within the remaining group. In this case, there is not even the excuse of a personal desire for advancement that may be advanced for Brackenridge.

Nor is this idea of inequality a simple one of the educated versus the ignorant. For, William Irving also seized on that problematic idea of the "sovereign people" which we saw Jefferson deploy in his letter to John Dickinson. Irving, here, recalled the previous letter's description of an election, and described the outcome:

> The result has been that the *people*, as some of the slang-whangers say, have obtained a glorious triumph, which however, is flatly denied by the opposite slang-whangers, who insist that *their* party is composed of the true sovereign people, and that the others are all Jacobins, Frenchmen and *Irish rebels*.

Here, equal treatment is denied to those who do not think the right way, just as, to parade the historical examples, it was denied to the Loyalists, the anti-Federalists, and, at different times, the Federalists or Democratic–Republicans. Even this is not the most serious aspect of the case. We noted in the fifth letter, the device in *Salmagundi* of not leaving any pauses, but rather piling thrust upon thrust. Now, after this endless parade of talk, we come to the result of the election. The letter stated:

> I, for my part, expected to see wonderful changes, and most magical metamorphoses.

It is difficult to avoid the echoes of Jefferson's ascension in 1801, or indeed the hopes of the Patriots in 1776. As in the latter occasion, so in the former, suggested Irving, "every thing remains exactly in the same state as it was before the last wordy campaign."[72]

Now this may seem to carry the comparison a little too far. After all, did not the Revolution remove an elected monarchy, and grant equality to White men? Did not Jefferson's ascension mark a true reversion to the principles of 1776? These claims, at least the former, seem unarguable. Yet, that equality excluded those who disagreed and, unless we are to dismiss the realities displayed by Brackenridge and Irving, neither economic nor political equality occurred. Or, as William Irving put it:

> The labourer still toils for his daily support; the beggar still lives on the charity of those who have any charity to bestow . . .

And, in the ascension of a new chief bashaw, is this society really so far from the pre-Revolutionary world?

> They will praise, idolise, and exalt [him] for a while, and afterwards, notwithstanding the sterling merits he really possesses, in compliance with immemorial custom, they will abuse, calumniate, and trample under foot.[73]

There is, it seems, nothing new under the sun. In the New World, the laws of the Old still apply.

Brackenridge persistently repeated his points. A strength of the authors of *Salmagundi* is their willingness to turn to other themes. The next, in "Salmagundi No. XVI," turns to the question of fame. Ascribed to Irving, it possesses something of the melancholy tone that is more pronounced in parts of the *History* and *The Sketch Book*. Again, America is placed on the same stage as other countries. Here, as elsewhere, those who hope for fame will be disappointed:

> The storied obelisk—the triumphal arch—the swelling dome shall crumble into dust, and the names they would preserve from oblivion shall often pass away, before their own duration is accomplished.[74]

But the melancholy is turned aside here in a mockery of a public dinner, the preferred device for such memorials in enlightened America where "every coward becomes a hero, every ragamuffin an invincible warrior."[75]

This lightness of tone persists through the remaining two letters. The first is occupied with the subject of women ("Salmagundi No. XVIII"), while the second is stated to precede some already printed and turns its attention back to society. This is in keeping with the overall thrust of the numbers. This chapter has focused on the sharpest satire; there is much more material that is gentler and more reflective. The mingling is the key point. We can see here, in a bizarre harmony, the collision between Irving's two literary tendencies, which he later described in *The Sketch Book* as the dilemma whether to please or to instruct.

But it was the sharp satire which dominated his next, and solo, work, the *History of New York* (1809). This is the most important literary work to emerge from America in the entire period.[76] Common themes resurface from the place of the Indians to the appropriate means of government. The unique quality of the work is the overall narrative within which these issues are contained, and the moral to which it points. That this narrative is deliberately mired in confusion and superfluous detail does not negate its existence, and the key points are elucidated with a clarity lacking in fellow writers.

The work remained popular throughout Irving's career, something few contemporary works achieved, and he revised it five times, increasingly omitting some of the more strident satire.[77] We focus here, solely, on the original 1809 edition.

The *History* possesses three interconnected narratives. First, the pseudonymous writer Knickerbocker, representative of the problem of being an American writer, an adoption of an American persona which recalls Crèvecoeur's Farmer James; second, the grand historical lesson within which the smaller narratives of the Dutch governors operates, and which they and other briefer internal stories illuminate, a device of cumulative effect recalling Farrago and Teague's endless adventures and the various representative colonists of Crèvecoeur's *Letters*; third, that smaller narrative history of the Dutch colony of New York, which is the purported subject of the book but which is also a history of American republic of Irving's own time and its various presidents. The focus on the presidential figure marks an awareness of the key role of that individual as a symbol of American character. The narrative is divided into a sequence of "books." The historical lesson is established at the outset by Knickerbocker's personal history, his account of his motivations for producing the *History* and a remarkable fable in "Book One," concerned with the Native Americans. The specific history of the Dutch colony occupies "Book Two," with its discovery, while "Books Three" to "Seven" explore the reigns of the various governors.

Irving experimented with authorial soubriquets from the beginning, most extensively with Mustapha in *Salmagundi*. It was also foreshadowed by his literary predecessors, particularly Crèvecoeur's Farmer James, and in the many political essays of their period published under a variety of classical pseudonyms. With Diedrich Knickerbocker, though, Irving developed the technique to new heights. As with Crèvecoeur\James, Knickerbocker was not precisely the same as Irving but a representation of an aspect of Irving. Thus, the disappearance of Knickerbocker, discussed in the following, represented an aspect of Irving's experience as an American writer.

Knickerbocker captured the sense in which America was written into existence, noting, "Cities *of themselves*, and in fact empires *of themselves*, are nothing without an historian."[78]

Without writers there can be no nation.[79] Yet, by a persistent self-deprecation, Knickerbocker undermined his own authority. Thus, in introducing "Book One:"

> Book I—Being, like all introductions to American histories, very learned, sagacious, and nothing at all to the purpose.[80]

This self-undermining sets Knickerbocker apart from previous pseudonyms like Farrago and James, who asserted, until the latter's catastrophe, that they fully understood what they described. Knickerbocker has no compunction about acknowledging confusion or uncertainty. Nor is his *History* to be a rose-tinted one:

> It is the patient narrator who cheerfully records their prosperity as they rise—who blazons forth the splendour of their noontide meridian—who props their feeble memorials as they totter to decay—who gathers together their scattered fragments as they rot—and who piously . . . rears a triumphal monument, to transmit their renown to all succeeding time.[81]

There are two implications here. First, all civilisations are going to fall, the grand historical lesson of his narrative, symbolised when he compares his *History* to "*Gibbon's Rome*;"[82] second, that in that grand rise and fall there are going to be smaller successes and failures. But in America this challenged the prevailing vision. Failure was either denied, or obscured by an optimistic narrative fashioned through documents from the Declaration of Independence to Jefferson's First Inaugural Address. Not only did Knickerbocker anticipate failure, he also denied American uniqueness, seeing that failure as symbolic of America's similarity to everywhere else:

> The same sad misfortune which has happened to so many ancient cities, will happen again, and from the same sad cause. . . . With most . . . the time for recording their history is gone by . . . and the same would have been the case with this fair portion of the earth . . . if I had not snatched it from obscurity . . . at the moment that those matters herin [*sic*] recorded, were about entering into the widespread, insatiable maw of oblivion.[83]

Knickerbocker's personal character possessed one more telling attribute. He stood above party, as his landlord, Seth Handaside recounted:

> [At] . . . election time . . . he did nothing but bustle about from poll to poll, attending all ward meetings and committee rooms; though I could never find that he took part with either side of the question. On the contrary he would come home and rail at both parties with great wrath.[84]

This railing is clearly ineffectual. His fate, also described by his landlord, further illuminated these points. For Knickerbocker has disappeared. If the historian is gone, so is his subject, an ultimate conceit on a country written into existence. That the book is being purportedly published to pay Knickerbocker's bills at his landlord's is only the most contemptuous of a series of swipes at American pretensions, a swipe compounded by Handaside declaring Knickerbocker eccentric or possibly mad.[85]

The introductions set up Knickerbocker's central thesis, but it is a remarkable fable in "Book One" which gives the book its power, a fable so devastating in its conclusions that it almost makes the rest of the narrative an irrelevance. The situation of American Indians was discussed in Crèvecoeur and Brackenridge but their morals become muddled. Through Knickerbocker, Irving boldly confronted the fundamental question:

> What right had the first discoverers of America to land, and take possession of a country, without asking the consent of its inhabitants, or yielding them an adequate compensation for their territory?

The immediate response is brutally mocking. Knickerbocker anticipates the ease with which he will solve this conundrum "which has so long been the terror of adventurous writers." The claim that numbers of writers are worrying about this question is itself questionable, as is Knickerbocker's assertion that the general population is concerned about it:

> Until this mighty question is put to rest, the worthy people of America can by no means enjoy the soil they inhabit, with clear right and title, and quiet, unsullied consciences.[86]

The illusory quality of the claim is precisely the point. They probably aren't worrying about it, but they certainly ought to be. Knickerbocker proceeded to apparently salve their consciences in reality little troubled. First, he advanced the right of "DISCOVERY."[87] This depends on disproving the very existence of the Indians, something the preceding chapter had provided innumerable proofs of. Untroubled by this difficulty, an equal number of sources on the other side are supplied which claim that "the two legged race of animals before mentioned, were mere cannibals, detestable monsters."[88]

These arguments are proved in the absence of the Indians having any writers to defend themselves. Irving took this question up again in two brief Indian sketches in *The Sketch Book*.[89] The tone of those sketches is visible here. What seems to be a damning indictment of Indian character is instead turned back upon its begetters. Quoting Vanegas, he noted:

> The objects of ambition with us, honour, fame, reputation, riches, posts and distinctions are unknown among them.[90]

With striking brevity, Knickerbocker drew the comparison between Whites and Indians that Crèvecoeur took pages of confusion to reach. More, Knickerbocker pursued the satire to ever more bitter ends, next striking a comparison with the slaves:

> [The savages] being of a copper complexion, it was all the same as if they were negroes—and negroes are black, "and black" said the pious fathers . . . is the "colour of the devil."

The consequence is "they had no right even to personal freedom, for liberty is too radiant a deity, to inhabit such gloomy temples."[91] Knickerbocker affected to be referring only to the Spaniards in South America, but the contemporary resonance is clear. The attack on the Indians next notes their failure to engage in cultivation, another familiar line of attack. The argument is here undermined as it is made by Knickerbocker's pointing out that the land entirely supported the Indian way of life. The distinction between civilised and savage works in the latter's favour:

> They were so much the more savages, for not having more wants; for knowledge is in some degree an increase of desires, and it is this superiority both in the number and magnitude of his desires that distinguishes the man from the beast.

The discussion next considers the attempted civilisation of the savages. The familiar civilising virtues of alcohol and disease are present, overshadowed by religion. Again, Knickerbocker extols the savages even as he seems to denounce them:

> It is true, they neither stole nor defrauded, they were sober, frugal, continent, and faithful to their word; but though they acted right habitually, it was all in vain, unless they acted so from precept.[92]

The settlers proceed from mere argument to attempted conversion by "persecution." Knickerbocker continued to cover American sensibilities by locating the consequent massacres in South America, but the parallel to his own nation remained unmistakeable. This persecution provides the basis of a fourth right to possession of the land, that of "EXTERMINATION" or the "RIGHT BY GUNPOWDER."[93] If you have killed all the former possessors, there is nobody to dispute your right to possession. The argument is crowned with a startling analogy. Knickerbocker noted that, "Argument is never so well understood by us selfish mortals, as when it comes home to ourselves."

Again with that degree of ludicrosity which makes for hard satire, Knickerbocker proposes the existence of inhabitants on the moon who have "arrived at an enviable state of 'perfectability.'"[94] This recalled Mustapha's descriptions of the American republic. These moon men are as superior to the Americans, as the Americans were to the Indians, a claim contradictory to the American myth that America was the last perfect country, its people the last perfect race. It is in this analogy of a new great people that Irving demonstrated the broader vision lacking in his literary predecessors. Crèvecoeur and Brackenridge grappled with their sense of a failing perfection, of a flawed people. Irving, clearer on this point, was able to see America within the natural historical cycle, of which that failing perfection is a perfectly natural component. Equally clearly, he acknowledged, in denouncing it, the capacity of his country-men for self deception:

> I warrant the poor savages, before they had any knowledge of the White man, armed in all the terrors of glittering steel and tremendous gun-powder, were as perfectly convinced that they themselves, were the wisest, the most virtuous, powerful and perfect of created beings, as are, at this moment, the lordly inhabitants of old England, the vola-tile populace of France, or even the self-satisfied citizens of this most enlightened republick.[95]

The Americans are here decisively in the same scale as all the other peoples, White and Red. Their fate is easily determined. The new race of moon men looked for new lands to conquer and civilise, just as the early colonists did. The Americans duly complain and receive a sharp response:

> They will turn upon us and say—miserable barbarians! ungrateful wretches!—have we not come thousands of miles to improve your worthless planet . . . [96]

By the introduction of this fable, Knickerbocker potentially made the actual history of the Dutch colony/American republic irrelevant before he even embarked on it. The device places governors and presidents within a larger historical wheel. The reader may note the smaller lessons of those individu-als, but must recognise their entrapment in a larger fated cycle.

Those smaller lessons are contained in the history of the three governors of the colony, Walter the Doubter (Wouter Van Twiller), William the Testy (Wilhelmus Kieft) and Peter the Headstrong (Peter Stuyvesant). The most obvious contemporary satire is here and this has raised confusions regarding Irving's intentions. Kieft is clearly Jefferson, with "Book Four" repeating sat-ires familiar from *Salmagundi*, and unsuccessful attempts have been made to cast the other two as satires on specific presidents. Irving compounded the problem by mischievously denying any contemporary connections:

> This hint will be of importance, to prevent my readers from being seized with doubt and incredulity, whenever, in the course of this au-thentic history, they encounter the uncommon circumstance, of a gov-ernor, acting with independence, and in opposition to the opinions of the multitude.[97]

Rather than see the other governors as satires on specific presidents, or get too hung up on the identification of Kieft with Jefferson, more is to be obtained from the book if they are taken as political types and their errors examined in this light, although aspects of Stuyvesant's reign do have interesting resonances to the presidency and character of John

Adams.[98] More, each reign is not a historically confined period. Instead, Irving ranged throughout American history for comparisons. Van Twiller at one moment looks like Washington, at another like Jefferson. The technique is suggestive of unchanging humanity. The names may change; the problems, and the ending, stay the same, a situation symbolised by the fact that all three governors fail. Further, by focusing on the governors, Irving recognised the centrality of this question of governance to the nature of America and Americans.

This problem of governance was anticipated in "Book Two" where the plodding council meetings of the burghers are described. Their incapacity to plan city development curiously seems to benefit the city:

> The town . . . increased as rapidly in importance, as though it had been burthened [sic] with a dozen panniers full of those sage laws, which are usually heaped upon the backs of young cities.[99]

This laissez-faire approach necessitates the deployment of governors by the mother country who seeing, the colony's success, are suddenly anxious to protect it; thus it carries within it the seeds of its own demise. This approach is in stark contrast to that of the governors, even during the golden age of Van Twiller, but those active governors are equally doomed, even the golden Van Twiller. Each successive failure, anticipated by the book's historical framework, was in defiance of the emerging American myth, but there was plenty of American reality to draw upon from the successive falls of George III, George Washington, John Adams, and Thomas Jefferson.[100]

Dealing first with Van Twiller, he presides over both a golden age and a disaster, demonstrative of the warring capacities of mankind. It is a curious golden age, since no gold is involved:

> Because the evils produced by the precious metals, such as avarice, covetuousness [sic], theft, rapine, usury, banking, note-shaving, lottery-insuring, and the whole catalogue of crimes and grievances were then unknown.[101]

The parallels to the world of Hamiltonian finance are clear. In addition, "the profoundest *tranquillity* and *repose* reigned throughout the province."[102] This means that personally people mind their own business, and nationally:

> There were neither public commotions, nor private quarrels; neither parties, nor sects, nor schisms; neither prosecutions, nor trails, nor punishments.[103]

The number of habitual human characteristics excised from the settlement in this era is quite remarkable and suggests further mockery on the very possibility of a golden age. This list also recalls the sort of proclamations made in the early 1790s. But Knickerbocker drew a more curious parallel in explaining the consequences of this golden age. Citing Jefferson and Paine, alongside a host of classical authorities, Knickerbocker dismissed the notion that "honesty is the best policy:"

> It might have answered well enough in the honest times when it was made; but in these degenerate days, if a nation pretends to rely merely upon the justice of its dealings, it will fare something like an honest man among thieves.[104]

This recalls Jeffersonian, rather than Washingtonian, foreign policy. A portrait that, in its inability to capture its subject fully because of "the facts" being "so scattered and vague," anticipated Cunliffe's Washington, now recalls Henry Adams' Jefferson.[105] Yet, this confusion is entirely logical. For both men in ascending to the presidency proclaimed a golden age of progress. The point is the cycle. All golden ages fail. Again, there is a parallel with Brackenridge and his endless versions of the same moral.

The depth of Van Twiller's failure is greater than that of either of his successors, partly perhaps because of the apparent extent of his golden age; the contrast is more striking. His fall is the result of a quite specific failing, connected to the policy of honesty analogy:

> The guileless government . . . like a worthy unsuspicious old burgher, quietly settled itself down into the city of New Amsterdam, as into a snug elbow chair—and fell into a comfortable nap—while in the meantime its cunning neighbours . . . picked its pockets.[106]

Those neighbours are the inhabitants of New England. Irving used this to draw another remarkable historical parallel concerning the founding of the American colonies. In doing so, he stood on its head the argument of a heritage of liberty deployed by men such as John Adams in the years preceding the American Revolution.[107] First, he outlined why these people were in difficulties in Europe:

> [They] . . . did most presumptuously dare to think for themselves in matters of religion, exercising what they considered a natural and unextinguishable right—the liberty of conscience.[108]

This liberty must be exercised in vocal debates and therefore requires also a *"liberty of speech."* To preserve these liberties, they embarked for America. But, once there, this liberty mushrooms into something horrific:

> The right of talking without ideas and without information—of misrepresenting public affairs; of decrying public measures—of aspersing great characters, and destroying little ones; in short, that grand

palladium of our country, the liberty of speech; or as it has been more vulgarly denominated—the gift of the gab.[109]

This liberty of speech has flaws enough, but the pilgrims pursued it to fearful ends:

> Having served a regular apprenticeship in the school of persecution, it behoved them to shew that they had become proficients in the art. They accordingly employed their leisure hours in banishing, scourging or hanging, divers heretical papists, Quakers and Anabaptists, for daring to abuse the *liberty of conscience*.

These actions, just like those of the Americans, more broadly conceived, against the Indians, demonstrate the absence of any new race. Irving next spelt out their ultimate interpretation of this liberty of conscience:

> [This] they now clearly proved to imply nothing more, than that every man should think as he pleased in matters of religion—*provided* he thought *right*.

Now the contemporary parallel gradually emerges, recalling the attitudes of our various disputants, Republican and Federalist in 1800, Federalist and Anti-Federalist in 1788–89, Loyalist and Patriot in 1776:

> As they (the majority) were perfectly convinced that *they alone* thought right, it consequently followed, that whoever thought different from them thought wrong . . . was . . . a corrupt and infectious member of the body politic, and deserved to be lopped off and cast into the fire.

Irving did not draw quite this parallel here.[110] Yet the sense of an historical cycle is plain, moving from first settlement, through inter-Colonial conflict to the present day, and the present day clearly implies Jeffersonian America:

> But . . . what are we doing at this very day, and in this very enlightened nation, but acting upon the very same principle in our political controversies. Have we not within but a few years released ourselves from the shackles of a government, which cruelly denied us the priviledge of governing ourselves. . . . And are we not at this very moment striving our very best to tyrannise over the opinions, tie up the tongues, or ruin the fortunes of one another? . . . Where then is the difference in principle between our measures and those you are so ready to condemn among the people I am treating of? There is none; the difference is merely circumstantial.—Thus we *denounce* instead of banishing—We *libel* instead of scourging—we *turn out of office*

instead of hanging . . . this political persecution being, some how or other, the grand palladium of our liberties, and an incontrovertible proof that this is *a free country*.[111]

Where Mustapha declared things straight out, Knickerbocker attempts to draw his audience to such comparisons before openly declaring them.

Confronted by a threatened invasion of New Englanders, Van Twiller expired, ushering in the second governor, William the Testy (Wilhelmus Kieft). As with Van Twiller, historical moments and presidential characteristics are intermingled. The main thrust of Kieft's reign is a satire on his passion for Economy and the effect of that upon his foreign policy. Kieft responds to the numerous external threats with a flurry of Proclamations,[112] which prove utterly useless:

> All that was wanting to secure its effect, was that the Yankees should stand in awe of it; but, provoking to relate, they treated it with the most absolute contempt . . . and thus did the first warlike proclamation come to a shameful end.[113]

The military disasters of the War of 1812 seem to be anticipated in the government's inability to organise itself to meet the looming threat. But, satirising Kieft's policy of educating the populace, leads the narrative to the Democratic–Republican societies of the 1790s[114] and here, and in considering Kieft's demise, parallels with presidents other than Jefferson suggest themselves. The societies make the whole population discontented, but also cause them to turn upon Kieft. This hardly reflected the 1790s, but may well have reflected contemporary feeling at the close of Jefferson's reign. Kieft's demise is occasioned by the utter rejection of his proclamations, a deluge of policies being proposed by the populace and "the refractory disposition of his council".[115] Elements here are equally suggestive of John Adams' fate.

The failure of Kieft ushers Stuyvesant, the final governor, onto the stage. In removing Kieft, Irving took a further opportunity to undermine the relevance of his narrative. Having emphasised the importance of the governors to history, he now suggested their ultimate irrelevance. The "good people of New Amsterdam" give all the:

> civil and affectionate speeches that are regularly said on the death of all great men; after which they smoked their pipes, [and] thought no more about him.[116]

Stuyvesant adopts a third approach to governance, that of disregarding the people, for, "he possessed a sovereign contempt for the sovereign people."[117] Instead, he follows his own unchanging inclinations, earning by so doing warmer praise from Knickerbocker than anybody else has yet enjoyed:

> The clock that stands still, and points resolutely in one direction, is certain of being right twice in the four and twenty hours—while others may keep going continually, and continually be going wrong.[118]

This and the additional characterisations of Stuyvesant as an "old 'seventy-six' of a governor" and a man "jealous of his personal and official dignity" are all suggestive of John Adams.[119] His great independent act further cements this, for Stuyvesant's grave error is to make peace, an act Adams had committed in 1799. Irving used this to show that between nations, as between individuals, quarrels are inevitable and endless, and unity or cooperation impossible, another pronouncement at odds with the American myth.[120] Stuyvesant's qualities are highly praised before this error, and Irving was clearly satirising the argument that it was an error. Stuyvesant does hold out against the encroaching enemies for longer than either of his predecessors, but the final result remains exactly the same. The book's historical law has predetermined Stuyvesant's fall.

In the failures of the governors, there is an underlying similarity; all in some way mislead the people. This might seem to offer a way out. It is the leaders who are flawed, not the people, but the people, in sleeping, proclaiming, or fighting as they are bidden, are equally contaminated with their leaders failings. They allow themselves to be bound by the "political vocabulary."

Yet, another possible way out does remain. The history of the New Netherlands was on the verge of oblivion but Knickerbocker recovered it. Knickerbocker has vanished but, like William the Testy (Kieft), if the myth is to be believed, may be only sleeping one day to reawaken and give the New Netherlands more history.[121] The United States, at the end, is distinguished from the New Netherlands, although still locked in the same historical cycle. Irving related the subjugation of the New Netherlands by Britain and the "glorious revolution" which freed the American colonies.[122] He also pointed out that the revolution did not halt the cycle:

> The successful revolution in America produced the sanguinary revolution in France, which produced the puissant Buonaparte who produced the French Despotism, which has thrown the whole world in confusion![123]

America, Irving suggested, hung in the historical balance. Nobody could say what might flow from renewed European meddling in American affairs. Its fate depended on either leaders or people finding a way out of the morass of disasters Irving had chronicled. That way was hinted in Stuyvesant's flaw, for, in his own way, however admirable, he was as deaf to alternatives as his predecessors, just as the people he rules remain helplessly susceptible to that abuse of the "liberty of conscience."

Irving's *History* was a defining moment in two ways. First, it captured an America in literature in ways none of his predecessors had succeeded in doing. Second, it was a last defiant wake-up call to the new nation to live up to its own rhetoric, indeed to see what that rhetoric demanded of it. Knickerbocker ultimately left the matter hanging in the balance, but that balance faced with the shadow of Gibbon's Rome and the illusions of Jefferson's Inauguration was heavily precarious. The true state of Irving's mind, which would lead to a decade of near literary silence, was indicated in one of Knickerbocker's most poignant laments. That lament might have stood for a good many fellow Americans, who knew the sham of "we have called by different names brethren of the same principle" for what it was:

> Luckless Diedrich! born in a degenerate age . . . a stranger and a weary pilgrim in thy native land . . . doomed to wander neglected through these crowded streets, and elbowed by foreign upstarts from those far abodes, where once thine ancestors held sovereign empire.[124]

CONFUSIONS

The publication of *A History of New York* marked a turning point in Irving's life, although this was clearly not absolutely apparent to him at the time, nor was it perceived as such by his public. The success of the work, which had surmounted so many of the difficulties bedevilling his literary predecessors, must have placed Irving at the head of the list of American authors of the day. Of the other major writers of the era, Brockden Brown was to die the following year, and had produced no literary works since the turn of the century; Brackenridge, now on the Pennsylvania supreme court, had last published an addition to *Modern Chivalry* in 1804; James Kirke Paulding, Irving's collaborator on *Salmagundi*, had yet to carve out a distinctive work of his own. In late 1809, there was every reason to assume that, at last, America had found the great native author for which the intellectual community had been clamouring since the foundation of the republic.

Instead, after his steady stream of work over the preceding three years, Irving now fell silent. His next major work, *The Sketch Book*, did not appear until 1819, and appeared to have adopted a more English style, and to deal with more English subjects. The American content was arguably its high point, but its quality was offset by its rarity. The purpose of this section is to explain why Irving found it impossible to produce a second masterpiece focused solely, like the *History*, on American subjects. It contends that this was the direct result of his abiding concern for the developing American polity.[125]

In reality, despite the sunny vistas opened by the success of the *History*, Irving already faced a number of personal and literary problems. His fiancée, Matilda Hoffman, had died in April, 1809. Irving had partially found refuge from his misery by throwing himself into the completion of the book, but with publication, that distraction was now lost to him. The family importation business was enmeshed in the chaotic international trading situation created by the Napoleonic Wars. This interfered with the early writing of the *History*, depriving Irving of his collaborating brother, Peter, sent to Liverpool to oversee the European side of the business in 1808. It would take Irving several times to Washington to lobby Congress, usually futilely, and to his increasing disgust, before finally contributing to his departure for Europe in 1815.

But these factors in themselves are insufficient to explain the disconsolate tone of Irving's letters of the time. The problem of career again reared its head. The difficulty was not new. Irving was a reluctant legal student, but the lure of Matilda Hoffman was strong, and Irving successfully qualified. That lure was now gone. He made an attempt in February, 1810 to secure a clerkship at the New York courts, but it came to nothing, and the letters to Mrs Hoffman, Matilda's mother, describing it are laced with Salmagundian scorn at the whole procedure:

> I . . . have been disgusted by the servility, duplicity and rascality I have witnessed among the swarm of scrub politicians who crawl about the great metropolis of our state, like so many vermin about the head of the body politic.[126]

Personal disappointment may have contributed to this attitude, and Irving does lament the absence of Mr. Hoffman at the crucial moment, but his jibes suggest a dislike of the whole procedure which seems beyond mere personal pique:

> I shall return to New York poorer than I set out, both in pocket and in hopes, but rich in a great store of valuable and pleasing knowledge which I have acquired of the wickedness of my fellow-creatures. That, I believe, is the only kind of wealth I am doomed to acquire in the world, but it is a kind of which I am little covertous.[127]

They are also coupled with reflections on the importance to the nation of nurturing artistic careers. Interestingly, Irving did not complain for himself, but wished he had money to support the portrait painter Anson Dickinson whom he met on the trip.

Irving was temporarily rescued from his dilemma by the generosity of his brothers who made him a sleeping partner, with a one-fifth share, in the family business, for which, for the moment, he had to do little in the way of work, although the connection would subsequently become a millstone round his neck. But this apparently satisfactory arrangement did not negate Irving's problem. By freeing him from the necessity of seeking work beyond writing, it only made the problem of writing more acute.

His difficulty was made clear in two letters from this period, one from September, 1810, the other from the following February. The recipient in 1810, John E. Hall, then editor of the *American Law Review*, had proposed that Irving produce a new literary journal. Intriguingly, Irving rejected the idea, not on grounds of nonprofitability but because:

> I do not wish to meddle with my pen for a long while—I would rather devote a year or two at least to study—as there are several branches of knowledge which I am but little acquainted with at present, which are indispensable to popular writing. Indeed I feel conscious that my mind wants improvement, and it is impossible to give it the regular cultivation that is necessary, unless I disengage myself from literary enterprises.[128]

He came close to indicting the policy of most of his fellow writers:

> I wish to proceed as cautiously as possible; and if my caution does not enable me to write better, it will at least preserve me from the hazardous error of writing a great deal. I know it is one of the difficult things of this world, to check and keep down an itching propensity to scribble, which every man has, who has once appeared in print.[129]

Irving was in a luxurious position to take such a high line. Ostensibly, he wanted to improve his style, as became evident in *The Sketch Book*, but the problem was also one of subject.

In the second letter written to his brother, William Irving, in February, 1811, after Irving had again missed out on preferment (on this occasion the hope of the secretaryship at the American Legation to France),[130] Irving expanded on the plan he previously proposed to Hall, focusing much more on subject:

> Should I not be placed in the situation alluded to, I shall pursue a plan I had some time since contemplated, of studying for a while, and then travelling about the country [USA] for the purpose of observing the manners and characters of the various parts of it, with a view to writing a work, which, if I have any acquaintance with my own talents, will be far more profitable and reputable than any thing I have yet written.[131]

No such work materialised from Irving's pen, nor do the letters directly address the reasons for its abandonment. Obviously, Irving wanted to produce another major work. The importance of his failure so to do demands an explanation. To do so, we must both make some connections between the subjects which do occupy his letters of this period, and the literary work he did undertake which was, in effect, a surrender to exactly the sort of scribbling he condemned in his letter to Hall. Further, these endeavours must be set in the context of events in the wider world.

Irving had not remained holed up in New York City during this period. We have noted his trip to Albany. He made a trip to Washington in the spring of 1811 mainly to lobby for legislation significant to the family business. Irving commented extensively on the political scene which confronted him in the state and national capitals. Again, there are echoes of *Salmagundi* satire in his description of his visit to Madison's White House, referred to as "the sublime porte."[132] Irving attempted at various points to declare that he had risen above any great concern for the factional disputations he witnessed. He stressed the many individuals who stood above the factional battle, but his continued concern escaped onto the page in despite of this, most strikingly in a letter to Van Ness:

> As to talking of patriotism & principle, I've seen enough of both general and state politics to convince me they are mere words of Battle— "Banners hung on the outer walls", for the rabble to fight by—the knowing leaders laugh at them in their sleeves—for being gulled by such painted rags.[133]

To a limited extent then, Irving was travelling and observing. For all his protestations to the contrary, sprinkled through these various letters, he could not lose the fascination that politics held, nor the concerns it evoked in him. The nature of the contemporary political situation is also significant, although beyond references to the effect of legislative acts on the family business, Irving's comments tend towards the broad brush. James Madison had succeeded Thomas Jefferson in 1809, at almost precisely the moment at which Jefferson's policy of using economic coercion to force concessions from France and Britain was coming apart at the seams. Congress and the Administration appeared at a loss as to what alternative policy they might pursue. The country remained divided between Federalists and Republicans; the former, though increasingly an isolated faction, still commanded considerable support in New England. To put it simply, the state of the nation was uneasy, and showed little sign of becoming any less so in the foreseeable future. Irving's previous writings had shown that he was an acute observer of the state of the nation. They had shown that it mattered to him. It is unlikely that this had ceased to be the case.

This uneasy state raised obvious difficulties for any such book as Irving had proposed to research. There is a hint in his remarks to Hall that he hoped to produce a work more reputable than anything he had yet published. Such a desire obviously depended on getting away from the political qualms documented in his early masterpieces and from the unsettling light they threw upon his countrymen. His experiences in New York and Washington made this extremely difficult.

These various concerns, personal and public, culminated in mid-1811 in a despairing letter to Henry Brevoort:

> Pleasure is but a transient stimulus, and leaves the mind more enfeebled than before, give me rugged toil, fierce disputation, wrangling controversy, harassing research, give me any thing that calls forth the energy of the mind; but for heaven's sake shield me from these calms, these tranquil slumberings, these enervating triflings, those syren blandishments that I have for some time indulged in, which lull the mind into complete inaction which benumb its powers, and cost it such painful and humiliating struggles to regain its industry and independence.[134]

It is clear that the plan for a new work had got nowhere. Irving had, so far, failed to find a way forward. For the next year, he retreated into the distraction of his old social life among the lads of Kilkenny,[135] and his letters appear to suggest a regaining of something of his old humour. The contention that this was but another, more extended, attempt to escape his contradictions, rather than an indication that all was now well, is strengthened by the contents of Irving's next literary production.

This is his editorship of the *Analectic Magazine*, which he took on in late 1812 and continued until the close of 1814. Irving's biographers have been unanimous in their dismissal of this literary production as mere hackwork or editorial "filler."[136] But the question then remains as to why Irving chose to undertake it. Literature had never left his mind during the preceding three years. Even during his retreat into a wilder social life from mid-1811 to mid-1812, he produced the first of many revisions of the *History*. The tangle of motivations visible in Irving's letters, veering from a carping dismissal of the magazine to an optimistic view of the financial rewards and the potential content, do little to clarify the situation. We are thus left with the actual content of the magazine, and of Irving's contributions. These point to more complex motivations.

Under Irving's editorship, the magazine broadly consisted of two sections: reprints of articles from leading British and European periodicals, and original material produced mainly by Irving himself, James Kirke Paulding,[137] and Giulien C. Verplanck, another of the New York literary coterie.[138] Verplanck contributed a number of biographical sketches of important, fairly recently deceased, political figures, including Samuel Adams, Fisher Ames, Oliver Ellsworth, and Joel Barlow.[139] Now there are some curious juxtapositions, bearing out the contention that Irving was selecting material at random from whatever came to hand. The January, 1813 edition, leading with the "Sixth Report of the Directors of the African Institution" followed by excerpts from Maria Edgeworth, a description of the Spanish peasantry, and a description of St. Petersburg is a particularly good example. However, two abiding and interconnected concerns, literature and politics, do emerge, and the examination of these through the selection of reprints and Irving's own contributions is vital in explaining Irving's journey from the *History* to *The Sketch Book*.

Literary pieces embraced reviews of old world writers such as Maria Edgeworth, Lord Byron and Samuel Taylor Coleridge and, perhaps most significantly, some rare British reviews of American publications (February, 1813—William Wirt's *Letters of the British Spy*,[140] January, 1814— Major Amos Stoddard's *Sketches of Louisiana*).[141] The review of Wirt is complementary of his work and, by extension, American literature.[142] This particular reprint may be an early indication of Irving's burgeoning desire, explored more fully in *The Sketch Book*, to bridge the gulf between America and Britain, the depth of which was later symbolised by Sydney Smith's acerbic comment concerning the reading of American books.

The political–historical articles are notable for a frequent recurrence to the issue of the relationship of government and society, and the problems of different forms of government (for example the review of the *Memoirs of Frederick the Great's Sister*, April, 1813 and the review of a *Historical Sketch of . . . The Reign of Gustavus the 4th*, October, 1813, both with themes of apparent lunatic monarchs).[143]

Most important are a third group of pieces which combine literary and political themes, as their fates were entwined in the American Revolution, and in Irving's career to date. Most significant here are a number of reprints of reviews of Madame de Stael's works, particularly a reprinted review of de Stael's *De La Litterature*, from the September, 1813 issue. The book, as discerned by the anonymous reviewer, suggests a role for literature similar to that which Irving practised in the *History*:

> The professed object of this work is to show that all the peculiarities in the literature of different ages and countries, may be explained by a reference to the condition of society, and the political and religious institutions of each;—and at the same time to point out in what way the progress of letters has in turn modified and affected the government and religion of those nations among whom they have flourished.[144]

This extract reflects confrontational concerns of the American literary community and its members, put simply, the desire for a national literature positively reflective of the nation, and the belief, held by Brackenridge, Irving, and others, that that literature could both reflect, but more importantly modify, that nation.

The publication of a European piece so brilliantly reflective of an abiding American concern is, in itself, striking, the more so when de Stael goes on to stress the importance of literature as a tool for educating public opinion.[145] But what follows is remarkable. De Stael asserted that this national literature and the society it was influencing, was in a continued state of progress and it was this fact which her anonymous critic seized upon and violently disputed. It was precisely this issue of the progressing American society with which Irving had been concerned in the *History.* It was a problem which, following the proposition's reassertion by Jefferson, and Irving's critique of the resultant regime, had become especially live with the commencement of the War of 1812, a dimension specifically addressed by Irving in his original contributions.[146]

Again, these pursue two concerns: the state of American literature, and biographical sketches of key naval personnel in the War of 1812, which expand to become assessments of the state of the nation. His reviews of American writers cover a collection of the verse and prose of Robert Treat Paine, Jr. (March, 1813),[147] Paulding's *The Lay of the Scottish Fiddle* (September, 1813) and the collected poetry of Edwin C. Holland Esq. (March, 1814). These are partially concerned with the parlous state of the nascent American literature and its nurturing towards a brighter future, with hints here of the Irving on the road away from the satire of his early writings:

> Absorbed in politics, or occupied by business, few can find leisure, amid these strong agitations of the mind, to follow the gentler pursuits of literature, and give it that calm study, and meditative contemplation, necessary to discover the true principles of beauty and excellence in composition.[148]

That personal dimension also comes out in discussing Paine's personal shortcomings. Paine both suffered from "irregularity of habits" and "want of application" in pursuit of his literary career, and failed at the law—charges which, although not so extreme, might have been levelled at Irving. Finally, the state of American literature is also clearly tied to the state of the nation. In Paine's case, Irving excerpts a lengthy section from a poem entitled "Rise Columbia!" which dwells on the merits of peace, perhaps hinting at Irving's uneasiness regarding the war:

> Nor yet, though skilled, delight in arms;
> Peace and, her offspring, Arts be thine;
> The face of freedom scarce has charms,
> When on her cheeks no dimples shine.[149]

The dimples suggest a kinship to the speckled nation Irving documented in the *History.* In Holland's case, the frustration of American shortcomings is heightened by celebration of American victories taking place in British literary forms, highlighting the very fragility of those victories:

> By tasking our own powers, and relying entirely on ourselves, we shall gradually improve and rise to poetic independence; but this practice of appropriating the thoughts of others, of getting along by contemptible

shifts and literary larcenies, prevents native exertion, and produces absolute impoverishment.[150]

These themes play out more extensively in the biographical sketches which investigate Captain James Lawrence (August, 1813), Lieutenant William Burrows (November, 1813), Commodore Oliver Hazard Perry (December, 1813) and Captain David Porter (September, 1814.)[151] Paulding would continue this series, after Irving severed his connection with the magazine at the close of 1814. Of these, the most interesting appeared during 1813, and show Irving wrestling constantly with the national question in long introductions before turning to the biographical specifics, his ostensible topic. The contradictions which litter these pieces are an instructive barometer not only for the state of Irving's mind but for the divisions and disputes occasioned by the War of 1812, of which the Hartford Convention was merely the most extreme expression.

Thus, these pieces are partially valedictory, seizing on the success of the Navy, and in particular it's leading commanders, as an indication of the salutary effect the war has had on national character:

> The idea of Lawrence, cut down in the prime of his days, stretched upon his deck, wrapped in the flag of his country . . . will form one of those talismanic [images] which every nation preserves as watchwords of patriotism and valour.[152]

On occasion he seems as mesmerised by the dream of a Canadian empire as the War Hawks of the Twelfth Congress:

> Those vast internal seas [the Great Lakes] will, perhaps, never again be the separating space between contending nations; but will be embosomed within a mighty empire.[153]

The rising prospects of the nation find an expression here previously denied them. But Irving was still Knickerbocker, too acute an observer to succumb wholly to the war fever. Just as Knickerbocker could not avoid the flawed characters of the great leaders he sought to celebrate, so Irving could not blind himself to the fact that, for all the flaws and arrogances displayed by the British, the Americans, too, often showed themselves no better. In the biography of Perry, Irving devoted his first two pages to a stark criticism of what he saw as the "boastful arrogance" the nation was displaying at its successes.[154] His reasons for this criticism hardly amounted to a ringing endorsement of his native land:

> We joy, indeed, in seeing the flag of our country encircled with glory, and our nation elevated to a dignified rank among the nations of the earth; but we make no boastful claims to intrinsic superiority, nor seek

to throw sneer or stigma on an enemy, whom, in spite of temporary hostility, we honour and admire.[155]

In consequence of this divided view of his country, both longing to celebrate its victories and conscious that the country was not always worthy of them, Irving's tone became pleading. As through Knickerbocker, now in his own voice, Irving admonished his countrymen's failings, whether ardent patriot, as above, or extreme Federalist:

> One of the dearest wishes of our hearts is to see a firm and well grounded friendship established between us [Britain and America]. But friendship can never long endure unless founded on mutual respect, and maintained with mutual independence. . . . There is an obsequious deference in the minds of too many of our countrymen towards Great Britain, that not only impairs the independence of the national character, but defeats the very object they would attain.[156]

Irving's problem was worse even than his unsurprising misery at the divisions that arose in the country. It is clear that he was by no means satisfied, for all his championing of naval heroics, that the war was really for the best, though whether this was the result of an unease about military confrontation or simply a sense that it was doing more harm than good to the nation cannot be stated with certainty. At the heart of this was Irving's abiding concern for what kind of nation was being forged by the war. He, like so many other writers and politicians,[157] saw the war, to begin with, as an opportunity to revitalize the national character, and the naval victories became, for him, the most hopeful sign that this might be possible. But, as the dissenting voices sounded louder, and Irving's own doubts about the "present unhappy war"[158] grew, it was the reverse of this belief which tormented him:

> There is no such thing as releasing ourselves from the consequences of the contest. . . . The disgrace of defeat will not be confined to the contrivers of the war, or the party in power, or the conductors of the battle; but will extend to the whole nation, and come home to every individual.[159]

As Irving's despondency increased, his active contributions to the periodical were reduced in number and scope. The last major piece is the critique of Holland's poems in March, 1814, and this, like the biography of Captain Porter, has none of the wide-ranging questioning introductions found in the earlier articles. This could simply be an indication that Irving was losing interest in an occupation never given his whole heart. Yet, the depth of concern revealed in the earlier pieces suggests an alternative explanation. Irving had stopped writing because he felt that his audience was paying him no attention and that he was simply repeating himself to no avail. Instead, he undertook practical action. Virtually abandoning the magazine, as he acknowledged during a subsequent dispute over payment, he joined the New York militia as an aide-de-camp to Governor Daniel D. Tompkins (later Monroe's Vice President). As a result of this commitment, the number of letters also falls off dramatically, although there are still revealing glimpses of the unsatisfactory military situation. During a visit to Sackett's Harbour in September, 1814, Irving commented caustically that, "there is a sad deficiency of arms and military munitions."[160]

His uneasiness with his country, and his need to wrestle with that uneasiness in print, is clear in the *Analectic* pieces. It was temporarily tempered, as his contradictory judgements in those pieces and his decision for military service showed, by the need for national survival, and, if possible victory. But the attainment of the latter only heightened the unease, as *The Sketch Book* makes clear.

That this relationship was central to his departure for Europe cannot be absolutely proved from his papers since, unfortunately, no letters survive for the crucial months between February and May, 1815 when he sailed. Announcing that departure to Brevoort, Irving confined himself to stating that his life had been "unsettled and almost joyless . . . for some time past."[161] Biographers duly emphasise personal motivations for this decision—the chaotic state of the family business, the illness of Peter (the brother in charge in Europe), and an illusive tale of a possible romantic attachment.[162] Rubin-Dorsky made a connection with the failings of the republic but couched it in personal terms, arguing that Irving did not wish to live in this environment and, therefore, sought escape in Europe. But, as this chapter has sought to suggest, the national problem was about much more for Irving than mere personal questions of his place in the nation. His concern was wider, and was centred on the type of nation being forged. He hoped the war would expunge some of the failings he had observed so brilliantly in the *History*. To a limited extent, he had used his original pieces in the *Analectic* to push along this process. The manner of the war's ending demonstrated that he had failed. The extreme Federalists had tried to drag New England from the Union, and victory had inspired an outburst of unthinking patriotism of precisely the kind Irving had worried about during the War itself. The end of the war, and the optimism which it produced only left Irving precisely where he had been before the conflict began.[163] Then, for two years, he had struggled to produce a new work on America, only to find himself confronted by exactly the same questions he had already dramatised. His response to the war had demonstrated that he could not leave hold of the national question. The personal and the public were inextricably linked within him. It was not to escape that link, by flight into a personal imaginative haven, as Rubin-Dorsky suggested, but to find an adjustment of perspective which would make it tolerable that he left America in 1815. *The Sketch Book* was the result of that quest.

RESOLUTIONS

Irving's departure for Europe would prove to be the first step on the road to a resumed literary career. But this road, in 1815, remained long. Initially, Irving faced in Europe only a resumption of the crisis which had confronted him in America. His commentary on that crisis through his letters provides further illumination of the motives which had impelled him to Europe, and which would culminate in *The Sketch Book*.

His situation in Europe quickly came to mirror his position in America prior to the temporary escape which the war afforded him. Thus, while he again found distraction in the soulless misery of trying to rescue the family business, he went on worrying about how he might resume his literary career. This quest for a means so to do was now additionally hampered by a trace of guilt, discernible in his letters during the early years of his stay. Almost from the moment of his arrival, Irving displayed doubts as to whether he had made the right decision in leaving America. His homeland haunted his correspondence, conveying a sense that somehow, perhaps in spite of himself, he felt that he had failed in leaving.

Before coming to this sense of failure we need to consider his actual activities in Europe at this period. In a much earlier phrase of the crisis, in 1812, Irving had contemplated flight to Europe. In his vision then, it offered the possibility of a series of distractions, an opportunity to find stimulation in "novelty and variety."[164] But if this was his anticipation when he actually departed in 1815, he was to be rapidly disabused.

From almost the moment of his arrival in Britain, he was plunged into the crisis bedevilling the family business. The business had been floundering for some time, under the pressures of the war and the illness of Peter Irving, the brother in charge in Europe. Because Peter's health continued to be poor, Irving had to take much of the burdens of the business on himself. A two-and-a-half year struggle to rescue it ensued. But it was futile, and in February, 1818 the business was declared bankrupt.

The struggle did nothing to improve Irving's taste for the business world, or his general morale, and his letters are littered with increasingly despairing comments:

> I am here alone, attending to business—and the times are so hard they sicken my very soul.[165]

If the problem had simply been dislike of business and frustration at his comparative confinement to English commercial cities such as Liverpool and Birmingham, the situation might have been less grave. But the imprisonment in the business world only masked the ongoing career crisis Irving had now been struggling with for over six years. This crisis was now become exceedingly complex. Irving still yearned after some kind of literary career, but he could not yet see what that would be and, meanwhile, he was trapped in the struggle to salvage something from the wreck of his family's livelihood. In addition, he increasingly displayed uneasiness as to whether he had made the right decision in leaving America. These thoughts are most clearly expressed in a July, 1816 letter to Henry Brevoort. Irving first spelled out his continued literary desires:

> I have attempted . . . to revive the literary feeling & to employ myself with my pen; but at present it is impossible—My mind is in a sickly state and my imagination . . . blighted. . . . Time & circumstances must restore them to their proper tone.[166]

Next he returned to the question of his putative return to America. He spelled out his sense of being cast adrift:

> I must wait here awhile in a passive state, watching the turn of events, and how our affairs are likely to turn out—"My bread is indeed *cast upon the waters*"—and I can only say that I hope to *find it after many days*.[167]

After meditating on this theme, Irving concluded with an insistent assertion:

> This you may be assured of—all my ideas of home and settled life centre in New York—and I have had too little pleasure or even comfort in England to wean me from this delightful spot of earth.[168]

This confusion as to where to reside physically is mirrored in his literary comments. During 1817, as the business wound torturously towards its dismal failure, the idea of *The Sketch Book* began to take shape in his mind. By July, 1817, he was asserting the existence of such a plan to Brevoort, while abandoning thoughts of returning home because the plan, it appeared, could only be executed in Britain. This was in stark contrast to the other literary comments which run through his letters. He showed a persistent concern with getting British culture across the Atlantic so that it might influence his homeland.[169] Further, a letter to Washington Allston (1779–1843), the painter, in May of the same year, finds Irving urging his compatriot to pursue his career at home:

> As to sending it to America . . . I would rather do so—as it is infinitely preferable to stand foremost as one of the founders of a school of painting in an immense & growing country like America, in fact to be an object of national pride and affection, than to fall into the ranks . . . of Europe; or perhaps to be regarded with an eye of national prejudice, as the production of an American pencil is likely to be in England.[170]

Thus did Irving urge his compatriot and namesake upon the path that he, himself, could not follow. To understand why, we must turn from his explanations to his friends and family, to the literary work in which he resolved the crisis, *The Sketch Book*.

This work, a collection of 34 essays, was composed between the years 1817 and 1820, with the exception of the two sketches dealing on Indian themes originally published in the *Analectic*,[171] and some early manuscript jottings of themes and ideas dating back to 1810. It was originally published, as *The Sketch Book*, in seven periodical numbers in America between 23 June, 1819 and 13 September, 1820. The choice to publish there first, and to do so in this format, suggests, again, Irving's desire to maintain his position at home and that the primary audience for which he wrote was his American one.[172]

The work, in particular the two American tales "Rip van Winkle" and "The Legend of Sleepy Hollow," is today Irving's best known, and perhaps the only one (barring *The Alhambra*) which is frequently reread. It was seen at the time, particularly by British reviewers, as the first American work to be worthy of placement in stylistic terms alongside the English greats.[173] Critics and biographers have tended to follow this line of argument, focusing on it in artistic terms.

Our concern here is less with this development of style, except insofar as it demonstrates Irving's movement from literature as a tool in the shaping of society, to literature as a work of art. *The Sketch Book* is relevant for its detailed dramatisation of the struggle which Irving's letters and other writings of the 1810s have borne witness to. It is a witness to his painful search to construct a world in which he could live, but which need not necessitate the total abandonment of his homeland, the choice which he faced because of the failings of that homeland and its populace. *The Sketch Book* replays and resolves that struggle, but it is a painful and provisional resolution.

That this struggle is central to the book is further indicated by the book's competing narrators: Geoffrey Crayon, Gent., the work's alleged author, representing Irving's expedition to Europe as he might have wished it, free to view its glories rather than enslaved to attend to family miseries; Diedrich Knickerbocker, who tellingly speaks from beyond the grave (directly in two stories, "Rip van Winkle" and "The Legend of Sleepy Hollow," and indirectly in "Little Britain" which, although ostensibly attributed to Crayon, is pervaded by Knickerbocker's warnings); and Irving himself, whose actual experiences and situation occasionally break through these masks. Additional confusion is created by the presence of the two essays on the Amer-Indians—"Traits of Indian Character" and "Philip of Pokanoket"—reproduced from the *Analectic Magazine*, but presented here as though written by Crayon.

Crayon represented the persona towards which Irving was reaching, who became in the course of *Bracebridge Hall* and *Tales of a Traveller* almost a mere sketcher.[174] Here, he is still in development, and embattled. While Crayon's voice seeks to banish America from view, Irving, haunted by Knickerbocker, is unable to leave it behind, a problem dramatised from the opening sketches, "The Author's Account of Himself" and "The Voyage." Here Crayon strives to justify leaving America and to establish his voice while periodically sounding very like Knickerbocker.

The sketch begins with an innocent explanation for the journey, but one which reverses the customary application of "new" to the New World:

> I was always fond of visiting new scenes and observing strange characters and manners.[175]

But the tone rapidly becomes almost apologetic, Irving going out of his way to stress the wonders of America, "never need an American look beyond his own country for the sublime and beautiful of natural scenery," as if a desire to write of other places naturally reflects ill upon his homeland. Irving's characterisation of America as unsurpassed in these terms is somewhat ironic given that many of the European sketches focus on the natural beauties of Europe. Having temporarily dismissed this quality, Irving must now advance another reason for his shift of focus to Europe:

> My native country was full of youthful promise; Europe was rich in the accumulated treasures of age.

Two things are striking about this statement: first, the reiteration of America's quality, suggestive of Irving's vulnerability on this point; second, the intriguing inference that Europe possesses an historical quality that America does not have. The passage that follows suggests the extent to which something of Knickerbocker lurks behind Crayon's more genteel mask:

> I longed to wander over the scenes of renowned achievement—to tread as it were in the footsteps of antiquity . . . to escape in short, from the commonplace realities of the present, and lose myself among the shadowy grandeurs of the past.

Irving's desire to escape the present is a paean of his letters of the period after 1809, and a key factor in the hopes fuelling his flight to Europe. Yet there is something more at stake here. Irving's last major work had centred on the creation of an (albeit fictionalised) history of his native land, designed as a means to comment on the present. But that work had also demonstrated the very richness of the American heritage which Irving's defensive tone here affects to deny.

And this is followed by an echo of the old satire. Irving now latches on to the familiar argument (which Jefferson had challenged in his *Notes on Virginia*), that all creatures, including man, degenerate in America. In Irving's hands, it becomes complex. At one level, Irving is here satirising this argument, and the "swelling magnitude of . . . English travellers" who stalk through America advancing it. But his comments also recall his own criticism of his native land:

We have, it is true, our great men in America. . . . I have mingled among them in my time, and been almost withered by the shade into which they cast me; for there is nothing so baleful to a small man as the shade of a great one.

Neither side, in fact, is getting out of this with much credit, for given Irving's view of the great men of America here alluded to, the claim that "a great man of Europe . . . must therefore be as superior to a great man of America"[176] has an uneasy hollowness to it.

The opening sketch then serves merely to show the confusion with which Irving is wrestling while pointing to the way out he intends to adopt.

Having set up the dilemmas in relatively straightforward terms, the second sketch, "The Voyage," adds a broader imaginative sweep to the narrative. Here the Crayon aim is brought centre stage. Irving emphasised the problem of travelling by land:

We drag . . ."a lengthening chain" . . . we can trace it back link by link; and we feel that the last still grapples us to home.

He contrasted it with the benefits of travelling by sea, "a wide sea voyage severs us at once." Ostensibly, the latter is Irving's desire as mapped onto Crayon, to escape the burden of America in the safer pasts of Europe, but Irving's anxieties immediately force a qualification:

It [a sea voyage] makes us conscious of being cast loose from the secure anchorage of settled life and set adrift upon a doubtful world. It interposes a gulph [*sic*], not merely imaginary, but real, between us and our homes—a gulph subject to tempest and fear and uncertainty, rendering distance palpable and return precarious.[177]

In the imaginative juxtaposition of the sailing ship as both a blessing which "has brought the ends of the earth into communion" and a curse because so dangerously prone to shipwreck,[178] Irving's dilemmas, chronicled in the scattered writings of the preceding decade, are starkly exposed. Indeed, the turmoil of fears that the talk of shipwreck awakens in Crayon might stand as symbol for that dilemma, from which Irving now hopes to escape. Duly, this nightmare concludes with the safe arrival of the ship, "lord[ing] it over the deep" and a remarkable reversal of the definitions given in the preceding sketch. Then, America was the land of "promise," now:

None but those who have experienced it can form an idea of the delicious throng of sensations which rush into an American's bosom, when he first comes in sight of Europe. *It is the land of promise*, teeming with every thing of which his childhood has heard, or on which his studious years have pondered.[179]

This expression of feeling might be taken as innocent pleasure in the possibilities of the new world before Irving, but it is vital to remember that it has to be true. Or, at least, Irving has to believe it, precisely because of what he has abandoned by the act of sailing away from home, and severing his ties to it. The fragility of this promise is underlined by the sketch's conclusion:

> I alone . . . had no friend to meet, no cheering to receive. I stepped upon the land of my forefathers—but felt I was a stranger in the land.[180]

Factually this is, as has been seen, wholly inaccurate. Irving had family to stay with and a business to tend. This was not even his first visit to Britain. But Irving was referring to an identity, a community more fundamental than this. It is that need for an identity, from which he claimed to have been severed by making the sea voyage, that underpins the work.

Yet, there is an self-deluded quality to this quest, since the severing upon which it is based, the forsaking of America, is an illusion, demonstrated not just by the ghostly presence of Knickerbocker but by the comparisons between Old and New worlds that frequent the later sketches.

The sketches "English Writers in America" and "Rural Life in England," printed consecutively, showcase this confusion. In the first, Irving attacked English accounts of journeys in the New World. In doing so, he presented a picture of America which appeared to contrast sharply both with that given in the *History* and, indeed, in the recent *Analectic* pieces. How dare these travellers not recognise, he complains:

> a country in a singular state of moral and physical development; a country in which one of the greatest political experiments in the history of the world is now performing, and which presents the most profound and momentous studies to the statesman and the philosopher.

On the surface, this appears a stunning contrast to the indicted politicos who were his targets in the earlier American works, but as the sketch proceeds, the odd hints of uneasiness surface, "The national character is yet in a state of fermentation: it may have its frothings and sediment, but its ingredients are sound and wholesome."[181]

Irving begins to sound again like a man trying to convince himself, while the next section knocks a famed American dream to pieces. Irving suggested that foreign travellers may have pictured America as El Dorado, but "there, as every where else, a man must sow before he can reap; must win wealth by industry and talent; and must contend with the common difficulties of nature."[182] This section again suggests a writer who cannot yet make up his mind what his aim is. The need to defend his homeland in a work to be published in the country that has often made the most strenuous attempts to destroy or dismiss her is clear, yet, even here, and despite his attempt to slough it off, Irving cannot resist comments which recall his views of 1807–9. There is a distant echo here of the pointed comparison between the New England Federalist extremists and Jeffersonian America even if it is now couched in rather more gentle terms. For all his pretence, he is still concerned to address both sides,[183] as well as his current hosts, a new, third side.

Thus, he concluded the sketch not in the forceful tones expressive of American glory which sound at least briefly in the opening section, but with another appeal, echoing that made in certain of his *Analectic* pieces, for a better mutual understanding between the two countries. Then, having again emphasised the need for America to "take . . . examples and models . . . from the existing nations of Europe," Irving presented a remarkable list of English attributes as examples "congenial to the American character:"

> The manners of her people,—their intellectual activity—their freedom of opinions—their habits of thinking on those subjects which concern the dearest interests and most sacred charities of private life.[184]

The third English characteristic is particularly striking, implying again that freedom may be improved upon in America. Thus we see that Irving is not yet wholly prepared to abandon engagement with his homeland. To support his argument, "Writers" is followed by "Rural Life in England," the first of such visions which came to dominate *Bracebridge Hall*. "Rural Life" begins the sustained quest for the English character, and yet Knicker-bocker quickly breaks in afresh with "Rip van Winkle."[185]

The tale is set among the descendents of Peter Stuyvesant, the heroic final governor of the *History*, and Rip, the protagonist, appears an excellent example of the inevitable degeneration of peoples, as he mismanages his farm and cowers before a termagant wife. Here the meaning of the overturning of British rule and the establishment of the American republic is openly at issue, where in the *History* its dilemmas were covered by the Dutch mask. Yet, the characterisation of the populace as descendants of Stuyvesant maintains the narrative within the *History*'s broader story of the rise and fall of nations, in contradiction to Jeffersonian and Monrovian expressions of rising glory. Moreover, whereas the *History* delights in the twists and turns of that inevitable fall, here it tends towards dream, a hint perhaps at the problematic consequence to clear vision from the illusory political statements of Jefferson and his successors.

Thus, in this revolution there are no grand battles, no gallant last stand by Governor Stuyvesant. The transformation occurs off-stage, while our hero sleeps. The change, the story suggests, is so insignificant, that one might as well sleep through it. Yet sleep is preceded by as stark a vision of reality as any the *History* presented. En route to his symbolic avoidance of the American Revolution, Rip stumbles into an ancient Dutch encampment, wherein the inhabitants "maintained the gravest faces, the most mysterious silence, and were, withal, the most melancholy party of pleasure he had ever witnessed."[186] Isolated and forgotten, they personify the price exacted by the Revolutions with which the story is concerned—a price which Rip at this moment of connection is oblivious to but which will shortly be exacted from him.

And so it proves. Oblivious to the consequences of his slumber, Rip stumbles back to his village where, at first, the revolution seems to amount to little more than an exchange of symbols. The old inn has become "the Union Hotel," George Washington has replaced George III on the inn-sign. Gradually the consequences widen, in less flattering ways:

> The very character of the people seemed changed. There was a busy, bustling disputatious tone about it, instead of the accustomed phlegm and drowsy tranquillity.

Among the disputants, one provides an echo of Salmagundian satire; "[he] was haranguing vehemently about rights of citizens—elections—members of Congress—liberty—Bunker's hill—heroes of seventy six . . .".

Abruptly, the darker side of this change emerges, as Rip tries unwittingly, to explain "whether he was a Federal or Democrat?"[187] Announcing himself "a loyal subject of the King," he immediately looks likely to be set upon by the mob as a Tory and a spy.[188] For a brief moment, we are in a world where only a violent response can ensure security, a world governed by the determining rubric: you are either with us or against us. This is no longer an innocent dreamlike transformation, confined to the obscured Revolutionary past. The connection with the divided polity obscured by Jeffersonian rhetoric is forcefully made, with one, critical, difference. Rip, unlike exiled Loyalists and increasingly silenced Federalists, is preserved. Authority steps in to hold off the mob, his daughter appears, and Rip is at last recognised for who he is. The moment this is established, beyond all doubt, by the respected local historian, Rip ceases to be of interest, as "the company . . . returned to the more important concerns of the election."

Life rapidly returns to its "old walks and habits." As if to shake off the unsettling impressions left by the election mob, we catch a glimpse of Rip's son, the image of Rip, who shows as little interest in farming as his parent.

The muddle is profound. On the one hand, there is an election system, a new United States sufficiently changed that Rip, unless he conforms. is to be set upon by a mob apparently created with them, a contrast to the old, peaceable village. On the other, once satisfied as to his identity, Rip seems able to slip back into his old way of life, for "Rip in fact was no politician; the changes of states and empires made but little impression on him . . .".[189]

Yet, beneath this slipping back, two profound changes have occurred. Rip's personal tyrant, his wife, has been removed. Ostensibly, this is cause for celebration:

Whenever her name was mentioned, however, he shook his head, shrugged his shoulders and cast up his eyes; which might pass either for an expression of resignation to his fate or joy at his deliverance.[190]

But there is a profound pain attached to this loss, demonstrated at the height of Rip's bafflement at his situation by his calling loudly for his wife and children.[191] Revolution is not the painless, dreamy transformation it might appear, the seamless continuum conjured by Jefferson and Monroe.

That agony is obscured, but through acceptance, rather than exile. Rip does not, in fact, slip back into his old obscurity. In striking contrast to the insults hurled at him when he first reappears, he soon grows into great favour among the rising generation.[192] He "was reverenced as one of the patriarchs of the village and a chronicle of the old times 'before the war.'"[193] As the Dutch persist in the hills, so Rip may persist in his village. His history, unlike so much elided by the dreamy transformations crafted by Jefferson and others, can be heard. In this imagined New York State, there are people prepared to listen to him. Rip can go home.

But the forward movement of the book paints the opposite lesson, as Crayon resumes his attempt to craft a fresh, Old World idyll. The sequence which follows musing on rural beauties, magnificent Old World ruins and still standing glories, and the importance of literature to society. But Knickerbocker is not yet exorcised. Crayon, musing on the tombs in Westminster Abbey, sounds uncannily like Knickerbocker musing on the fall of New Amsterdam:

History fades into fable, fact becomes clouded with doubt and controversy; the inscription moulders from the tablet; the statue falls from the pedestal.[194]

This voyage culminates in the extended sequence of sketches describing an old-fashioned English Christmas, sketches which seem to mark a decisive distancing from the problematic world of the American republic. Instead, they conclude with the clearest discussion of all, decisively in Irving's voice on the very problem they have apparently banished:

Methinks I hear the question asked by my graver readers, "To what purpose is all this—how is the world to be made wiser by this talk?" Alas! Is there not wisdom enough extant for the instruction of the world? And if not, are there not thousands of abler pens labouring for its improvement?—It is so much pleasanter to please than to instruct— to play the companion rather than the preceptor. What, after all, is the mite of wisdom that I could throw into the mass of knowledge; or how am I sure that my sagest deductions may be safe guides for the opinions of others? But in writing to amuse, if I fail, the only evil is my own disappointment. If, however, I can by any lucky chance, in these days of evil, rub out one wrinkle from the brow of care, or beguile the heavy heart of one moment of sorrow; if I can now and then penetrate through the gathering film of misanthropy, prompt a benevolent view of human nature, and make my reader more in good humour with his fellow beings and himself, surely, surely, I shall not then have written entirely in vain.[195]

All, it seems, is to be for the best, in the best of all possible worlds. Irving will, finally, surrender his clearer gaze to the rising vision of the Jeffersonians. In fact, as it proves, the authorial conflict cannot be so suppressed, as it could not be for the less public Jefferson, concerning which the warnings about the Missouri Compromise were only an especially outspoken example. We should also note that there remains an element of instruction here. Irving's particular complaint had been the failure of his contemporaries to live in harmony with one another. His "benevolent view of human nature" recalls the acceptance of Rip's New York State, against the mob, and, more politely, but no less troublingly, the exclusionary character of certain key Jeffersonian statements. This pleasure still contains the possibility of demands upon his countrymen. It is not completely the easier, rising road.

In any case, it is no more a severing of the instructing need than the sea voyage severed Crayon from home, for it is immediately followed by a fresh eruption of the former. Instead of continuing the English idyll, after another brief sketch of a corner of London, the sketch of "Little Britain" is set out. Here, Janus-like, Crayon speaks with Knickerbocker's tones, deploying, as the *History* persistently did, instruction in government.

"Little Britain" is the only sketch referring directly to contemporary British events. We are in the world of the death of George III and the Cato Street Conspiracy, of radical meetings and bloody violence, events tied by the local prophets to a broader sense of impending doom for the nation. These events are examined, and the future of them foretold, in one small quarter of London, entitled, tellingly, Little Britain, intended as a microcosm for the nation:

> Little Britain may truly be called the heart's core of the city; the strong hold of true John Bullism.[196]

But this fragment of Britain soon emerges as yet another mask for the troubled American republic. Here, as there, this core is suffering the horrors of factionalism, although they are described in gentler terms than in the earlier satires:

> Little Britain has occasionally its factions and divisions, and party spirit ran very high at one time in consequence of two rival "Burial Societies" being set up in place.[197]

This idea of disputation, apparently focused on minor details regarding burial procedures, is duly ridiculed, but the strategy of Rip's return is now deployed in tandem:

> Besides these two funeral societies there is a third of quite a different cast, which tends to throw the sunshine of good humour over the whole neighbourhood.[198]

Thus does Irving show his strategy operating in practice, with, it appears, a fair amount of success:

> I have pleased myself with considering it [Little Britain] as a chosen spot, where the principles of sturdy John Bullism were garnered up, like seed corn, to renew the national character. . . . I have rejoiced also in the general spirit of harmony.[199]

But neither resolution or escape is yet possible. Knickerbocker's baleful tones will not go away:

> All empires . . . are doomed to changes and revolutions. Luxury and innovation creep in; factions arise; and families now and then spring up, whose ambition and intrigue throw the whole system into confusion.

In keeping with the lighter, fanciful tone, of this version of the story, the villain here is merely "the aspiring family of a retired butcher,"[200] and the row one over questions of fashionable society. Yet, this does not negate the fact that the new plan has failed. Rip may have been able to go home to his village; Crayon's home, and behind him, Irving's, is still uncertain. The quest goes on:

> I have determined . . . to beat a retreat . . . and am actually looking out for some other nest . . . where old English manners are still kept up.[201]

Crayon will find this in *Bracebridge Hall* (1822), but *The Sketch Book*, while anticipating the possibility, keeps repeating the lesson behind it. Indeed, in this last portion of the work, the idyll is disrupted more than ever, by both the republished Indian sketches "Traits of Indian Character" and "Philip of Pokanoket," and "The Legend of Sleepy Hollow." The Indian sketches are almost a greater disruption of Crayon than Knickerbocker's interventions. For they are placed under his name, contradicting his professed desire to sever his ties with America, and they are a firm, rather uncomfortable reminder of a particular conflicted aspect of the new republic. In the *History*, as we saw, Knickerbocker is incandescent regarding the treatment of the Amer-Indians. Now Irving, having acknowledged that ill-treatment, tried not altogether convincingly to defend the American government, praising their treatment of the Indians and blaming the less reputable White men on the frontiers.[202] America is still not spotless with all the problems of observation that entailed, and yet America cannot be left alone. The problem appears as insoluble on personal and national levels as it was in 1809.

Yet solution there is. *The Sketch Book* concludes with a story more dreamlike in its ultimate meanings than Rip's, where the fate of the central character remains obscure.[203] Yet, on close examination, it places contending Americas and Americans in precarious yet sustained balance. Though Irving remained in exile, he did not end, as he had done in the *History*, by dooming his homeland. The story which achieves this is, of course, the second from Knickerbocker's pen, "The Legend of Sleepy Hollow."

The story takes place "in a remote period of American history, that is to say, some thirty years since."[204] Thus, we are in the year 1789, the moment of the refounding of the republic. Ichabod is the schoolmaster of Sleepy Hollow, a town which is haunted by the ghost of a headless horseman, said to have been a Hessian trooper, who fell in the Revolutionary War.[205] It gradually becomes clear that this area was contested ground during the Revolution, and there is some hint that the many ghostly apparitions said to haunt the locality are connected to the atmosphere engendered by that contest.[206]

Ichabod possesses a good position among the women of local society, being considered superior, by virtue of his learning, to "the rough country swains."[207] He is a fan of all the local myths and legends, which he enjoys retelling at the firesides of his acquaintances, only to suffer terror on the way home. All would have been well, had not Ichabod fallen for a worse demon, a woman, the local heiress, in whom he glimpses a far brighter future in the unexplored Western reaches. Ichabod then might be named a typical rising American, looking out for the best chance of a prosperous future, perhaps on the frontier.

But Ichabod's dream is not realised. He departs late from a party at his beloved's house, with the imputation that something has gone wrong between them, much scorn having been heaped upon her coquettish ways. On the way home, he passes the tree where Major André was captured, and soon imagines, or possibly really is, pursued by a headless horseman. The next morning Ichabod has vanished. Several years later, a farmer visits New York, and reports back that Ichabod left in dudgeon at his rejection by the heiress but "had been admitted to the bar, turned politician, electioneered, written for the newspapers" and generally been a thorough success. His rival, who successfully gains the heiress, is also suspected to know something of the truth, but has not revealed it.[208]

The old themes are very clear, the neglect and failure of the educated in the new republic, the ease with which a beloved object may be lost. Again, too, the story reminds us of the disputed character of the Revolution, particularly acute in New York State. Unlike the potential traitor Rip, the actual traitor Major André cannot go home. But the central conundrum then remains. What are we to make of Ichabod's experience, and should the news from New York be taken as the truth? Both Rip van Winkle and Sleepy Hollow are more than ghost stories to beguile an idle hour. Like the rest of the book, they show their author wrestling with the nature of America and Americans, and pressing his countrymen to do likewise. Rip's Revolution depends on the death of his wife, this Revolution upon the death of André. The latter has become a means of humour for the rest of the village, but it is deadly serious for Ichabod as the former was, at the critical moment, for Rip. Both are needed for the success of the story, its chronicler, and the nation for which it is a microcosm. Similarly, the farmer's story posits a success, but the villagers' superstitious belief that Ichabod "was spirited away" reflects a reality. Ichabod can only achieve success by remaining away from the village, just as Irving can only achieve equilibrium through exile in Europe. The darker side, whether glimpsed in Jeffersonian rhetoric, or seen in revolutionary ghosts, remained present to them both. The escape, the possibility of the "land of promise," is permitted. The recognition that the darker side, the fate of all nations, could not be endlessly paraded is allowed. By this balancing act, Irving located a hope which Crèvecoeur and Brackenridge failed to find. Yet that very balancing act meant that Irving's chain was only weakened, remaining to lead him home 17 years later, ultimately to conclude his career struggling to finish a huge biography of George Washington, a corroboration of the burden of his country. Equally, the chain remained in the story. For it does not end with the report of the farmer but with the image of the haunted, ruined schoolhouse, another reminder of the *History* and the fragile method by which Irving maintained hope in his country:

The schoolhouse being deserted, soon fell to decay, and was reported to be haunted by the ghost of the unfortunate pedagogue; and the plough boy, loitering homeward of a still summer evening, has often fancied his voice at a distance, chanting a melancholy psalm tune among the tranquit solitudes of Sleepy Hollow.[209]

4 The Fragments
Minor Writers, c.1810–1824

In reviewing the scenes through which it [the peace] has been attained we can rejoice in the proofs given that our political institutions, founded in human rights and framed for their preservation, are equal to the severest trials of war as well as adapted to the ordinary periods of repose.[1]

[This book is] as genuine, and the facts which it records as true, as that a great, valiant, and pious president of these United States, has ably conducted our late glorious war with England to a most honourable conclusion, and for ever secured "free trade and sailor's rights."[2]

The end of the War of 1812 saw renewed expressions of America's rising glory, that abiding American conviction that all was for the best in that best of all possible worlds. Key politicians led the way, but for some writers, notably Irving, this optimism remained illusory.

Irving's retreat to Europe, away from direct engagement with America, in retrospect marked a crucial moment in the developing American literary quest for a country. For, no major writer emerged to fill the gap. The uneasy line traceable from Crèvecoeur to Brackenridge to Irving is broken after *A History of New York*. Instead, a strange cacophony of publications occurred, borrowing haphazardly from their predecessors, but lacking that earlier intensity of vision. There was an ultimate failure to engage with the question as those predecessors had done. Significantly, the loudest voice to emerge from this, James Fenimore Cooper, would, in his works of the 1820s, make a decisive turn away from critical literary engagement with America's problems. The three writers examined here demonstrate this transitionary moment, for while they did dimly grapple with the quest, they pointed also to Cooper's path.

The three writers are James Kirke Paulding, Irving's collaborator in *Salmagundi*; John Neal; and the almost unknown Jonas Clopper. Despite a recent new biography of James Kirke Paulding, all three are neglected by critics.[3] Their various literary endeavours drew on a variety of their predecessors. Two key strains not yet discussed are present, the seduction novels, and the work of Charles Brockden Brown (1771–1810), concerning which a few words must be said.

Really? Not writers about Brown

The seduction novelists, such luminaries as Susannah Rowson, Hannah Webster Foster, and William Hill Brown to name but three, might be considered the founders of the American novel. Their works usually track the ruination of a flower of American womanhood at the hands of some blackguard male. Although they do provide useful comment on societal mores and notions of sexual morality in post-Revolutionary America, their grasp on the nature of the wider polity is limited. Put simply, they did not ask the kinds of questions asked by writers like Irving and Brackenridge, and those questions were broader and more significant to the nature and development of America, than which spotless maiden might have been foolishly lured into bed. These questions about appropriate behaviour towards women resurface at length in several of Neal's novels.

The case of Brockden Brown is more complex. Now canonised, Brown can certainly claim to be the first major American novelist, producing six novels, and a variety of fragments and magazine pieces during his brief life. He has recently enjoyed an extensive critical renaissance, and monographs now exist covering almost every aspect of his life. Brown did glimpse the wider questions central to the work of Brackenridge and Irving, although discussion was embroiled in unfortunate romances and characters never able to make decisions, all of which did not advance much on the world of the seduction novelists. But there are significant problems with these glimpses. Brown presented the confusion theme in embryo. Frequently he lighted on important ideas and themes, the nature of authority in *Wieland* (1799), problems of social position in the pell mell world of the emerging capitalist America in *Arthur Mervyn* (1800, 1801), the Indian question in *Edgar Huntly* (1800). But these ideas are presented from a profusion of opposed positions and those positions are enmeshed in complex plots driven by characters behaving with the utmost stupidity. Moreover, Brown's glimpses of the broader polity are precisely that, contrasted with Brackenridge's travelogue which literally and figuratively possessed a wider focus.

Since Neal's six early novels partially invoke Brownian confusions, his inclusion might be questioned on the same grounds. Neal merits inclusion because this study is both thematic and chronological. Brown's confusions do not have the same significance for this narrative in the late 1790s which Neal's possess for it in the 1810s and 20s. Further, Neal ultimately grasped at the broader questions in a more sustained way than Brown, and he was clearer in what he wanted to say about them. In Brown's case, it was never entirely clear whether the nature of America and Americans was in question and, if so, what Brown intended to say about it. Critics have appropriated him to support a variety of positions precisely because of this confusion. Neal dimly glimpsed a problem, and struggled to find a solution. His quest for America was a peculiarly literary one, as Brackenridge's and Irving's were not, but it raised the familiar questions. His quest was also oddly personal. It can, at first sight, appear that his vigorous, even vicious, attack on Cooper was fuelled by purely personal motives, the jealousy of a man who thought himself equally entitled to fame. But the contrast between a Cooper novel ending in a happy marriage and a Neal novel ending in a pile of corpses is significant.

Paulding and Clopper are more simply explained. Paulding maintained a fading strain of satire, increasingly dominated by the strident nationalism of the British–American literary quarrel. Yet, in 1824, he returned to satire full blast in an American Indian saga in striking contrast to Cooper's, *Koningsmarke, or the Long Finne.* Clopper was the loneliest voice of all. In his extraordinary *Fragments*, he produced a work in direct descent from Brackenridge and Irving. The book satirised the history of the republic from the discovery of America (Bawlfredonia) to the presidency of John Adams. It reiterated a need for realism to a public about to be swamped in the wild but ultimately reassuring world of Cooper.

While these writers borrowed, cannibalised, and confused, their countrymen, if the President was to be believed, were ascending to ever nobler heights, a rise immortalised in that unintentionally ironic name "The Era of Good Feelings," with which one newspaper baptised the Monroe era.[4] Monroe, in his First Inaugural Address, encouraged such a description, replaying the old themes as vigorously as his more literary contemporaries.[5] Again and again, Monroe repeated the adjective happy: "the present happy condition," "the happy government," "no country was ever happier," "the present happy state," "a people so prosperous and happy." This reiterated insistence on mood was accompanied by the customary paeans to the unity of the people and the growth and prosperity of the country. The polity and its chroniclers were out of joint with one another, the question was slipping through the cracks.

RAMBLINGS

> All his late productions had a scope and purpose in them—a steadiness and unity—far more serious, than were ever attributed to them, at the time; nothing less, I believe, now, than to effect a revolution in the literary taste of the age.[6]

> [Neal] learnt ... how to ... pass counterfeit money—if occasion required—as it would, sometimes, in a country, where that, which was counterfeit, and that, which was not, were exceedingly alike, not only in appearance, but in value.[7]

Neal and his twin sister Rachel were born on 25 August, 1793, in Portland, Maine. His father died a month later, an event possibly preceded by ghostly portents. He was educated at the Quaker boarding school at Windham, but like many contemporary writers was dissatisfied with his education. Also, similarly to contemporaries, he was an early, wide-ranging reader. Like Irving, he was sucked into the commercial world during the War of 1812, but, unlike his more fastidious compatriot, he embraced the seamier side of the business. He was a notably unsuccessful businessman, all three of the operations going bankrupt, but there is less anticommericalism in his writings than one might expect. Again, following fellow writers, he studied law, but was rapidly distracted by the possibilities of writing. Now living in Baltimore, he was a leading light in the Delphian Club, a collection of aspiring writers fired by the resurgent American nationalism of the post-War world. This group included Hugh Henry Brackenridge's son, Henry Marie, Paul Allen, whose *History of the American Revolution* (1819) Neal completed, and John Pierpont, author of the epic verse tribute to sacred music, *Airs of Palestine*. Neal began to contribute to periodicals, and produced his first novel, *Keep Cool* (1817).

Critical consideration of all of Neal's novels, with the possible exception of *Rachel Dyer* (1828) is limited. Fortunately, Neal was endlessly self-referential. In 1825, in his most famous exploit, he attempted a review of American literature in four essays for *Blackwood's Magazine* (published in Edinburgh and enjoying wide influence in the States), concealing his identity under the pseudonym of Carter Holmes.[8] Nothing if not immodest, Neal proceeded, in the fourth essay to invite Neal, himself, to critique his literary productions to date. This self-reviewing repeated a device employed at the outset of *Keep Cool*, and it is the comments on that novel which concern us here. Neal paved the way for contemporary critics to emphasise the antiduelling aspect of the novel[9] by stating that it was "a paltry, contemptible affair. . . . It was written chiefly for the discouragement of duelling."[10]

Neal made a similar claim for the book in his autobiography, published in 1869. Given Neal's concern, by the mid-1820s, with the production of original American work, his dislike of his first novel is partially explained. *Keep Cool* hoovered up the array of American literary antecedents. The seduction novelists are recalled in the complex plot of the loves of three soldiers, Charles Percy, James Earnest, and Colonel Sydney. Both sexes come in for an equal share of criticism, with attacks on male and female coquetry. These sorts of themes become more prominent in the novels of the 1820s, where Neal's protagonists are perennially having the cup of happiness dashed from their love-hungry lips through failings of their own. This aspect of the novel, as of those similar episodes in Neal's later doorstoppers, contains elements of autobiography drawn from Neal's own highly turbulent romantic career.

In isolation, this theme, even augmented by the odd bloody duel, would merit as much attention in this study as the seduction novels it draws on. Two points lift it above its origins: first, Neal's inability to take himself entirely seriously, a handicap which faded with the later novels; second, the fact that the novel also addressed more significant themes, in particular the American Indian problem.

The strain of self-mockery, clearest in the early part of the novel, recalled *Salmagundi*. Thus, when the hero has followed the girl he presumes is his mysterious beloved, only to discover she is a total stranger, Neal reflected caustically:

> Here I know I ought to give a bit of a description about the morning, and the dew, and the clouds . . . about his suffering, and his prayers, and his dreams, and his tears; but all that is quite too common: any body can be eloquent on the subject of a dirty morning, hard beds, and Albany fare, and therefore—I leave it to *anybody*.[11]

This self-mockery, lightening the plot, is joined by Neal's grappling with two issues familiar to previous writers. First is the role of the writer and the novel in America, pursued both through the narrator and the character of Echo, an epic poet also embroiled in the book's duels and love affairs. The second is the collision between savage and civilised worlds, dramatised by the character of Sydney, prominent in Volume Two of the novel.

Neal borrowed from *Salmagundi* in addressing the role of the writer, affecting to undermine himself by opening the novel with a self-penned review. Neal based the piece on what he called the customary critical practice of contradicting every utterance in one paragraph in the following paragraph. This also recalls Brown's confusions. Neal has almost become a one man logocracy, a point clarified in the review. Here, Neal did not simply assume a reviewer's persona, instead reviewer and author battle each other, apparently fighting for control of the pen. The battle moves beyond the relative merits of the novel to reflect on the national literary culture, represented by the novel, and the political nation within which that culture is embedded.

Thus, the reviewer begins by criticising all authorial attempts, excepting his own commentary, to fashion great American literature:

> There seems to be a curse resting on American scholarship and taste . . . [of] a preposterous and idle ambition of doing something for the literary reputation of *our* country. True patriotism would inform *us* that the only way to do honour to *our* country is to be silent.[12]

He gleefully indicated that Neal's attack on reviewers, made in introducing this very review, was extremely unwise:

> It will not be for *his* interest, or his booksellers', in a country where people never make up their minds on the merit of any work, till *we* have placed *our* mark upon it.[13]

We are poised, it might appear, for Neal's work to be brutally dissected, but the authorial personality abruptly reasserted itself over the reviewer in Neal's fevered brain, to condemn his rival:

Reviewers suppose themselves to be, in the republick of letters, what our legislators are, in our national assemblies; the collective wisdom of our country;—the representatives of opinion and intellect;—the concentrated majority of opinion. The body of the people are their slaves.[14]

The overt political parallel is striking, demonstrating again the entanglement of politics and literature, of the rising nation and its culture. There is also a hint of Brackenridge's concerns about tyrannies of the ignorant though here transposed onto a new segment of society. But the central problem is older and more serious; where does authority lie? Who can speak for America? This is starkly displayed by this juxtaposition of two minds in one, each questioning the other's authority, a more extreme version of the multiple personas displayed by Crèvecoeur, Franklin, and others. Their personas may argue within their texts, but they do so with a little more decorum than this. But both also claim to be spokesmen for the wider American polity. Here it is not so much what they say as their manner of saying it. The very fact of their dispute undercuts their claimed authority. Almost as a by-product, it also undercuts the authority of "our national assemblies." This is in striking contrast to the most obvious rival spokesman, President Monroe. His Inaugural Message is produced precisely on the premise of the reviewers. It endeavours, by speaking in one voice, to personify the unity of the country to which it lays claim. That unity, built on the back of the attempts at New England's secession, the wider disputes over the war and the burning of Washington, was as illusory as Jefferson's claims to it had been in 1801. Neal's divided self was but another reflection.

But the reflection is a clouded one. The writers of the earlier period, Irving and Brackenridge being the key examples, reflected that illusion with clarity. In Neal's case, although the muddle is less tangled than in Brown's fiction, there are contradictions left unresolved. For, even as he, at war with himself, called national unity into question, he gave voice also to the reborn American literary nationalism. The English and Scottish writers are condemned for taking so long to achieve any literary success, in stark contrast to the rise of the Americans: "We, with the characteristick [*sic*] genius of our countrymen, for improvement, rather than invention, *we* have alighted on, its very summit at a bound."[15]

Further, the reflection is becoming more personalised. The importance of the dilemmas of Knickerbocker and Brackenridge was in balance with the wider fate of their society. Each needed the other. Here that relationship shows hints of becoming unbalanced. There is a sense that if Neal could be confident of triumphant reviews, his worries might dissipate, prefiguring his 1820s assault on literary Britain. Neal's concern, again and again, is with the success of Neal, whichever thin character he is concealed behind.[16] Further, his success remains possible, as that of Brackenridge and Irving did not. The contradictory restatement of the rising glory dream which forms the penultimate paragraph of this peculiar pseudo review hammers these questions of authority:

> The time will arrive, when the production of American science and genius, will bear some proportion to the scale of their inspiration. The time will arrive when these slanders, and these aspersions will be forgotten; when our posterity will wonder that we could have ever doubted the everlasting charter of greatness that is written upon our barriers;—our cataracts—our rivers—and our mountains.[17]

While it is significant that the time has not yet arrived, it is equally so that the possibilities still resonate in contrast to Knickerbocker's doomed empire, or Brackenridge's ignored narrator. Yet, what one ultimately returns to in these opening pages is the sense of the quest in flux. Neal more than honoured his claim to pile contradiction upon contradiction. He concluded the review with a reiteration of doubt:

> Reader!—this novel was written when the author felt that occupation was happiness;—when he felt that dreams may answer all the purposes of reality; it was written too; . . . but no matter—if you have courage, read it and you may not find your time wasted![18]

From this melée of an introduction, we proceed to the melée of the novel proper, and the various themes and characters already noted. In this narrative proper, characters persistently question each other's authority, while the whole is undermined by the unreliable narrator with his frequent pronouncements on the irrelevancy of his own text. Thus, after a series of poetical scraps, of the usual standard for the period, he declared:

> *Keep Cool*, Reader; the rest is illegible. I had no other way of showing that I *could* make rhymes.[19]

Among these characters, a detailed examination of two—Echo, an epic poet, and Sydney, who becomes the leading protagonist—is necessary. Although all the characters, in their different ways, demonstrate the confusion of authority, Echo is the most obvious example since, as Harriet, one of the lovely ladies, explains:

> I have heard him defend a position with such plausible earnestness, that his whole frame would shake with illustration; and if any person else agreed with him . . . he would shift to the other side of the question with such consummate dexterity, that you would overlook the tendency of his movements.[20]

This is a more forceful version of the confusions created by Neal's two personae in the introductory section. It calls into question Echo's integrity just as the integrity of those two personae is called into question. Yet, what Echo has to say in this instance goes some way to explaining Neal's attitude in the introduction and is in contrast to earlier writers often nervous in their profession:

> What folly for a man after he has published, to mince about a little flattery, to apologise, to declare that his book was a trifle, full of errors, written in a hurry, out of town when it was printed, never saw a proof sheet. He is either a liar, or a fool. . . . First he does not believe his book is a trifle; he says so, and he is a *liar*. He expects the public to buy a book that the author himself declares is full of errors, etc. and therefore he is a *fool* to say nothing of the complement he pays the publick.[21]

Echo's blunt argument is that a man should not be shy of celebrating his work and that society is wrong to condemn him for doing so.[22]

Echo makes interesting points about some of the problems facing American writers in this period, but is undermined by his evident contradictory character. Yet, from the cacophony produced by Echo and his colleagues, one forceful voice does emerge, that of Sydney. Sydney is shown to stand apart from the other characters. Echo's reaction is particularly striking:

Henri Sydney is the only man I ever saw that I could not laugh at.[23]

This reaction finds justification in the familiar stigma that Sydney's blood may not be racially pure, an easy brush with which to tar the man who stands outside society's conventions. Sydney, unsurprisingly, gives them further ammunition in this first significant outburst about himself:

> For seven long years have I withstood the influence of fashion, the provocation of fools and madmen. My principles have been unshaken; and I am wild, haughty and ungovernable.[24]

It is an arguable point whether the reader is expected to admire or despise Sydney. Certainly, when he is finally compelled to duel, the narrative condemns him, but his evils in this respect are no worse than the fashionable fops who dominate the rest of the plot. More, Sydney, in his attempt to rise above the dreadful practice of duelling, is more American than the others, combining the characteristics that mark out and exclude the emigrant, with those which mark the excluded Indians. Sydney's dream of a fresh start is familiar:

> I came here, to America, in the hope of finding *here*, among a nation of brothers, of brave men, some, whose hearts were not the receptacles of foreign vices and foreign fashions.[25]

It is the old familiar plea for difference; the old familiar disappointment. This time Sydney is driven to battle. The battle occurs, significantly, near that same location that marked the most notorious duel of all, "where the great Hamilton expiated his only weakness with his heart's best blood."[26]

Sydney is the recipient of a hollow victory, immediately and acutely conscious of his moral bankruptcy at having finally given way to fashion. The approbation he receives in society only rubs salt into the wound, as the narrator comments caustically on the kind of society that approves such acts:

> Sydney did not know, reader, that here, in America, a *gentleman* may cut another's throat, or blow out his brains with complete impunity, there, the vulgar only are hanged for murder.[27]

The illusion of all men are created equal, the flaws of those more equal than others are again exposed. As with Crèvecoeur and Irving, this is given added punch by the comparison with other societies. For, in his misery, Sydney now gives his life history, expanding on this very different experience sensed by Echo. Sydney fought at a high level under Wellington, with the Russians, in South America, and among the Indians.[28] What began as soldiering for fortune led to steady disillusion. South America seemed quite hopeful:

> In that country I have felt a sensation of liberty—of unshaken independence—a land of expansion of the spirit, that I cannot describe; and never felt anywhere else.[29]

Unfortunately, the movement turned out to be led by dubious leaders with dubious aims. And, lest his readers deceive themselves, North America is little different:

> After her countless battles, her hardships, her sacrifices, though peopled with adventurers, with Englishmen, strong with the soul of unanimity and resistance: even North America produced but one WASHINGTON, and was *but* independent![30]

It is worth noting the confusion evident here, in this use of the term "Englishmen" alongside "independent." The question of American character, at least for this would-be American, and despite a second War of Independence, still seems open. And yet North America is different, because of the presence of the Indians. Sydney lavishes praise upon them, while openly confessing a racial prejudice in spite of that admiration:

> He [an especially close friend] was much lighter than the common copper of his people, scarcely darker than a Spaniard, and indeed, sister,

I am not wise enough to conceal that I loved my Indian brother the better for it.[31]

This admission lends weight to the testimony that precedes it. Sydney begins by praising the Indians as soldiers,

[I led them] with the proud certainty that I led braver and better men, then ever followed me before . . . and I found them less savage than the refined Europeans.[32]

He condemns European judgements of the Indians, challenging the designation "cowardly:"

The White soldier has innumerable protections, that an Indian can never have: his officers, science, and discipline. The latter is never so safely screened behind his tree, as the former is in his platoon.[33]

Thus, as in Crèvecoeur's and Irving's writings, the civilised and the savage are transposed. But Sydney then makes a further connection, drawing in the slaves:

It is said they [the Indians] are treacherous; unfaithful to their *brothers*, the Americans. Their brothers! Ask the Carolinian slave who is *his* brother—*there* is the stamp of fraternity![34]

The slaves and the Indians are the true brotherhood, Sydney argues, and an open rebuke to American requests to God for "a blessing on their efforts to be free."[35] Sydney proceeds from this to a long list of the crimes committed against the Indians by the White settlers, comparing the failings of the Whites at every turn with the noble characteristics of the Indians.

The purer world of the Indian stands as a vivid contrast to the corrupt fashions of the white world which have so far dominated the novel. Sydney, just as much as Crèvecoeur, is caught between the two. For all his repudiations of that fashionable world, he is drawn back to the ties of family and the ties of love, not to mention the temptation to duel which produces the fatal event of the novel.

His membership of two worlds reaches a climax after the fatal duel. He flees back to the wilderness, lamenting that he ever left it:

Why did I leave thee? . . . thou last retreat of Freedom! thou rugged wilderness! virtue's own home."[36]

But this utopia is promptly snatched from him. At the anticipated sanctuary, Indians turn on him, including one he thought a friend. The dream crashes about his ears, as the narrator recounts with a certain mockery to his tone:

> To be deceived—by an *Indian*! to give his hand to an *Indian* and be stabbed; to have his proud, heaven-inspired belief in the generosity of these rude sons of nature *so* smitten, by one blow.—He felt so humbled. Here was another glorious fabrick [*sic*] of his imagination crumbled by a touch.[37]

He is eventually rescued by "his" Indians, but it is proved, irredeemably, that the Indians are no more a single perfect race than the White Americans, or, indeed, anybody else. Moreover, Sydney, unlike Crèvecoeur's literary persona, returns to live among the Whites. He has taken what he needed from them:

> He had no longer that air of conscious superiority; he no longer *talked* eloquently, or imperiously of the duty of a Christian; but now he *did his duty in silence.*[38]

There is, in this conclusion, a belittling of the earlier rage. Sydney surrenders more obviously than Irving or Crèvecoeur, acquiescing in the compromises of his society. He marries one of the coquettes, and ceases to indulge in diatribes against the society he once rejected. His earlier diatribes are, in any case, undermined by the difficulty in determining precisely how important they are intended to be against the cacophony of subjects from which they emerge. Yet, the stark message does still emerge in this novel, a message akin to that conveyed by Crèvecoeur and Irving. At this starting point of Neal's career, it is clear that the principle of "instruction" was not yet dead.

Keep Cool sounded a last trumpet. Neal proceeded from it down familiar paths of authorship, for all his bluster that he was doing any number of new things never before attempted. He made the customary attempt to produce an epic poem, *The Battle of Niagara*, published in 1818. He wrote a variety of magazine pieces and part of a hack history of the American Revolution. Finally, and again the connection with Brockden Brown is apposite, he embarked on the production of a sequence of five doorstop novels, *Logan* (1822), *Randolph, Errata* and *Seventy-Six* (all published in 1823) and *Brother Jonathan* (1825). They were written with a zany rapidity which shows in their muddled plots and volubility of language.[39] *Keep Cool* possessed at least one clear voice. Cooper, as will be seen, was fashioning, at the same time, an equally clear voice. Neal was conflicted by his multiple inheritances. In *American Writers*, Neal claimed them, excepting *Brother Jonathan* as:

> a complete series; a course of experiment, as the author himself declares, upon the forbearance of the age.[40]

Randolph, an epistolary novel, bears the closest similarities with the seduction novelists, apart from some early workings out of the literary criticisms Neal developed more fully in *American Writers*. *Errata* is a kind of cross between a Gothic horror story and a picture of Dickensian slums in America, ending with a typical array of madness and death engulfing principal characters. *Brother Jonathan* returned to the era of the American Revolution, but with an even looser focus than that of *Seventy-Six*. All three drift, albeit in various intriguing directions, away from the main question of American character and are not discussed in detail here.

Logan showed Neal wrestling with his conflicted literary heritage, being part Brownian character study set in convoluted plot, and part authorial digression on various themes including religion, love, and the fine arts. These digressions recall Brackenridge but lack the underlying philosophy binding his thoughts together.[41] The book also features less lively admonishments to the reader from the narrator recalling a technique of *Keep Cool*.

Amid this chaos of discussion, one central theme is visible in the first volume. This is Neal's continuing concern with the problem of the American Indian. *Logan* is set in a pre-Seven Years War world of shifting empires, where the position of the Indian, foreshadowed in Sidney's collapse when the Indians turned on him, is here expanded to new levels of entanglement and confusion. *Logan* lacks a moral compass. Each time we think we have a handle on a moral, it slips from our fingers. Sidney's disappointment, glimpsed in the confusion between "his" and the "other" Indians, is now centre stage. There are the typically flawed Whites, in this case the aged governor of the frontier town in which the scene is laid. He represents the mistreatment of the Indians at the hands of the Whites. But the Indians are conspicuously no better. Three of their number, delineated Mohawks, strike down Logan during the first volume of the novel, despite the fact that Logan is a staunch defender of Indian rights. The governor's fear of Indian violence is not entirely unreasonable:

> The red Indian let loose on us again. Again the mother and babe to feed the flame. The land of the pilgrim again to be polluted with the blood of the innocent and helpless.[42]

Indian vengeance may be justified for White occupation of their lands, but the governor's lament, and his designation of the looming conflict as "another civil" war[43] forces us to question at what point the retribution becomes more criminal than the original crime. This passage, and the entire career of Harold, Logan's son, raise the further problem of exactly how far descendents can be held responsible for the crimes of their ancestors, or burdened with their bequests. The babes, in particular, have been born into a situation they did not create.

This compass is further confused by the centrality of a mixed race family, or rather a family which acts as though it were of mixed race. This is the family Logan of the title, consisting of the Logan apparently killed by the Mohawks, Harold, who is about as close to a hero as the novel allows, and his brother Oscar. It is, perhaps, necessary to note that these various family ties are only revealed gradually and with a considerable amount of attendant confusion. Nor is their mixed blood status a simple matter. Logan (the father) is an Indian by marriage only. Harold, although Logan's son, has been brought up as a White, imagining himself to be the son of the governor. All these protagonists are locked in a struggle over possession of the country in which they all find themselves. All consider themselves entitled to a dominance of that possession. The crusade of Logan, apparently high-minded, tends as dangerously to a new tyranny as the dominance of the Whites he seeks to overthrow. This is revealed not only in the Mohawk attack on him, but in his own plea to his newly discovered son as he lies, apparently dying:

> Be thou the Indian leader. . . . Unite them; heed them; perfect their confederacy. Drive the Whites back to the banditti of Europe—back to . . . to—back to England! . . . Rescue thy inheritance, avenge thy mother. . . . Harold, remember England. Thou hast great claims, great pretensions there. Learn all that White men know. Return and emancipate the Indians."[44]

Logan escapes his confusions by a degree of madness, and because his racial split is one he has bought, into rather than been born into. Harold's situation is a great deal more confused. His very blood and soul are split between his half-Indian birth and his White education. This is also expressed in the divided bequests of his parents, his father commanding him to war, his mother to forbearance:

> Hence these eternal contradictions in his movement. There was a perpetual warring of the elements in his head and heart.[45]

The problem is partly Harold's fate as an individual. His Ambition, another dubious quality and as confused as the rest of him, is driving him to some great act:

> Where should he look for that enobling intercourse, which, should fit him for command and companionship with the captains of Europe? That discipline which should make his name terrible, when generation after generation had passed away? Where that high and polished chivalry of deportment which should sustain him, as an Indian Prince, in his future intercourse with the whites?[46]

This personal fate is here, as in Logan's dying commandments, tied to a racial fate. Harold accepts Logan's view that the only way to save the

Indians is to adopt the methods of the Whites, but the consequence is very clear:

> But how, if he went away, how should he retain that overwhelming influence over the Indians, so indispensable to his purpose? Would they resign him? Would they receive him again? Would they not feel jealousy, distrust and apprehension? They would.[47]

So far, Harold sees. But his justification contains a problematic rebuke of the race he desires to save, "better . . . if he came qualified for their redemption, than that he should risk among them the wasting away of his faculties, ineffectually."[48]

There is, here, an assumption of superiority. The Indians can only be saved, in this analysis, by accepting the ways of their conquerors, by accepting a half-Indian overlord, as opposed to a pure White. As Harold explains to a passing French governor (he has, by this point, contrived to arrive in Quebec),

> [I plan] to fit myself for a captain and a statesman, in the schools of Europe; to return, to establish a confederacy among all the tribes of America—wrench back a part of our possessions from the English—and prevent all further encroachments.[49]

The Frenchman naturally offers to help him from his own selfish motives.

The Indian theme is striking, and dominates the first volume of the book. Unfortunately, in the second, it becomes enveloped in the tangled family history of the Logans. This history envelops Oscar (Harold's full brother);[50] Harold's two women, Elvira (the intellectual love) and Leona (the simple Indian love); a small child by the name of Leopold (who turns out to be Harold's and Elvira's illegitimate son); and the miraculously revived Logan. The Gothic overtones of spectres and daggers become pronounced. The whole complex tapestry of intrigue now begins to be told through various papers and letters, recalling the techniques both of the seduction novelists and the abandoned manuscript of Knickerbocker's *History*. Harold's original mission is almost completely obscured. This part of the book effectively becomes simply another slice of Gothic lunacy, much of which takes place in England, rather undermining Neal's later calls for American fiction on American themes.

But the second volume does contain certain twists. Harold's original mission briefly resurfaces when, as a representative of Logan, he appears before a parliamentary committee to plead for his people. Because this is entirely surrounded by the increasingly incredible familial intrigues, it is extremely difficult to know what Neal's intention here was. It seems likely that, in the confused composition, an idea, originally intended, suddenly resurfaced in his mind. The fact that Harold's speech is mostly a reiteration of earlier arguments supports this contention. Yet, at the end of the speech, the opposed races, and indeed Harold himself as personification of their interconnection (and imagining himself here as channelling Logan's spirit), are put on an entirely new, more equal footing:

> Your Creator is our Creator. Of the same elements, the same materials, as you are made, we are made. We have the same passions, the same infirmities, and are accountable to the same God.[51]

Of course this is, again, to see the Indians in White terms, for they would have seen themselves as children of quite different Gods, and yet it is a step towards a moderating of the extremes of Logan and the Whites that there is only one righteous path, a dilemma which Harold never resolves.

The ending of the novel may also be significant. It is here that the most significant divergence from the Brown influence occurs. Consistently, in the Brown world, the leading protagonists, for example Arthur Mervyn, Clara Wieland, and Edgar Huntly, survive. For all the catastrophes that befall them, there remains the possibility of starting over. Frequently, in the case of Neal's characters, there is only darkness and despair. In none of the novels is this more clearly displayed than *Logan*. At the conclusion here, three deaths (of Harold, Logan, and Leona) occur in rapid succession, and the implication is that they are followed by those of Oscar and Elvira. There is a deadening horror to this conclusion, in stark contrast to the mitigated tragedies of early Cooper.

Seventy-Six, Neal's next novel, focused on the most important history of all, the Revolution. Its opening chapter gave promise of a rich source to come. Introducing his fictional memoirs, the book's narrator, Jonathan Oadley, writing presumably in old age (though no date is given) admonishes his children for not knowing enough about this important event of their past.[52] His sense of the burden of that struggle is a heavy one:

> We wrestled, children as we were, for eight years, with armed giants: and wrenched—*wrenched*! with our own hands, the spoil from the spoiler—overcame them all, at last, after eight years of mortal trial.[53]

He also worries that that past is too easily forgotten, lamenting the situation of the remaining heroes of that struggle, condemned to wander America, now, apparently, the residence of a "degenerate people."[54] There is that sense of something lost in Revolution also encountered in Crèvecoeur: "You see none of the old fashioned kingly-looking people in this generation . . . nothing of their high carriage and attitude—hear nothing of their powerful voices, and regal tread."[55]

The tone is reminiscent of the innumerable dismissals of Congressmen. How can they, or a "withered little apple-john"[56] in the White House, compare with the kings who are foresworn, become giant in memory. Whatever the truth of this hint at monarchical nostalgia, they certainly cannot compare with the giants of the revolutionary struggle:

> Hold what there is left to you, of other days, as the regalia of giants; to be visited only, by torch light, with downcast eyes and folded arms. Ye are a fettered people—fettered too, by manacles that would have fallen from the limbs of your fathers like rain.[57]

What initially follows is similarly interesting. In the opening chapters, Neal captured the fragile moment Crèvecoeur gave firsthand witness to. The narrator's father, (also, confusingly, called Jonathan), has been hanging back from the conflict. Pressed by his sons (the narrator Jonathan and Archibald) he declares himself, witnessing the divided polity:

> Our cause *must* perish, if all abandon it, as I have done. No, I will mount and ride, tomorrow, through all the neighbourhood, and never rest, till I have stirred up some of our substantial men—for they are the most backward, after all—they have nothing to gain, and much to lose—and they, like me, have been lying by.[58]

The narrator recalls the opportunity presented by the conflict, the meaning the Revolution gave to their lives:

> The war of the revolution . . . gave to our characters . . . a strange, unexpected power, revealing many deeply hidden properties, that might have been . . . buried for ever, but for the events I am now about to relate.[59]

From this high point, the novel rapidly descends to the level of a seduction novel. The reader is treated to the interminable romantic disasters of Jonathan, Archibald, and a number of minor characters. Techniques and themes of past and future Neal work appear, duels occur[60] and are condemned, the narrator drifts into reflections on a variety of subjects of no particular relevance to the plot.[61] Loosely attached to this is a narrative of the Revolutionary War, presented both through rapid summary, "Then came the treachery of Arnold; the execution of André; the trial of General Gates; the operation of Greene at the south,"[62] and via a succession of bloody and confused battle sequences. The intention seems to be to demonstrate the author's grasp of historical accuracy, into which he has merely invented the characters of his story, but the details are muddled, and too often simply provide a slightly detached background for the romances to play out upon. There is also much familiar lauding of the incomparable Washington.[63]

The original intention outlined in the early chapters becomes, as in *Logan*, almost wholly obscured. Yet, underneath all the intrigue, the blood and thunder, two significant reminders of the unease occur. As in *Logan*, where the anonymous narrator, though a member of the Logan family, lived to tell the tale, so here, this unease is signified not by Jonathan, but by his far more highly strung brother, Archibald. This, in itself, is significant because it was Archibald who was least fit, through ill-health, and most desperate to fight. And it was Archibald who, from the very outset, appears more aware of the implications of the war, who, effectively, puts that war above his own romance. By the opening of the second volume, he is deeply uneasy about the entire enterprise. This is partly the consequence of the duel he has just fought with his rival in love, and thus a repeat of Sydney's agonisings, but it is not merely Sydney's personal character, but the character of a country at stake here. His exchange with Jonathan is worth quoting at length because it recovers the central question of the Revolution which Crèvecoeur posed: at what point does a virtuous war cease to be so?

> "How atone for them [our transgressions]? . . . how recover our name? By spilling more blood! fighting more battles! killing more human creatures! Brother, I am not very sure—not so sure, as I have been, that this war is a righteous one?"   [Archibald]
>
> " . . . for shame! would you have your children slaves!"   [Jonathan]
>
> "God can make them free . . . and they were better and happier, as *slaves*—than if their freedom—that priceless heritage, were bought with blood."
>
> "But God will not, cannot be hoped to work miracles for us—we must labour?"
>
> "God hath said—thou shallt not kill; we dare to say thou *shallt* kill?"[64]

Jonathan feels the burden of the war far less profoundly than his brother. Arguably, the whole tenor of his feelings is strung at a lower pitch. He is able to trifle with the affections of women in a way impossible to his more fastidious brother. Archibald is essential to their participation in the Revolution. It is Archibald's pressure[65] which compels his brother into battle, Archibald who really believes. This, too, recalls Crèvecoeur, who also possessed, as we saw, a profound belief in the more perfect America. Archibald, like Crèvecoeur, cannot sustain it. Archibald's demise is the more appalling. Slowly, as the second half of the novel progresses, his loss of faith eats away at him, until, at the very moment he utters his wedding vows, he collapses dead on the ground. This is hardly ringing endorsement of the glorious cause and contrasts sharply with the appropriate marriages which conclude Cooper's *The Spy*.[66]

Yet Cooper, with his revolutionary novel *The Spy*, enjoyed far greater success than Neal, who, following the failure of *Brother Jonathan*, returned to the States, and although he continued as novelist and editor, no longer did so at the feverish pace of the 1820s, and never enjoyed Cooper's reputation. The comparison in their later careers must await another study, but the contrast in tone and reputation in the 1820s is revealing, and caught be Neal himself. His discussion of Cooper damned him with faint praise, as lacking the "extraordinary power"[67] which Neal clearly considered he himself possessed. The analysis of Cooper suggests a concern with style, but both have weaknesses there, what burns through Neal's early novels is a sense of the uncomfortable realities of the new America, which Cooper, by contrast, would gloss with the sheen of rising glory.

AN IMPORTANT HISTORY

Jonas Clopper is shrouded in mystery. The only existing biographical sketch appeared in a reprint of *Fragments* published in 1969, and identified him as a Baltimore clergyman. This sketch is chiefly concerned with what it views as the anti-Jeffersonian bias of Clopper, personified in his references to Jefferson's supposed relations with a black slave girl. Since the Scholar's Commission report, this whole question looks quite different. Moreover, Clopper's attitude to the slavery question is far more complex than this allows. Put simply, he recognises the contradiction involved in revolutionaries championing liberty while preserving slavery. It is intriguing that in the 1960s, such a recognition should be dismissed as mere scandal-mongering. Parrington made a brief critical comment on the book in his study of American utopias.[68] Neither of these are able to give clues as to Clopper's literary influences or his reasons for writing the book. All we have, then, is the text itself and, perhaps, one significant fact that, yet again, a vision of America in literature should emerge from one of the middle colonies.

This text is remarkable and strongly suggests that Clopper was familiar with Irving's *A History of New York*, both in its content and style. There is the familiar confusion of authority. Clopper claimed to be passing on a translation of an original French manuscript by a man named Herman Twackius. Clopper went to some lengths to establish Twackius's genuine existence before completely undermining it with the swipe at the conduct of the late war printed at the head of this chapter. Equally customarily, Clopper denied that he, or rather Twackius, intended satire on contemporary great people of the most enlightened commonwealth:[69]

> The immaculate purity of the characters, the transcendent intellectual powers which all our great men have possessed, both for civil and martial government, and the unparalleled prosperity to which they have, especially of late years, raised this flourishing commonwealth; all these, I say, set them far above the loftiest flights of the shafts of satire.[70]

Clopper also grapples with that other abiding problem of American writers, the need to encompass all of America, to produce a complete history. His work is necessarily incomplete because it came to him in fragments. But these fragments possess, Clopper claims, an important unity:

They must be supposed to embrace the most important periods of the history of Bawlfredonia, passing over those epochs in which there were few events to court the attention of the historical muse.[71]

Given that the fake quality of the fragments is exposed at the outset, that is, we know that Clopper has fragmented them rather than the sea, the selection is clearly deliberate. This is key because of the events Clopper chose to select. But this selection is only half the story for, within it, Clopper raised a barrage of familiar concerns.

Fragment I begins, in sub-Irving manner, with the history of the discovery of the continent, undertaken by two rival travellers, Fredonius and Bawlfredonius, of very different character. To further complicate matters, these two pseudonyms are used twice to denote different people. In the early Fragments they refer to the rival explorers, in the later Fragments, to George Washington and Thomas Jefferson. It is impossible to know if this was deliberate or accidental, but it raises the intriguing suggestion that Clopper was attempting to tie the acts of his explorers to their descendents more deliberately than even Irving had done. Clopper certainly recalls the freewheeling style of *Salmagundi* in his use of this loose framework to attack a whole sequence of issues. Thus, the escape of Fredonius's initial expedition from a violent storm occasions a discussion on whether they possessed God's blessing. Clopper admonishes, unusually for a clergyman:

To enter on such inquiries, investigations, and metaphysical subtleties in a history of a civil empire, is *to mix very improperly, civil and religious things together.*[72]

Clopper condemns a late attempt to do precisely that. He also suggests that the storm may prefigure "the storms of faction which were to reign in Bawlfredonia,"[73] but then gives the necessary denial, though in a footnote, that these factions even exist. It is here that his unsubtle mask slips, openly exposing Fredonius as Columbus:

I will further remark, that we may felicitate ourselves that the storm which assailed Columbus, did not meet him until he was on his return to Europe, so no one can possibly imagine anything portentous in the matter. Our remarkable exemption from the *storms of faction*, from *windy orators* etc. puts the matter beyond all doubt.[74]

Beyond these increasingly standard mockeries, although that standard shows all too clearly the fallacies of Monroe's claims of happiness and unity, Clopper also used his explorers to dramatise, anew, the Indian question. This is particularly worthy of emphasis as in the cases of Neal, Paulding, and, indeed, Irving and Crèvecoeur, because of the lingering idea that, somehow, Cooper lit on the Indian as literary subject first. Not only was he nowhere near the front but, as we shall see, his romantic view of them is fraught with problems.

Here Clopper ties the Indian question to the broader theme of the lure of America. Fredonius, convinced of its existence, struggled for years to obtain finance for the voyage. His treatment of the Indians upon his arrival perhaps reflects this:

> Commodore Fredonius . . . ordered his people to treat the native inhabitants of this strange land with every mark of kindness.[75]

Fredonius is careful to ensure that his crew only act on land with the permission of the native ruler, but even under such a captain, the clash of civilisations cannot be wholly postponed, nor subjective judgements avoided. Fredonius is no more capable than anybody else of leaving the Indians to their own devices. On this first voyage, he interferes with an attempted human sacrifice by pretending to be able to darken the sun, aided by a convenient eclipse. On his second voyage, he tries to encourage agriculture and Christian teaching, the twin pillars of civilisation. Fredonius is, however kind, just as certain that he knows how the Indians should be treated. Yet his kindness is a point in his favour, contrasted by Clopper with the rival explorer, Bawlfredonius, "a noisy young man,"[76]

The points are necessarily against him from the outset. He only troubles himself wit the new world once Fredonius has proved its existence, and incidentally, the presence of gold dust. Bawlfredonius's expedition ravages the land, killing the savages on the grounds of their savagery and their copper-coloured skin. It is the same old depressing story, though; in this case, Bawlfredonius gets his comeuppance, being slain by the natives on his second voyage. It is instructive that this should be so in the light of the latest expressions of rising glory from the mouth of the president. Clopper reminds the reader of the country's highly questionable past. It was a past, in the Indian context, still to be played out to its bitter resolution. But Clopper also, like Irving, used his pseudo-history to fire salvos at other aspects of his America. For Bawlfredonius also produces a book, celebrating his achievements and castigating Fredonius at every turn. The emperor of their homeland commands his arrest and Fredonius dies in prison. Bizarrely, the origins of the explorers being somewhat confused, this leads to a monument to him being erected in Delhi. But the point of this lies in Clopper's biting footnote:

> This is a tribute of respect seldom paid in Hindustan, and which the rulers of this country have never paid to the memory of the GREATEST and BEST of our heroes and statesmen although it has long been demanded by the voice of every *patriot* in the nation.[77]

It is regrettable that Clopper did not spell out precisely what heroes he meant, although the vexed problem of the Washington Monument springs immediately to mind. There is a further point of nomenclature here. The difference between Fredonius and Bawlfredonius is a tiny one, a linguistic distinction which might recall Jefferson's Inaugural. It is also a distinction which might seem to imply that there is more unity between these two than their differing actions at first sight suggest, that it does not take much to transform the one into the other. But if this is the moral, it is a most unsettling one. It is Fredonius who opens the door to Bawlfredonius. The violence of the latter lurks in the cunning of the former. What Fredonius would have done if the eclipse had not halted the intended human sacrifice is not recorded. Bawlfredonius has Fredonius' blood on his hands as much as that of the Indians. Once again, in this America, the playing field is a depressingly level one, expressed in Clopper's conclusion to the first Fragment. He justifies the lengthy discussion of Bawlfredonius because "one of his descendents was afterwards a king of this country." This will prove to be Jefferson, recalling Irving's windy William the Testy. Clopper then acknowledged:

> some may suppose that this had some effect in making us a noisy, vociferous, talking, and *bawling* people.

Clopper here, still slightly hedges his bets, but there is no equivocation in the denouement:

> It is true we do bawl no little upon a variety of subjects, especially respecting the superiority of our political institutions over those of every other nation. But then all other nations do precisely the same.[78]

Monroe's most perfect nation here goes up in smoke. The significance of Clopper, here, is not that he was saying anything new, the parallels with early Irving are particularly obvious, but that he was saying the same things in 1819 that Irving had said in 1809. Apparently, nothing had changed. It is this sense of a rather questionable equality which pervades *Fragments*. In this retelling of American history, everybody appears equally ghastly. This is to recall something of Brackenridge's tyranny of the majority, dragging the exceptional down to the level of the gutter. Clopper can even give the impression of rising glory while sticking the knife in:

> There were few poor amongst these our ancestors, and not many rich. A golden mediocrity was the common condition.[79]

Mediocrity, however golden, is hardly sufficient for the most perfect society. Further, as in Neal's tangled world, this mediocrity is founded on moral chasms, principally and unsurprisingly, centred on slavery.

This forms the principal subject of Fragments II and III. They move to the next stage of American history, establishing more secure colonies. One colony, in this case of Christian refugees from Arabia, establishes itself in the north, while a rival colony sets up at Blackmoreland Bay, subsequently revealed, unsurprisingly, to lie in the south. The latter is the central focus, with its White colonists displaying a striking mediocrity:

The young nabobs were both too proud and too lazy to work.[80]

From this they are rescued by tobacco, here "STINKUM-PUFF," and slavery. This indictment of slavery is particularly damning because a decision about it has to be reached by the colony's council. The atmosphere in which this decision is to be made is already determined by the attitude of those shipping the slaves:

They either thought, or pretended to think, that the devil must have the sole government of these people who were of his own colour.[81]

But the council clouds the moral position still further. A leading member advances a sequence of justifications for their importation. First, they are clearly animals, therefore there is no question to answer. Second, even if they are human beings, it was not for the council:

to consider the sin or the duty of the matter, but the policy.[82]

Policy in this particular case appears to signify whatever is politically expedient. The significance of this episode lies in both the contemporary resonances and the role that such councils are supposed to play in national life. It seems likely that Clopper would have had the initial skirmishes over the admission of Missouri as a slave or free state in mind since these occurred in February and March, 1819, provoked by Representative James Tallmadge's amendment prohibiting slavery in the state. But there were plenty of other examples of such councils avoiding such questions. Yet, these councils are the uniquely American bodies, supposed to be above such technical avoidances, particularly of so morally clear an issue as slavery. Again, such satire breaks against the façade erected by Monroe, who protested that, in respect to the government, there was no improvement to be made.[83]

Nor does the trade confine its corruption to the politicians, or the southerners. The northerners, denoted Asylumorians, scenting the financial benefits, sometimes get involved while two clergymen are shown debating whether the morally correct position is to shun the trade utterly or buy slaves to better their situation.[84] In Fragment III, the southerners deterioration under slavery leads to their repudiation of the Bible because it will prevent their illicit relations with their Black slaves, and the consequent foundation of a society, the Bacchesians,[85] dedicated to the corruption of Christianity, in which Tom Anguish (Paine) takes a leading role.

Fragment III also brings on the Revolution, in this case at the hands of the tyrannous Arabian Emperor. This sets up an intriguing set of contradictions. Having spent the first part of the fragment continuing to cast scathing comment on the overly-religious Asylumorians and the slave-owning southerners, shades of rising glory are suddenly inserted:

> Notwithstanding these vices, which were productive of much evil, the people of the Bawlfredonia settlements were, upon the whole, in a highly flourishing condition.[86]

Such a claim hardly seems justified when set against the previous sections of invective. But the claim which follows is even more markedly at odds with the existing reality. The narrative explains that what has really offended the Arabian Emperor is the "golden mediocrity," the lack of castes or classes:

> for these odious distinctions had entirely disappeared in the new world of the South Sea. Every man was noble or ignoble there, in proportion to his real value.[87]

Leaving aside the rather odd oceanic locale, this is flagrantly contradicted by the denunciations of slavery and the situation of the Indians recounted in the earlier sections. The question, undeterminable on the basis simply of the text itself, and the text is all we possess, is whether Clopper was aware of the contradiction he created. Some light is thrown on this by the way he then celebrated the republicans of that era, in comparison to Madison's unloved administration:

> In those days there was no king in Bawlfredonia, and every man did that which was right in his own eyes. Fortunately for the liberties of our country, every man did that which was right in the eyes of all prudent statesmen. And here I cannot but remark the great contrast between the conduct of these republican sages, and that of the late Pigman Puff who, whilst contemplating war, adopted every measure which could tend to deprive his subjects of the means of carrying it on to advantage.[88]

It is as if, despite the dubious aspects exposed by his founding of the two colonies, Clopper has suddenly remembered that the Revolution is sacred. This peculiar mental divide persists through the rest of Fragment III, peopled mainly by various incompetent generals, with the army finally rescued, as usual in such retellings, by General George Fredonius, quite obviously Washington. The narrative here is further muddled, a point excused by a footnote explaining Twackius's illness. This has a hint of the contemporary complaint, that Neal fell victim to in *Seventy-Six* and John Adams lamented, of the impossibility of writing a history of the Revolution. Clopper has the grace at least to admit when he is beaten, since his attempt is brief and certainly not serious.

Fragment IV is similarly brief. It sets up satire of Jefferson in a flurry of Salmagundian wind. His undignified flight, when Governor of Virginia, from the state capital during the Revolution is noted:

> He asserted that his soul was brave, and panted for the fight, but that in spite of every opposition, his cowardly legs had carried him off the field of honour.[89]

His penchant for the colour red is commented on, and his ultimate destination undermined, "as their friend Tammany was no hero, he must, according to the immutable laws of nature, be a most accomplished statesmen."[90] Such a view of statesmen rather undermines the foundations of the American body politic.[91] It is supported by assaults on Jack Headstrong (John Armstrong, Secretary of War 1813–1814, blamed for burning of Washington during the War of 1812), General Philio Canio (probably representing the double agent General James Wilkinson), and Thomas Paine.

Fragment V moved on to the fragility of the post-Revolutionary world. Clopper addresses the need to arrange a new governmental settlement, which must unite North and South, and the Constitution is revisited. The representatives of Asylum Harbour and Blackmoreland duly collide over the twin issues of religion's place in the new order, and the maintenance of slavery. Clopper's intention is, again, to attack the extremes of both sides. The Asylumorians lay too great stress on religion:

> Was it ever heard that a nation settled a form of government without the least mention of heaven, or recognition of its authority?[92]

But they are redeemed by their attack on slavery:

> I wish to see the importation of black slaves entirely checked by an article in the fundamental laws of the kingdom; and if possible, freedom granted to all who are among us.[93]

The Bacchesians, to whom the response is given, enjoy no such redemption. Instead, they call on liberty to justify slavery:

> I invoke the genius of liberty to preserve to his Blackmorelanders the right of doing as we please.[94]

It is the familiar Irving "liberty of conscience" thesis replayed. A satire on the Virginia Plan follows, as the Bacchesians seek dominance of the gathering and duly attain it. Partial responsibility falls on the flawed people, recalling Brackenridge:

> Many of the lookers on were too indolent to think for themselves, and readily adopted, without examination, the sophistical arguments, and enormous conclusions of the orators.[95]

The remainder of Fragment V and the final two Fragments carry the story through the 1790s. What Clopper had thus far established was the fraudulent dimensions of American history, from first discovery through the illusions of the Revolutionary period. In these final sections, he turned directly on the Adams administration. Brackenridge had fallen silent during those critical years. Irving faced them only obliquely. Clopper dealt with it head on, and, again, with striking even-handedness. Jefferson's faults having been much chronicled, King John of Onionville (Adams) is similarly mocked:

> He was an insufferable egoist, and was vastly proud of his acquirements in jurisprudence and theology. His proud and haughty airs, caused him to quarrel with Alexander the cofferer, Timothy the scribe, and many others of the old and confidential counsellors of King Fredonius.[96]

Clopper not only recognised the divisions within the Federalist Party, but he attacked the Democratic–Republicans on the crucial point. He argued:

> No sooner was John seated in the car of state, than his hypocritical friend . . . Thomas Tammany Bawlfredonius . . . began to plot in secret how they might dethrone him.[97]

He also advanced the argument that Adams was monstrously treated by the press:

> His most meritorious conduct was grossly vilified, his most upright intention called in question, and every effort made by him, to secure the rights and liberties of our country, were represented as the most wicked machinations for engineering and oppressing his subjects.

The relative merit of these claims is still, as Chapter Two hinted, a matter of dispute among historians. But it is significant that Clopper gave voice to them, and that he gave voice to them alongside a not inaccurate assessment of Adams' flaws. A final jibe at the Jeffersonians is also significant. Clopper argued that, whenever a lie was set forth by Jefferson, Madison, or one of their followers, the whole party took it up:

> The maxim of the bawlers was, 'A public favourite can do no wrong.' It therefore mattered not, whether such an one spoke false or truth. It was enough for him to speak, and every member of the faction was bound to support the assertion, whether true or false, upon pain of expulsion.[98]

The dangers of unthinking factionalism are clearly exposed, but Clopper also asserted that the Jeffersonians may not always have been telling the truth. There was, as Chapter Two showed, a convincing case for that accusation of Jeffersonian blindness, but no one else made it in literature as openly as Clopper.

It is here that the manuscript abruptly halted, and the most likely explanation is that Clopper simply ran out of inspiration, although without further evidence no absolute conclusion is possible. But this does not diminish this striking ending. For the collision between Adams, Jefferson, and the High Federalists was a crucial moment in the unfolding American narrative. Adams recognised political realities in a way that neither his predecessors nor his successors did. The depth of the illusion perpetrated by Monroe showed how much that recognition was still needed. By concluding his history at that moment, whether accidentally or by design, Clopper emphasised the point. There is no evidence that he, like any of the other satirists, was particularly heeded.

A GENTLER SATIRIST

> My head is just now full of the future destinies of this noble young country, and I mean to empty it, destinies and all, if the rain only lasts long enough.[99]

James Kirke Paulding's early career was noted in Chapter 3. Unlike Irving, he continued to write in the satiric vein which *Salmagundi* pioneered, producing a stream of works throughout the 1810s and 1820s. His connections and the breadth of his career give him an interest similar to that of Brackenridge. But where Brackenridge and Irving maintained a sharpened satire, Paulding's mockery became increasingly gentle. Despite an increasing tendency to propaganda, itself a revealing contrast to the Paulding of *Salmagundi*, he could still produce biting satire, in this case on frontier America.

His background may be significant, although it makes his gentler tone more surprising. Born on 22 October, 1778, Paulding entered a family caught in the chaos of rural New York State during the Revolution. This was the area immortalised by Cooper in *The Spy*.[100] At the time of his birth, the family were in retreat from the violence at the Pleasant Valley. Later, his father served as supply commissary for Patriot troops and, during one of the periodic currency crises, had to assume personal responsibility for congressional debts to keep supplies flowing. At the war's close, Congress refused to pay the bills and William Paulding was jailed as a debtor.[101]

Paulding moved to New York in 1796, taking up a position at the U.S. Loan Office, where he served until 1815, eventually becoming head clerk.

He was active in the lively society group which included Washington and William Irving, the "Lads of Kilkenny," and a participant in many New York literary societies. His early literary career was often collaborative. *Salmagundi* was preceded by work on Peter Irving's newspaper, the *Morning Chronicle*, and *The Corrector* to both of which Irving also contributed. We saw the extent of his contribution to *Salmagundi*, something he felt was later unfairly forgotten. His also read the manuscript of Irving's *History of New York* and was involved in the publicity campaign surrounding its publication. When he published his first major solo work in 1812, he had more literary experience than any other writer in a similar position in this study.

The literary works following that debut fall into three main groups. First, a series of works satirising the Anglo-American relationship, increasingly imbued with patriotic fervour. These included the satire, *The Diverting History of John Bull and Brother Jonathan* (1812); a pamphlet, *The United States and England* (1815); and two pseudo-travel narratives, *A Sketch of Old England by a New England Man* (1822) and *John Bull in America* (1825). The *Sketch* is a pale shadow of Irving's sketches of the old world. Second, various collections of essays, including a second series of *Salmagundi* (1819), generally lacking the bite of the first, and *Letters from the South* (1817). Third, the remarkable novel satirising frontier life, and particularly Cooper's versions of it, *Koningsmarke, or the Long Finne* (1824).

Of the Anglo-American works, *Diverting History* is the strongest. It began with a brief retelling of the American Revolution. This is done from first settlement onwards, but no mention is made of the Amer-Indians or the European dimension. A standard geographical satire of America is also included, with the Southerners being lightly attacked over slavery, the New Englanders for their rapaciousness,[102] and the Middlelands enjoying warm praise. Paulding also noted long-standing quarrels between North and South:

> From a certain little petty opposition of interests. I mean those little every-day interests which lead little men by the nose, in direct contradiction to their permanent and lasting happiness.[103]

Paulding became increasingly concerned about this quarrel, which he recognised as being centred on slavery. In *Slavery in the United States* (1837) he attempted to justify the institution, a position anticipated in *Letters from the South* (1816).

The majority of the narrative is concerned with the foreign relations leading to the 1812 War, with the background set by the Revolution. For all these quarrels Britain is made clearly responsible, while Jonathan's good nature is stressed; he is "a peaceable sort of careless fellow, that would quarrel with nobody if you only let him alone."[104]

The rising glory theme is also clearly evident:

> Still you could see he [Jonathan] had not come to half his strength, as yet, and that when his sinews were a little more strengthened, and his joints

stronger knit, woe be to the blockhead that should wantonly provoke him to raise his fist, for it would come down like unto a sledge hammer.[105]

Most of the satire lacks the bite of Irving's *History*. Indeed, Paulding recalls it several times, satirising both the New Englanders and historians.[106] One particularly effective jab is made on the failure of Americans to stand up for themselves:

> Brother Jonathan had in general no great stomach for fighting, was not easily provoked to extremity, and loved profit rather better than honour.[107]

This expands to a comment on the misuse of words, which also recalls Irving:

> He used to say . . . that this same honour was in general nothing else but ambition, revenge, envy, malice, interest, or some other scoundrel passion, the owner of which knowing that if he came out with it in its naked deformity, he would be turned out of all good company, did dress it up in the likeness of something respectable, and pass it off upon the world.[108]

The anti-English bias became increasingly strident in the subsequent works of the series, centred on attacking the Tory and anti-American *Quarterly Review* (founded in 1809 to challenge the Whig oriented *Edinburgh Review*). In *The United States and England*, Paulding was responding to two unfavourable pieces published January, 1814, one criticising his poem *The Lay of the Scottish Fiddle* (1813), the other a review of Charles Jared Ingersoll's *Inchiquin's Letters*.[109] The attacks were followed up in *Letters from the South*, which made glancing references to the *Quarterly*'s iniquities, while *John Bull in America* sends a writer from the publication round America ostensibly to insult it. The first of these Paulding works, especially, is a rather depressing piece of propaganda with all the failings of the war laid at Britain's door:

> It [her wartime conduct] has been such as to outrage every rule and practice of civilised nations, and almost every principle and feeling of common humanity, a war carried on in fellowship with pirates of Barataria, runaway negroes of the south, and savages from all points of the compass, backed by the scum and offscourings of Europe.[110]

Notably, Paulding, rather than disproving American flaws, focused on simply demonstrating the British to be more flawed. American rising glory is again declared, rather than explained:[111]

> Our difficulties have not yet been altogether overcome, but they assuredly must be, and the victory will be one of the noblest ever achieved by human nature.[112]

Letters from the South showed the dual effects of Paulding's patriotism, and increasingly lightened tone, in another direction. Pursuing national unity, Paulding attempted to prove the merits of the South to doubting northerners. This expanded, when not extolling the natural and man-made beauties of the South, into attempts to deal with all issues that might divide the nation. In "Letter XIX," a sequence of issues is dealt with, interspersed with especially ecstatic paeans to American glory. Paulding dismissed demagoguery by recalling the Tenth Federalist:

> A widely diffused republic like this, must have many demagogues, who will become rivals instead of coadjutors, and consequently be incapable of any general conspiracy against the rights of the people, or the safety of the state.[113]

The prospect of the federal government tramping on states rights is regarded as so unlikely as to be hardly worth discussing. He regarded the people as so united that the growing western states were unthreatening. American expansionism calls for some of his most joyful phrases:

> But it was our happy destiny to grow up and to increase as one nation, speaking, thinking, reasoning, believing, and feeling, with a degree of similarity scarcely paralleled. . . . As we extend with the rapidity of a torrent, we incorporate with no adverse tribes, nor force any nation into an unwilling fraternity with those they hate. It is the same people, carrying with them the soul and the intellect of Americans—bearing the very nation on their shoulders wherever they go.[114]

Finally, Paulding turned to inequalities of wealth, where he claimed that people gained wealth in America either through "industry" or "talents," therefore, nobody could get too rich or too poor, a somewhat flimsy analysis. This is somewhat weakened elsewhere by the actual poverty Paulding perceives, but by blaming this on speculation, or the folly of charitable institutions, or the failure of men to stick to agricultural pursuits, he is able to turn away the evil.[115]

This knack of turning problems aside rather than coming properly to grips with them has its most serious effect when Paulding confronts the issue of slavery. Given the work is concerned with the South, the topic ought to feature prominently. Instead, the tone is set with a brief early comment, "Since their lot [the slaves] is beyond remedy, it was consoling to find it mitigated by kindness and plenty."[116]

Here he also tried to throw the blame for the institution onto the British (following Jefferson in his original draft of the Declaration of Independence), an argument taken up by Cooper in *The Spy*. The topic is then discussed in "Letter XI," and otherwise ignored. This letter showed Paulding caught tortuously between the desire to celebrate his country and the reality of slavery:

Don't mistake, and suppose that I am an advocate of slavery; for I hate it: and wish most sincerely and ardently, that there was not a man in our country that could stand up, and with his black fingers, point to the preamble of our constitution, which declares—all men are born free and equal—and swear it was not true. But yet I am grateful when I can persuade myself, that a race of men which is found in this situation in almost every Christian land, is not without some little enjoyments, that sweeten the bitter draught of slavery, and prevent its being all gall.[117]

Here, Paulding made the customary defences: the comparison with other countries (forgetful of the fact that America is not supposed to be like other countries), together with a faint declaration of his own antislavery credentials (which will not be practised because the slaves are really not so badly off). Paulding further weakened those credentials by the familiar claim that nothing can be done, "until they can be freed, without endangering the community, infringing the established rights of property, and rendering themselves even more wretched."[118]

He did condemn a slave trader, only to concede that, had the trader been American, he would have "suppressed this story,—for such a monster is sufficient to disgrace a whole nation."[119] His wishful thinking climaxed with the claim that flaws such as the slave trade need only to be pointed out to legislators and action would be taken.[120]

The second (now purely Paulding) *Salmagundi* (1819) contained equally disturbing satires on slavery. In one, pack horses are to be replaced by velocipedes, and the horses sent by a colonisation society back to their homeland to run wild.[121] In another, a dying Negro slave puzzled over how to occupy himself in heaven, realises, "I can wait upon the angels."[122]

Finally, in *A Sketch of Old England*, Paulding's racism is openly declared. Attacking the British for only seeking to help some oppressed peoples by prevention of the slave trade, he made a clear moral judgement between oppressed Greek Christians and the slaves stating:

The interests of humanity would be better served by [aiding] the former than by the latter.[123]

The slaves, at least, are addressed. The Indians are almost completely ignored, despite Paulding making several explorations concerning American origins. He did revisit one familiar theme:

For it is to be recollected that the first settlers of an Indian country not only take away from the copper coloured villains their lands and rivers, but give them new names, like the gypsies who first steal children, and then, to disguise the theft, christen them anew.[124]

Perpetual circle.

Again the satire is not sustained, and his references to the Indians as savages in *The United States and England* are equally suggestive.[125]

This firm adherence to the rising glory perspective makes the power of *Koningsmarke* the more surprising. The novel captures the racial turmoil of colonial America, in conjunction with mockery of White pretensions. It may be that the Whites come out on top but it is without the self-delusions, at least on the part of the narrator, seen in Cooper's romances. Indeed, the novel specifically satirised *The Pioneers*, published in the previous year. Paulding mocked Cooper's habit of concealing key plot points.[126] The Long Finne becomes a sort of medley of Cooper characters. His name obviously recalls Leather-Stocking, as does his initial account of himself:

> I am an outcast from my native land—a hunted deer, to whom neither woods, the waters, nor the air afford a refuge.[127]

But this, his romance with Christina, the governor's daughter, and his hidden secret concerning which Bombie is continually warning recall Edwards. He anticipated David, the tedious divine of *The Last of the Mohicans*, in his possession of a little flageolet.[128]

The novel also recalled Irving, setting up the rise and fall of a Swedish colony on the Delaware River in the sixteenth century. Paulding took on not only the familiar satire of the institutions and personages of government,[129] but also renewed Irving's argument of cyclical history:

> If we examine, aided by the light of history, the course of human events, we shall find that everything moves in a perpetual circle.[130]

The happiness of one is always balanced, argued Paulding, by the sorrows of another. It is this attempt at balance which underpins the narrative, or as Paulding put it, "we have endeavoured . . . to . . . please all sorts of people, whether lovers of hard or soft eggs."[131]

The treatment of slaves and Indians makes a sustained attempt to follow this through. In contrast to Cooper, Paulding introduced a major black character, Bombie, who rules the governor's household, and possesses a weighty lineage:

> We also claim the benefit of sublimity for the effusions of Bombie of the Frizzled Head; who, as before stated, was the wife and daughter of an African monarch, superior in state and dignity to any European legitimate; because he could actually sell his subjects, whereas the latter are only entitled to pick their pockets.[132]

Although this is an obviously barbed comment, it stabs both races. Koningsmarke ("Thou art a slave, and canst not witness against him that is free.")[133] and the governor ("But thou [Bombie] shalt pay for this, thou and all thy accursed race . . .")[134] keep the racial flag flying. The status quo is further maintained with Bombie's death and the disproving of her prophecies. Yet her death speech, calling for vengeance, is telling:

> The pile of oppression you [Whites] have reared to the clouds shall fall, and crush your own heads. Black men and Red men, all colours, shall combine against your pale, white race; and the children of the master shall become the bondsmen of the prosperity of the slave.[135]

Paulding probably intended this as another indication of Black instability, but this does not remove the fact that he permits a Black character to voice such opinions, which is more than any contemporary American writer had done.

Paulding's treatment of the Indians operated in similar fashion. Again, there are clear limits. A possible interracial relationship between Koningsmarke and Aouetti, an Indian maiden, has to fail. There is the customary comment on the exigencies of disease and alcohol. Emphasis is also laid on the savagery of the Indians, as against the violence of the Whites, with some particularly vivid torture scenes, and the slaughtering of a mother and child. Yet, in the midst of the interracial conflict, Ollentangi, the Indian chief, attempts to explain his people to Koningsmarke, urging that they learn from each other:

> We shall teach you a little of our ignorance in these matters, that you may comprehend us; and you shall teach us some of your wisdom, that we may comprehend you. This will be proper and neighbourly.

Unsurprisingly, Koningsmarke resists the argument, arguing that the Whites cannot be taught ignorance, and Ollentangi responds:

> You have just acknowledged what I want you to believe, namely, that we Indians are wiser and happier than you. I have known several white-men become Indians, but I never saw an Indian turn white-man. Therefore, if the human mind never goes backwards, 'tis a proof that the state of nature is better than the civilised state.[136]

Koningsmarke's response mirrors a Cooper technique from *The Spy*, where protagonists turn from the actual point of contention. He, and the narrator, take refuge in the claim that:

> Koningsmarke undertook to explain all these matters, but they were beyond the reach of the old man's philosophy, although one of the most acute Indians of the new world.[137]

The status quo is maintained, but it is again a nice point to determine which voice possesses the more convincing argument.

Paulding's voice was compromised, even in *Koningsmarke*, which culminates in a marriage between the Long Finne and Christina every bit as appropriate as those which graced Cooper's conclusions. Yet the other view is present in a way which it was not in Cooper. Paulding championed rising glory. He overrode the flaws of the new nation, yet those flaws still featured in his pages. Slaves and Amer-Indians were permitted to give voice to them in a manner Cooper did not permit. And Paulding remained aware of Irving's *History*. He mocked his own happy ending because he knew that reality rarely reached such resolutions. The fevered rhetoric of his propaganda demonstrated that he, like Irving, knew that America still hung in the balance.

5 The Illusion Ascendant
James Fenimore Cooper and the Art of Reconciliation

As far as I am acquainted with the writings of Mr Cooper, they uphold good sentiments, sustain good morals, and maintain just taste; and, after saying this, I have next to add, that all his writings are truly patriotic and American, throughout and throughout.[1]

Men live by lies.[2]

Clopper, Neal, and Paulding tried in their different, fragmentary ways to come to terms with aspects of their present. Cooper turned to the creation of an American past, although only after a curious Austenian foray into the world of the English aristocracy. Although he later addressed the contemporary scene, and there are inferences and implications to be drawn about that scene from his early romances, they do not directly face it. It would be impossible from Cooper's novels, prior to his 1826 departure for Europe, to gain the same sense of the state of the nation available from the work of Crèvecoeur, Brackenridge and early Irving.

These early novels fall into two groups, with the exception of the first, *Precaution* (1820). The first is the Leather-Stocking series comprising *The Pioneers* (1823), *The Last of the Mohicans* (1826), and *The Prairie* (1827), which explored American history through the lens of that most famous of Cooper characters. The second comprised a series of romances of the American Revolution: *The Spy* (1821), *The Pilot* (1823) and *Lionel Lincoln* (1825).[3] A similarity of approach unites them all. While acknowledging trouble, dispute, and doubt, these are invariably quelled by convenient marriages and contrived happy endings. Cooper constantly permitted conclusions corroborating the rising glory vision contained in documents like Monroe's First Inaugural. This permission is doubly problematic because Cooper gives an impression of attempting to confront troublesome issues, most particularly the fate of the Indians, only to acquiesce in the status quo. In the Indian case this is particularly important because Cooper is regarded as a pioneer in raising the topic. Crèvecoeur and Irving preceded him, and Cooper's moral compass was significantly looser than theirs.

But this loose moral compass is set in a series of ambiguous narratives such that it has been possible to read Cooper as either firmly patriotic or deeply subversive, or at points in-between. On this point, Cooper's choices of endings to his novels and the complicity in those choices of key characters are highly significant. Again and again, fictional characters, and Cooper as narrator, acquiesce in triumphant conclusions. In addition, even the exploration of conflict is kept firmly in the past. Whatever happens, the Revolution is shown triumphantly succeeding; whatever happens, the pioneers march on. Cooper was either incapable of fully facing the realities he chronicled, or chose to turn from them to sunnier vistas. Ultimately, his America, unlike that of Crèvecoeur, Irving, or Neal, cannot fall.

As with Irving's decision to please, rather than to instruct, there was plenty of justification for this (although Irving had, of course, first chronicled a fall of America). Cooper, in a different way from Crèvecoeur, had lost an inheritance. It was all the more necessary to cling to a country. Cooper also expressed a national need. The founders, the living exemplars of the glorious American prospect, were passing from the stage, a process decisively marked on 4 July 1826 by the deaths of Jefferson and Adams.[4] Cooper personally, and the nation he believed in, needed reassurance. But renewed acquiescence in the compromises of 1776 and 1800, a renewed turning from the realities of the 1820s came at the price of an obscured conflict with the very ideals thus espoused. With Cooper, as in those earlier cases, it remained an open question whether that acquiescence came at too high a price.

A CERTAIN VAGUENESS[5]

In tracing the problem of Cooper's agenda, the background to his initial literary endeavours is useful. Literature was not a vocation for him as it was for others in this study. Thirty years elapsed between his birth, on 15 September 1789, and the publication of his first novel in 1819. There is no sense in his letters before that of an unachieved vocation. The claim that, dissatisfied with an unidentified contemporary novel, he threw it down and informed his wife that "I could write a better book than that myself"[6] may be apochryphal. He may have gathered material for some time prior to commencing the task. A haphazard quality still remained, as though, having contemplated pretty much everything else, he now came to novel writing.

His family background and early career are also suggestive. His father grabbed the opportunity of the Revolution to raise himself, seizing tracts of land, often at the expense of ruined Loyalists, to establish himself as the patriarch of Cooperstown in upstate New York. His father also avoided any direct involvement in the fighting. After the Revolution, for over a decade, centred on the 1790s, William Cooper held a position as leading landowner, judge, and United States Congressman in the Cooperstown area of New York State he had developed. Unfortunately, the Revolution had opened doors to all potential upstarts, while also maintaining an older sect of gentlemen, so that Cooper found himself caught between the two and gradually fell into failure.[7] He hoped to establish his sons where he failed, but, at least in James's case, the early career was far from illustrious. His schooling may be significant. Fenimore Cooper was a boarding student at a school run by the Reverend Thomas Ellison, still apparently, in 1801, a devout Loyalist. As Cooper later recounted:

> He entertained . . . a most profound reverence for the king and the nobility . . . was particularly tenacious of . . . all the decencies of the church, detested a democrat as he did the devil.[8]

The presence of such a man is a significant reminder that the Revolution did not remove all Loyalists from the new republic even if, on the whole, it silenced them. It also raises questions about the focus on a British aristocracy which pervades *Precaution* (1820), and *Lionel Lincoln* (1825). Cooper followed this dubious beginning with a disastrous period at Yale where, proceeding rather too closely in the footsteps of an elder brother, he got himself expelled. He then went to sea, first in the merchant navy which took him briefly to London, then in the United States Navy, which kept him almost entirely on shore. In 1811, he married a wealthy heiress with a Loyalist background and set himself up as a gentleman farmer. Her family restricted his access to her fortune, however, and his situation was compounded by the gradual collapse of his father's estate after William's death in 1809. The precarious condition of the estate, hampered by dubious land titles, was exacerbated by the deaths of all four of Cooper's brothers, leaving their spouses and some seventeen children dependant both on the failing estate and on James. The years after 1811 were a continued struggle both to shore up the estate, ultimately unsuccessful, and to find means of bringing in money, which included a share in an unsuccessful whaling venture.

This heritage is suggestive about the fiction that immediately followed. First, novel writing as a possible money spinner was clearly a factor in Cooper's decision to attempt a first novel in 1819.[9] Second, his tangled heritage, particularly his wife's Loyalist antecedents, made him well placed to tackle the revolutionary themes. His grasp of them is quite different from Irving's "Rip van Winkle" or, indeed, Neal in *Seventy-Six*.[10] The occasional bloodiness of *The Spy* lacks the chill of Neal's ferocious battles; we listen in vain upon Cooper's middle ground for an echo of Rip's cry of loss.

The absence of such a cry is bound up with another problem, that of Cooper's style. It is useful to turn here to Mark Twain's famous critical judgement on Cooper, published in the *North American Review* in 1895. The title, "Fenimore Cooper's Literary Offences," reveals much, and an early sentence reveals more:

> There are nineteen rules governing literary art in the domain of ro-
> mantic fiction—some say twenty-two. In Deerslayer Cooper violated
> eighteen of them.[11]

Twain was responding to a comment on Cooper from the British novelist Wilkie Collins, who had stated, "Cooper is the greatest artist in the
domain of romantic fiction yet produced by America."[12]

Both claims have merit. Taken together, they raise an important possibility. Cooper, in a more sophisticated way than Brown, reflects a variety
of perspectives in his early texts. His correspondence is thoroughly unil-
luminating as to what his agenda may have been in the introduction of
crucial themes such as American patriotism or the fate of the American
Indians. We have only the novels, and the novels are frequently confused,
partly by the very style Twain complains of. This chapter makes two suggestions. Cooper does, frequently, reflect two sides of an issue; for example,
the Americans versus the British in *The Spy* and *Lionel Lincoln*, or the fate
of the Indians, in the Leather-Stocking series. In this sense, he captures
American moments. But not only are these moments confined in an historical timeframe, from which the only escape is to reflect happily on American
glories to come, but because they are romanticised, Cooper actually glided
over the surface of issues that pinned down his predecessors. The subtleties
are certainly there, but the analysis is clouded and the moral judgement
compromised. The key novels go deeper into the issues than, say, Monroe's
paean to his nation, but they do not go really deep.

Exceptionally, Cooper's first fictional attempt is not even set in America,
but in a world of English aristocrats and their tortuous love affairs. Now it
may be, as Robert Lawson-Peebles has argued, that this novel does reflect
America because, "Many in the United States would continue to retain the
shadows of English hierarchical structures."[13] *Precaution* may, in this sense,
be a preliminary exploration of the world of *The Pioneers* with its similar
concerns about the status of property and appropriate marriages. But to
assert this novel's importance in this way is to ignore significant issues.
It is still set in an English world, or at least a world with a thick English
veneer. Whatever else America may have possessed, it did not possess a lot
of disguised genuine dukes wandering about. Those hierarchies which had
endured the Revolution were, as Cooper's own experience demonstrated,
crumbling before a new wave of upstarts. More, when those concerns do
surface, there is something of a detachment in their expression. This early
passage may be a reflection on Cooper's own experience:

> The evening passed in the tranquil enjoyment of the blessings which
> Providence had profusely scattered around the family of the baronet,
> but which are too often hazarded by a neglect of duty, that springs
> from too great a security, or an indolence which renders us averse to
> the precaution necessary to ensure their continuance.[14]

But this reflection lacks bite, and is subsumed in the tedious tangle of on-again, off-again relationships more reminiscent of the seduction novelists than even Charles Brockden Brown.

The same problem presents itself with *Precaution*'s occasional political comments. A number of characters have served in the British parliament, and comment occasionally on aspects of that august body:

> "I remember when I sat in the House, there was a party who were fond of the cry of this said liberty; but when they got the power they did not seem to me to suffer people to go more at large than they went before; but I suppose they were diffident of telling the world their minds after they were put in such responsible stations, for fear of the effect of example."
>
> "Most people like liberty as servants, but not as masters, uncle."[15]

This is a familiar and hardly unreasonable moral, but it is quite impossible to know on the basis of its utterance whether Cooper conceived of its having any applicability to America. The abstract quality of *Precaution*, in terms of its subject matter and locale, is of relevance because of what it indicates about Cooper's intentions at this start of his career, and the contrast between those intentions and fellow writers. None of the others, not even Brown, had thought it necessary to commence an American literary career with a tale of aristocrats whether English or not. For no one else does the state and nature of America seem to matter so little.

Cooper did, of course, move from this world of dukes and daughters to a specifically American novel with his second attempt, *The Spy*, published in 1821. This was the first of three novels dealing with the American Revolution published before his departure for Europe in 1826. It was succeeded by *The Pilot* (1823), the first sea novel, and *Lionel Lincoln* (1825), the only one of an intended series of Legends of the Thirteen Republics published.

The Spy is set in rural New York State during 1780–1 recalling the disputed country documented by Irving in "The Legend of Sleepy Hollow." Cooper makes frequent reference to the case of Major André, as he documents his own, rather more complex, Spy. Wayne Franklin explored Cooper's debts to various genuine stories of the Revolutionary War, not the least of which was his close connection with the Jay family, whose leading light, John, was apparently a keen expounder of war stories at any and every available opportunity.[16] Where Cooper got his stories from is not of the first importance for this enquiry. The way he deployed them is. This deployment has sharply divided critics. Cooper is either taken at face value in his claims to be writing a patriotic novel, or he is seen as already hinting at the deep ambivalence concerning his country which became a key feature of his later novels. What in Irving is shadowy, almost mystical, in Cooper (despite twists and turns and twists again), will be explained by the conclusion of the narrative.

The plot explores the responses of a group of characters, of whom the central element is the Wharton family, to the situation in the neutral ground. This situation is laid out in the opening chapter in cool, almost historical tones:

> A large proportion of its [the county of West-Chester's] inhabitants, either restrained by their attachments, or influenced by their fears, affected a neutrality they did not feel. . . . Great numbers, however, wore masks, which even to this day have not been thrown aside; and many an individual has gone down to the tomb, stigmatised as a foe to the rights of his countrymen, while, in secret, he has been the useful agent of the leaders of the revolution; and, on the other hand, could the hidden repositories of divers flaming Patriots have been opened to the light of day, royal protections would have been discovered concealed under piles of British gold.[17]

This measured explanation is framed by an approaching storm obviously intended to mirror the chaotic political character of the times, through which rides a stranger, who will turn out to be Washington in disguise, to meet with his Spy, the peddler Harvey Birch. This contrast of violence and measured tones is one significant aspect of the book. It is a reminder that the storm is going to pass, a point hammered home by the triumphant final chapter when we find virtually everybody doing well some twenty-five years after. It is in this triumph that the illusion of the book lies. Cooper pretended to show the relative merits of the two sides, and did show some of the demerits of the Patriots, but the outcome is not only beyond question but warmly celebrated. The fundamental issues slip away and there remains a section of American society who is unrespected.

This section is comprised of those who actually attempt neutrality, personified here by the Mr. Wharton, head of the family whose fate is entwined with the eponymous Spy. Mr. Wharton, a "devoted loyalist," is in agony because of the divided state of his family. His elder daughter, Sarah, is in love with the British Colonel Wellmere; his younger daughter, Frances, with the American, Major Dunwoodie. The immediate crisis is precipitated by his son, Henry, a Captain in the royal army, who, having made an ill-advised journey in disguise to visit his family, has been captured. Wharton, already engaged in a difficult balancing act of trying to keep in with both sides, a reminder of how perilously unclear the situation was, is condemned for precisely such an attempt, "He sat gazing on the movements without, with a listless vacancy in his countenance, that fully denoted his imbecility of character."

To the extent that part of Wharton's concern is his own livelihood:

> The fact of his having a son in the royal . . . army, had very nearly brought his estates to the hammer.[18]

This denunciation may be justifiable. What is money against the fate of one's country? But Wharton's fears are at least as much for his family as for himself. He has already lost his wife to the shock of Revolution; whichever way things fall, he must also lose a child, and it seems more than a little harsh to condemn a man for hesitating over so appalling a dilemma.

The British perspective meets much the same fate. Sarah backs the British, and, in a manner repeated by the two young women of *Lionel Lincoln*, agrees firmly with every word falling from the lips of officers,

> "When the really British regiments come in question, you will see a very different result."
>
> "Of that there is no doubt," cried Sarah . . . hailing already in her heart, the triumph of the British.[19]

Colonel Wellmere is rapidly shown to be an inadequate character. When Dunwoodie, "a fine young man,"[20] appears in the sisters' salon, and commands his eventual bride to be true to America, the Colonel spends several sentences struggling with his obvious, unfair disgust:

> "His money appears to have been thrown away," observed the Colonel, betraying the spleen he was unsuccessfully striving to conceal.[21]

Moreover, Cooper is reluctant to seriously engage the issues behind the conflict. This is made clear in one of the few extended discussions between two opposed protagonists. The circumstances surrounding this discussion are additionally curious. The British, inadequately led by Wellmere, have been defeated. This has placed the wounded Colonel; a wounded American, Singleton; an American officer, Lawton; and an American surgeon, Sitgreaves, together in the Wharton house. Even in the manner of his wound, Wellmere is stripped of dignity, as the narrative all too plainly implies that he is malingering. Once a sufficient time has been allowed for the injured to recover, a dinner party is held. Everybody dresses in appropriate regalia, and the group meet under a veil of civility. Once the ladies have retreated, this is lifted by Wellmere and Sitgreaves, who proceed to dispute the merits of the conflict. Wellmere has already displayed his customary British manners during a toast to the absent Dunwoodie:

> The health was drunk cheerfully by all but Colonel Wellmere, who wet his lips, and drew figures on the table with some of the liquor he had spilt.[22]

Having been bearded by Sitgreaves's personal obsession (that the cause of war would be better served and considerably less bloody if the enemy were only maimed, rather than killed) Wellmere gets onto his high horse:

> I have yet to learn that the cause of liberty is in any manner advanced by the services of any gentleman in the rebel army.[23]

A spirited exchange ensues:

> "Not liberty! Great God, for what then are we contending?"
> "Slavery, sir; yes, even slavery; you are putting the tyranny of a mob on the throne of a kind and lenient prince; where is the consistency of your boasted liberty?"

Now, it was precisely such a danger that Brackenridge, not unreasonably, devoted much of his writing to warning about. But Cooper's manner of deploying the argument robs it of power. This is not simply a consequence of Wellmere's questionable character, but the way he argues. Having condemned Sitgreaves and the rebels for lack of consistency, the Colonel, nevertheless, shifts his own ground:

> "Ay, sir, your consistency. Your congress of sages have published a manifesto, wherein they set forth the equality of political rights."
> "'Tis true, and it is done most ably."
> "I say nothing of its ability; but if true, why not set your slaves at liberty?"

The issue of slavery and the issue of mob rule are two separate questions. The latter disappears completely from the dispute and is not touched on again. Indeed, it is substantially confuted by the later annihilation of the obvious representation of the American mob in the narrative, the unruly Skinners. Meanwhile, the debate turns on the slavery question. Cooper characterises Sitgreaves, and by implication American feelings, thus:

> Every American feels humbled at the necessity of vindicating his country from the apparent inconsistency and injustice of the laws alluded to. His feelings are much like those of an honourable man who is compelled to exonerate himself from a disgraceful charge, though he may know the accusation to be false.[24]

The language deployed here is really quite extraordinary. The charge is hardly disgraceful, or the accusation false. Regardless of the character of the accuser, who in his own morals will prove to be just as bad, the accusation is perfectly reasonable. But this cannot, obviously, be admitted. Nor does Sitgreaves seem much humbled by the burden of having to respond to this. He first lays out the reasons for the Patriot revolt, coming across more coherently than Wellmere's slashing one-liners allow him to do. When he does move onto slavery, he shifts the blame in a remarkable way. Slavery, argues Sitgreaves, is present in every nation, moreover:

I cannot except Great Britain. It was her children, her ships, and her laws, that first introduced the practice into these states; and on her institutions the judgement must fall.

Wellmere ought, if he were a remotely competent antagonist, to point out that the colonists, if they felt strongly about it, were perfectly capable of turning away the ships, or freeing the slaves and, in any case, whoever brought them there is hardly the issue. But Wellmere is incapable of engaging in argument beyond interjections and Sitgreaves is allowed to continue unchecked. Now, his next point may be slightly more valid:

So long as we were content to remain colonies, nothing was said of our system of domestic slavery; but now, when we are resolute to obtain as much freedom as the vicious system of metropolitan rule has left us, that which is England's gift has become our reproach.

Sitgreaves is brilliantly shifting the argument, and is quite correct in his claim that the British were largely untroubled by the institution in America prior to the present conflict. Wellmere's silence in the face of this condemns him as having deployed it as a mere pawn in a more important argument. But Cooper's allowing Sitgreaves to carry the day in this way is to miss the key moral point. The issue with slavery is not whether the British are justified in criticising the Americans, but whether the Americans, making claims for themselves, are justified in ignoring it. Sitgreaves does conclude with some slight acknowledgement of the point and, in so doing, gives voice to that vain hope of the founders:

We must come gradually to the remedy, or create an evil greater than that which we endure at present: doubtless, as we advance, the manumission of our slaves will accompany us.[25]

This is, on one level, an accurate reflection of the state of affairs at the time in which the novel is set. There was reason to hope that slavery might wither away, although Sitgreaves's failure to explain why immediate manumission would create so great an evil ought again to be exploited by Wellmere. Wellmere, long since retreated from the argument, now retreats from the room to the more pleasant company of the ladies and an attempt at judgement is left to our narrator:

It will be remembered that Doctor Sitgreaves spoke forty years ago, and Wellmere was unable to contradict his prophetic assertion.[26]

So much has already been allowed to slide in this ostensible argument that we must be careful to give Cooper his due in acknowledging that Sitgreaves's prophecy was not fulfilled. But an acknowledgement is all this statement is.

There is no real attempt to question whether Sitgreaves was justified then, or to delve into the moral ambiguities of the present situation, recently dramatically exposed in Congress. The issue must have been in readers' minds, yet Cooper substantially has little to say about it, setting up the argument such that it is actually never engaged, an action compounded by the subsequent exposure of Wellmere as a would-be bigamist.

Now it is possible that Cooper intends Sitgreaves to be condemned out of his own mouth, that this exchange is, in fact, a subtle comment on the failings of the Patriots and Americans of Cooper's own time. The book possesses one main black character, Caesar, a servant of Mr. Wharton, who might give some further clue as to Cooper's views on the institution. Here there is some evidence to support a more enlightened view on Cooper's part. The first brief authorial comment seems to be attacking the institution of slavery:

> The faithful old black . . . as if in mockery of his degraded state, had been complimented with the name of Caesar . . . [27]

A fuller description follows, with some similar comment:

> The race of Blacks of which Caesar was a favourable specimen is becoming very rare. The old family servant, who, born and reared in the dwelling of his master, identified himself with the welfare of those whom it was his lot to serve, is giving place in every direction to that vagrant class which has sprung up within the last thirty years, and whose members roam through the country unfettered by principles, and uninfluenced by attachments. For it is one of the curses of slavery, that its victims become incompetent to the attributes of a freeman.

The bottom line of this would seem then to support the argument of Sitgreaves. There may be flaws in slavery but they cannot simply be made free, as the institution has unfitted them for that position. Yet Caesar implies the opposite. Although Cooper has stigmatised him as an "indulged servant"[28] and one expects a degraded sense of self as a result, Caesar persistently utters sentiments of equality. Perceiving an insult to his race when Harvey Birch refers to an American general living among the "niggars," Caesar boldly takes on Birch and Sarah:

> "A Black man so good as White, Miss Sally . . . so long as he behaves heself."
> "And frequently he is much better . . . but Harvey, who is this Mr. Sumpter?"[29]

Caesar possesses a freedom of commentary, but the Whites may rapidly move the conversation, and, in the case of Harvey Birch, seem dismissive of the servant:

> The pedler [*sic*] . . . continued as if the discourse had met with no inter-
> ruption from the sensitiveness of the domestic.[30]

The dismissal repeats itself when faced with a skirmish outside his kitchen,
and the disdain of a dragoon at his obvious desire to escape hurt, Caesar
retorts, "A bullet hurt a Coloured man as much as a White."[31]

The dragoon promptly proposes to experiment by shooting the servant,
and Caesar rapidly retreats. In this subserviency is a key to Caesar's character. His main function throughout the novel is to obey his orders, to do as
his White superiors command him. Despite his pretensions to equality his
true, for Cooper, character, is exposed when he has helped Henry Wharton
to escape from prison. Caesar remains in his place and at the moment of
exposure is thrown to the ground:

> Happily for himself, he had alighted on his head, and consequently
> sustained no material damage.[32]

Caesar is, in the end, a tool in White hands and that is, ultimately, all he is
fit for. His incapacity is further demonstrated by his support for the British. It is notable here that it is usually the less able who are portrayed as
remaining loyal. We observed Wharton's "mental imbecility;" we observed
Wellmere's incapacity for argument. It is also to be seen in Henry Wharton's helpless adherence to rules of war completely out of place in the circumstances of America, and his inability to believe the worst of any of his
fellow soldiers. These positions will be repeated, at least to start off with,
in the character of Lionel Lincoln. Caesar, too, anticipates that novel. He
views the Skinners with absolute detestation, but is unable to conceive that
the British may be employing similar bodies of irregular troops. He cannot
believe the rebels to be competent soldiers and is duly surprised by their
success at the skirmish outside the Wharton property.

This loyalty to the British may be related to the other key attribute of the
servant. Cooper often refers to him as "The African."[33] This is significant
in a narrative dominated by questions of nationality where other Americans are at pains to emphasise their American credentials. A statement of
Caesar's throws further light on this point:

> If dere had nebber been a man curious to see Africa, dere would be no
> colour people out of deir own country.[34]

Cooper, then, has his one significant Black character describe his entire race
as belonging to another country. This is the key to Cooper's attitude on the
question in this book, a question, at best, subordinated to the more important romances. There may be good Blacks, but the race as a whole is not
equipped for freedom. Whether or not if we could prepare them the benefits of it is questionable, for they are not really Americans, but Africans.
This also further illuminates Sitgreaves's anti-British diatribe. It is the British

in this narrative who are responsible for saddling the Americans with this un-American race, this viper in their midst. If only they had never gone to Africa. If only they had never tried to tyrannise over the loyal colonists.[35]

For this theme of British responsibility is also tied to the main shadow lying across the American cause in the narrative, the character of their irregular allies in the neutral ground, the Skinners. These irregular soldiers are "the natural consequences of the possession of a military power that was uncurbed by the restraints of civilian authority."[36]

In other words, it is the British example which has created this American evil, not some inherent flaw in the American character.

The limitations of these arguments are complicated by a further point. Such discussions are subsumed by a text dominated with chases, battles, rescues, and love scenes. The only significant deaths will be of Americans, such as a rival for Dunwoodie's love, who dies proclaiming:

> I have the consolation of knowing . . . that what woman could do in such a cause, I have done.[37]

—and Captain Lawton, killed leading his men in battle. Everybody else, even the multitudinously threatened Birch, survives. Moreover, these momentary outbreaks of discussion, the hints at the complexity of Caesar's position, are enclosed in the old narrative of rising glory. Harper [Washington] hovers over events like a guardian angel, whether smiling on Frances for her treatment of Caesar, or pledging himself to the country through her as symbol:

> But you are my child: all who dwell in this land are my children, and my care; and take the blessing of one who hopes to meet you yet in happier days.[38]

And Harper [Washington] pardons Henry Wharton, an important point of magnanimity. Other more general paeans to American prospects also insert themselves. Harper's treatment of Frances contrasts sharply with that of Wellmere's behaviour to Sarah, a point emphasised by the narrator:

> The good treatment of their women is the surest evidence that a people can give of their civilisation; and there is no nation which has more to boast of, in this respect, than the Americans.[39]

Now this is not to say that there is no violence in the novel, or that the Skinners do not behave utterly reprehensibly, or that Sitgreaves and others do not lament the evils occasioned by war. But, not only are the evils ascribed to the British quite conspicuously the heavier, and the Americans' mitigated by their having been influenced by those evils, but the end term of the narrative is established from the outset. It is here that the point of history is crucial. History requires that it is Dunwoodie and Frances, and not Sarah and Wellmere, who will marry in the penultimate chapter. American victory is certainly not, and American worthiness is substantially not, in question. It is more a case of distinguishing who is really contributing most to it.

The culmination of this is the concluding chapter, set some thirty-five years later on another Anglo-American battlefield. Fortuitously the pedlar Birch, still loyally serving his country, encounters the son of Dunwoodie and Frances and gives a suitably glowing exclamation, lest we be in any doubts as to the lad's merits:

> "'Tis like our native land! . . . Improving with time—God has blessed both![40]

Such a glowing testimonial hardly seems necessary, given what we know of the marvellous qualities of his parents, themselves forcefully resurrected by Birch, soon referring passionately to the absent Frances as "an angel."[41] The narrator is additionally careful to show this war as a continuation of the earlier one, and Dunwoodie Jnr. as keen to earn renown in memory of the departed Washington. The British are duly repulsed. The work of the Revolution is symbolically completed. Birch, dying on this final battlefield, can at last be revealed in his true character, the only man present already worthy of Washington's testimonial before a shot is fired. America's glory continues its inexorable rise.

But the inevitable outcome leaves a critical problem. Was there a deliberate agenda in Cooper's inability to get to grips with the arguments of the war? Did Cooper, like Wellmere, quail before the dispute, retreating to the pleasanter company of the ladies? Either his agenda was to obscure the argument and write a patriotic romance, or there is an element of accident involved. In *The Spy*, it seems possible that Cooper was indulging in a not unreasonable bit of illusion. For all the claims to the contrary, it may still be that the neutral ground is too tortured to bear a really close examination. Even after nearly fifty years, it is still too painful really to ask what might have been lost there.

Before leaving the Revolution (a shadowy event in *The Pioneers*), we may say a brief word about the other two revolutionary novels of this period. *The Pilot* drew on Cooper's experience of the navy and the story of John Paul Jones. It is more overwhelmed by its battle scenes than the earlier romance, and its politics replays the themes of *The Spy*. Here, the principal Englishman, Colonel Howard, is again socially flawed, locking up his nieces to prevent them marrying rebels. He also capitulates to the Revolution at the moment of death:

> Perhaps I may also have mistaken my duty to America—but I was too old to change my politics or my religion—I—I—I lov'd the king—God bless him.[42]

The novel is also framed in the now familiar historical terms, stressing the importance of the period at the outset:

> [The period] has a peculiar interest for every American, not only because it was the birth-day of his nation, but because it was also the era when reason and common sense began to take the place of custom and feudal practices in the management of the affairs of nations.[43]

Again, as in *The Spy*, the plot raises some doubt about this. Again, those doubts are glossed with ultimate American success, although the character of the Pilot is a little more questionable than Birch.

Lionel Lincoln, like *The Spy*, has been interpreted as a deeply ironical portrait of the Revolution.[44] The internal treatment of the Revolution, the farcical plot, and its conclusion problematise such an assessment. The treatments of the battles of Lexington and Concord show the British persistently underestimating the Americans, and portraits of historical British commanders are pretty unflattering. As an aside, the connection between these historical events and the main plot is tenuous, an important point given that Neal has been criticised for a similar problem in *Seventy Six*. That main plot follows Lionel Lincoln, our hero of Anglo-American origins, who returns to America as a British soldier to quell the rebellion. On the boat he encounters a mysterious aged man named Ralph who indicates his possession of vital information concerning the Lincoln family. He naturally cannot reveal this for two volumes. Meanwhile, Lincoln falls in love with his cousin Cecil Dynevor, and the war proceeds. Ralph and an apparently idiot boy named Job Pray are persistently implicated in revolutionary activity, but Lincoln refuses to accept the possibility that Job may not be the idiot he claims. This refusal reaches depths of incredibility reminiscent of a Brockden Brown character. This incredibility is reinforced by a plot which initially suggests that Lincoln will be convinced of the error of his ways and become the true American he ought to be, and ends with a series of aristocratic dark sheep being hauled from their shadowy attic as Ralph is exposed as Lincoln's insane father, temporarily escaped from his asylum, and Job as Lincoln's illegitimate brother. Both father and brother conveniently expire and Lincoln marries the loyalist Cecil and retires to his English castle. This hokum raises various problems. Is the Revolution damned by its principal exponents in the novel being the supposed idiot and a madman? Is it a Revolutionary failure that Lincoln ultimately remains loyal? These questions seem more open than those of *The Spy* but an attempt to read the answers as subversive suffers because the revelation of Ralph's madness, and the claim of Job's idiocy, are both so unconvincing. Further, though Lincoln cannot revolt, it is equally possible that this is a consequence of too much British corruption in his upbringing, just as Ralph's madness is essentially the product of the actions of the staunch loyalist and lover of all things aristocratic,

Mrs. Lechmere. Moreover, once again the Revolution endures, and the conclusion presents a happy tableaux of English and American characters enjoying rosy futures. Assertions of amity, influential mansions whether in England or America, override the memories of war. Lincoln, unlike Rip, fails in the end to scream.

A DELIBERATE DECEPTION?

The Leather-Stocking tales are the books upon which Cooper's reputation centrally rests. This chapter has to deal only with the first three, *The Pioneers* (1823), *The Last of the Mohicans* (1826), and *The Prairie* (1827).[45] Although there is no evidence that Cooper originally intended a sequence, they represent an attempt at a history of America from the Seven Years War to the early 1800s. Such an overview was not new. Brackenridge had performed it in more detail by virtue of living through a similar period and continuously writing about it. Irving used history to inform the present with a much sharper vision than Cooper. These are important points because of a critical tendency to regard Cooper as having done something new and uniquely American. As Francis Parkman put it in 1852, "Of all American writers, Cooper is the most original, the most thoroughly national."[46]

Cooper may have been the first to forge fully Indian characters, although Neal and Paulding's works of the same period raise some question about this. He may have crafted a new character in Natty Bumppo, the Leather-Stocking, although there are certain parallels to the experience of Crèvecoeur in the American Revolution, and to Harvey Birch, although Natty is rather less spotless. But the key themes of these novels are familiar ones. Brackenridge had grappled extensively with the problem of which Whites should rule at home; Irving and Neal dealt with the question of Indian dispossession and extermination. Crèvecoeur explored the dilemma of being trapped between the savage and the civilised. Yet Cooper's books sold and Cooper achieved American celebrity. This raises two problems. First, what had Cooper done with these themes to make his work readable and popular? Second, was there a change in attitude to these themes which made them more palatable? For, it seems clear that contemporary readers thought that Cooper had crafted magnificent American romances, and many critics have seen him as a thoroughly patriotic writer. At the same time there are in the Leather-Stocking novels, as in *The Spy*, scenes which seem to upset the patriotic applecart. Geoffrey Rans' study of the five Leather-Stocking novels is illuminating here. Rans argued that by locating the novels squarely in the past, as *The Spy* was, Cooper's readers were able to face the challenging issues portrayed with equanimity. Again, there may be a suggestion that perhaps things could have turned out better, but the reader knows they did not. Rans concluded that, "His contemporaries found in him what they wanted to find."[47]

But this statement implies a wilful blindness on the part of Cooper's readers, which may have been at variance with Cooper's intentions. Rans does, indeed, advance this argument, but the problem of Cooper's intentions remains. Rans can only resolve this by arguing for the existence of a paradox whereby "Cooper's artistic resolve to embody the truth was at odds with the truth he would have liked to express."[48] But Cooper persistently ends by accepting the glorious harmony and granting permission to his readers to accept it, and there is a disturbingly artificial cast to certain of his conflicts.

The position of Natty Bumppo is key. Although he denounces the destruction of the Indians, his language and conduct is often as racist as the next White. Moreover, he is an agent of the very march of progress destroying both the Indians and, to his wail of complaint, himself. Cooper never really faces either Natty's complicity in these acts or the fundamental question of his right to the wilderness against either Indians or the other Whites, if he is, at bottom, as racist as they.

Before turning to the detail of the novel, it is worth noting some points concerning its origins and construction. We noted how little information is to be garnered from Cooper's letters. The only statement concerning intent in this case comes from a letter masquerading as preface, where Cooper claimed that:

> [*The Pioneers*] has been written, exclusively, to please myself: so it would be no wonder if it displeased every body else; for what two ever thought alike on a subject of the imagination?[49]

There was a particularly personal quality here. For the setting, and the key character of Judge Temple, Cooper drew on his family background and his father's role in carving out the settlement of Cooperstown during a period similar to that covered in the novel. Cooper also alighted on a principal drive of fellow writers from Crèvecoeur on; the need to somehow capture America on the page. In Cooper's case, he did so by capturing the detailed life of a developing settlement in upstate New York in 1793. It is in this sense, and more deeply than *The Spy*, a slice of personally witnessed history, which accounts for the frequent digressions from what may pass for the main plot which is either, depending on one's point of view, the disputed right of Natty to maintain his traditional way of life, or the disputed claim of Edwards to the lands occupied by the Judge. That the plots are concerned with these two individuals and their struggle with fellow Whites is the final crucial point. Just as in *The Spy*, the Loyalist perspective is set up for equal consideration only to be demonstrated as the less worthy, and thus excluded, so with the Indians here. Cooper's America is, again, a partial world.

Three aspects of the novel are important here. First, the way Cooper establishes his setting, and the implications of that establishment. Second, the central questions on which the plot turns, the character of the mysterious Edwards and the conflict between Natty and the law. Third, the relationship between these characters and the overall portrayal of the Indians in the narrative.

The opening of *The Pioneers* recalls *The Spy*. Again, Cooper carefully establishes the historical frame. He sets up the rich environment of the present day in no uncertain terms:

> In short, the whole district is hourly exhibiting how much can be done, in even a rugged country, and with a severe climate, under the dominion of mild laws, and where every man feels a direct interest in the prosperity of a commonwealth, of which he knows himself to form a distinct and independent part.[50]

The focus narrows to the specific period under examination, the year 1793, beginning with an encounter between Judge Temple (arriving with his daughter Elizabeth for the Christmas celebrations), Natty Bumppo, and the mysterious Edwards. There is a collective shooting at a deer, and the victor is disputed. We may note here that there is no Indian present; from the very outset the dispute about ownership is between Whites and, moreover, between Edwards and Temple, who turn out to be of the same class. The conclusion is also anticipated when Elizabeth intercedes to persuade Edwards, at this point unidentified, to accept Temple's offer of aid for his wound. This is a wound, incidentally, which Temple has inflicted by accident. This is precisely the state of affairs in their propertied relationship and Elizabeth proves a key agent in removing it, although the reader knows none of this.

The narrative then turns to Temple's background, and his friendship with the Effingham family. The relevance of this, beyond exploring Temple's somewhat dubious title to the land, is only clarified when Edwards is finally revealed as an Effingham. Again, the portrayal of the revolution is significant. It is *The Spy* in miniature, with Temple showing a certain dubious quality in his acquisition of crown lands, and the possibly illustrious Loyalists being swept away. But the tone is crucial. In the course of the discussion, Cooper raises the question of the Quakers. Recalling Franklin, the Effingham of the day is shown despising the Quakers for their refusal to organise the military defence of the colony. The narrator's comment is revealing in its detachment:

> It is not our task to explain what is, or ought to be, the substance of Christianity, but merely to record in this place the opinions of Major Effingham.[51]

The view is now further narrowed to the village of Templeton itself and its inhabitants, and Cooper's aim is further clarified. The diversity of such a settlement is demonstrated by the introduction of a Frenchman, a German, and a local priest. Equal consideration is given to their origins as to Mohegan's, and a considerable amount more to a discussion of religious history. Cooper's aim of capturing America is clear, as is the comparative position of the Indians in such a picture. The key question continues to be: which White will dominate? The complexity of Templeton's population, and the particular flaws of Temple's steward, Richard Jones, and the failed house he designed for the judge, do raise concern. The flaws in that construction are described at length, but the narrative also explains that Jones, although initially "his failure produced a . . . degree of mortification,"[52] subsequently, "grew better satisfied with his labours, and instead of apologising for the defects, he soon commenced praising the beauties of the mansion-house."[53]

This is further worrying because of its effect on the rest of the populace:

> He soon found hearers; and, as wealth and comfort are at all times attractive, it was made a model for imitation on a small scale.[54]

But this warning is negated by its context. The chapter concludes not with this questionable success, but with the reactions of Elizabeth, Edwards, and the Judge to the overall view. For all three, the individual flaws cannot mar that overall telling image of civilisation. The description is applied to Elizabeth, but the effect is similar, if reduced, for the others:

> Elizabeth . . . saw only in gross, the cluster of houses that lay like a map at her feet; the fifty smokes, that were diagonally curling from the valley to the clouds . . . [55]

Edwards's reaction is most significant considering that some effort is being made in the course of the narrative to present him as kin to Natty, as outside the civilisation, "[he] . . . cast one admiring glance from north to south, and then sunk his face again beneath the folds of his coat."[56]

The inter-White power struggle is next renewed when Edwards rescues Jones' sleigh from going over a cliff, a deed Jones later belittles to one of his passengers:

> Now mark my words: there will be a story among the settlers, that all our necks would have been broken, but for that fellow there—as if I did not know how to drive.[57]

By the end of this short speech, Jones' agile mind is already blaming Edwards for the mishap. These opening chapters not only set up Edwards as a key heroic figure, but also place Natty in a distinctly subordinate, almost irrelevant, role.

Nevertheless, their parts are more equal in the balance of the narrative. Edwards is torn between his allegiance to Natty and Mohegan, and his obscure relationship with the judge, coupled with his obvious attraction to Elizabeth. Natty battles to maintain his freedom to hunt from the encroachments of the Judge's law, and his freedom to privacy from the inquisitiveness of the questionable White element. The law will, unsurprisingly, act against him. Certain critics have laid great stress on Natty's fate in this regard.[58] But this is to ignore two points: first, the thin line that separates Natty from those who torment him, and, second, the remarkable deception Cooper perpetrates regarding Edwards' character.

The threat to Natty's freedom may well symbolise the dangers of a law supposedly civilised but left to the hands of Jones and his questionable associates, even if those associates are tempered by the presence of the Judge. But the question of Natty's right to special treatment remains. Jones's characterisation of him is useful, "a lawless squatter and professed deer-killer."[59] Allowing for Jones's bias, the underlying question remains: why should Natty be more entitled to the land than the Judge, Jones, or the other settlers? There is a selfishness in this implication that Natty should enjoy the wilderness but nobody, or hardly anybody, else, a strain of his character reinforced by his attitude to Mohegan's death.[60] Natty's claim rests on his treatment of the wilderness and his relationship to the Indians.

He does attempt to live more in harmony with nature than the other settlers, although they are excluded from that harmony. Yet Temple is, however misguidedly, attempting legal conservation, and Natty's harmony contains deceits as selfish as Temple's. When the court officers arrest him, he rhapsodises about an idyllic past:

> You've driven God's creaters [sic] from the wilderness, where his providence had put them for his own pleasure, and you've brought in the troubles and divilties [sic] of the law, where no man was ever known to disturb another.[61]

The Indians and the Indian wars are wholly excluded from this narrative. The problem of Natty's entitlement is excluded from this discussion, even though, as he has elsewhere admitted, his freedom is of a duration only slightly longer than the Judge's, "Game is game, and he who finds may kill; that has been the law in these mountains for forty years."[62]

The Indian claim underlies all of this. Given Natty's apparent affinity with Mohegan, and Edwards' supposed Indian blood, his right might derive from the same basis as theirs, the original Indian claim to the land. Three main problems exist here. First, the ambivalent attitude to the Indian question displayed by Cooper as narrator. Second, the highly murky, and frankly deceptive characterisation of Edwards' background, and third, the attitude of Leather-Stocking to the Indians.

We noted Cooper's supposed credentials in Indian portrayal, succinctly summed up by Kay Seymour House, who stated that, Cooper "set the pattern for writers who would treat of the Indian."[63] That he created a new type of fictional Indian is probably true, but their resemblance to the real thing is questionable. More, the way he deployed them, whether intended or not, possessed a duplicitous dimension.

In *The Pioneers*, no Indian character, or discussion of the Indian aspect of settler expansion, occurs until Chapter Seven. The Indian who appears is Chingachgook, here designated as John Mohegan, or Indian John. Here, Cooper freely acknowledges the European, or Christian, dispossession of Indian land, and there is almost a hint of satire in the opening sentence that recalls Irving, "Before the Europeans, or, to use a more significant term, the Christians, dispossessed the original owners of the soil. . . ."[64]

But Cooper simply, or rather not at all simply, submits the reader to another history lesson, concerning the earlier Indian wars. When the question of the White role recurs, it is almost matter-of-fact. The narrator notes two confederacies centred on the Chesapeake and New England and remarks, "of course, these two tribes were the first who were dispossessed of their land by the Europeans."[65]

It is as if the sole purpose of this lengthy introduction of Mohegan's ancestry is to demonstrate that Cooper has done his homework and is introducing the correct Indian for this historical situation. Furthermore, Mohegan, similarly to Natty, is self-compromised:

> He had, for a long time, been an associate of the White men, particularly in their wars; and, having been, at a season when his services were of importance, much noticed and flattered, he had turned Christian.[66]

If Mohegan and Natty give way to civilisation in this way, do they really deserve to be exempted from its evils? Cooper expands on this by firmly making Mohegan stand for his race, "In common with all his people, who dwelt within the influence of the Anglo-Americans, he had acquired new wants."[67]

There is a definite sense that their glory, remnants of which are still present, has been lost at least as much through Mohegan's racial flaws as through the acts of the Whites. Cooper's view of the Indian is particularly suggested by his use of the title "child of the forest."[68] This could simply refer to Mohegan's place of birth but, given Cooper's treatment of non-White races elsewhere in his early novels, there seems a strong case to suppose that this is meant to indicate inferiority. This introduction of the Indians is a rare case of exterior comment on them. Most of the rest of such discussions are performed through either Natty or Edwards, whose cases are complicatedly interconnected. To deal with Edwards first, it is persistently implied that he is contaminated with Indian blood. Mohegan first announces this, "the 'Young Eagle' has the blood of a Delaware chief in his veins: it is red."[69] This immediately places Edwards in a subordinate position. When he loses his temper, the Reverend Grant explains to his daughter Louisa:

> He is mixed with the blood of the Indians, you have heard; and neither the refinements of education, nor the advantages of our excellent liturgy, have been able entirely to eradicate the evil. But care and time will do much for him yet.[70]

There is a sense of caring for, of civilising the wayward child. This supposed Indian blood colours Elizabeth's attitudes to the young hunter. She is perennially surprised, although the fact should warn the reader of the truth, at Edwards' display of genteel qualities which, given his blood, he should not possess and which, in one case, she ties to the miraculously developing country:

> Every thing in this magical country seems to border on the marvellous . . . and among all the changes, this is certainly not the least wonderful.[71]

But this capacity of the hunter is partially explained by the history with which, without the slightest shred of evidence, Temple's household allow themselves to endow him. The explanation is that he is only partially Indian on his mother's side. There is, thus, more reason to suppose him redeemable than were he a full-blooded savage. Elizabeth here goes even further, crediting him with an appropriately rich Indian heritage, "I suppose him a descendant of King Philip, if not a grandson of Pocahontas."[72]

Edwards's genteel capacities and the interaction between Elizabeth and Edwards over the Indians ought to alert the reader to the truth. Here Louisa Grant points out that Edwards' eyes are not even so black as Elizabeth's and Elizabeth seizes eagerly upon her possible possession of Indian blood:

> It would be a great relief to my mind to think so, for I own that I grieve when I see old Mohegan walking about these lands, like the ghost of one of their ancient possessors, and feel how small is my right to possess them.[73]

This statement seems to seriously excite Edwards, and Elizabeth expands on her theme:

> But what can I do? What can my father do? Should we offer the old man a home and a maintenance, his habits would compel him to refuse us. Neither, were we so silly as to wish such a thing, could we convert these clearings and farms, again, into hunting-grounds, as the Leatherstocking would wish to see them.[74]

Elizabeth is clearly trapped by her heritage. It is unimaginable to her that the life she enjoys could be altered. Elsewhere, she has already shown herself a fervent supporter of the area's further civilisation. Her pity for Mohegan is quite genuine, but distinctly limited. Cutting responses from Edward, and Natty were he present, seem appropriate. In fact, Natty's response when it comes is not so clear-cut as his Indian relationships would imply, and Edwards' response is equally at variance with what one would expect an Indian sympathiser, never mind a man of mixed blood to argue:

> But there is one thing that I am certain you can and will do, when you become the mistress of these beautiful valleys—use your wealth with indulgence to the poor and charity to the needy;—indeed, you can do no more.[75]

This practically excludes the Indians altogether. Arguably, on a purely factual level, this is quite fair. The clock cannot be put back; Whites and Indians are incompatible in their ways of life; the two cannot live side by side. But whether this is accurate or not, it is clear that, in the world Cooper is recreating, it is not a matter of pressing concern. Recalling Wellmere confronting Sitgreaves, Edwards simply does not query Elizabeth on her use of the word "silly" to describe any possibility of undoing the march of civilisation. Instead, after a few more exchanges, he is lavishing praise upon her. Edwards, if he is of mixed blood, as the narrative continues to imply, inclines far more to the civilised than the savage side. This leaves Natty alone to stand by Mohegan's side.

   Yet Natty's principal concern, to maintain his accustomed way of life, is peculiarly personal, and Mohegan, though he partially shares that life, is absent from the crucial confrontations, including Natty's escape from prison. Furthermore, Mohegan, in his championing of Edwards, is further complicit in his own disinheritance. Their alliance here is considerably more limited than in *The Last of the Mohicans*. It hinges on their support for the rights of Edwards, the major topic of conversation in their various scenes together.[76] We shall come to the final exposure of the true nature of these rights in a moment. But a word has first to be said about Mohegan's most extended scene. This complex discussion of Mohegan's past and Elizabeth's attitude to it recalls the complex view of Indian–White relations implied both by Edwards' position and by the first introduction of Mohegan. Here, though, Mohegan is permitted to talk about more than simply the disinheritance of Edwards. Elizabeth first wonders where Mohegan has been, pointing out that she had various treats prepared for him. Mohegan stresses his illustrious past when he could shift for himself without such assistance. Elizabeth then argues, one imagines with relief given the bloody note of Mohegan's discourse:

> Those times are gone by, old warrior . . . since then, your people have disappeared, and in place of chasing your enemies, you have learned to fear God and to live at peace.[77]

As when confronting Edwards, she attempts to make acceptable the fate of Mohegan's people. But where Edwards accepted her argument without comment, Mohegan responds forcefully:

> Daughter, since John was young, he has seen the White man from Frontinac come down on his White brothers from Albany, and fight. Did they fear God! He has seen his English and his American Fathers burying their tomahawks in each others' brains, for this very land. Did they fear God and live in peace![78]

As with Natty's idyll, Cooper here glosses over the violent aspects of Mohegan's heritage, but it is nevertheless a telling argument. Yet Cooper compromises the Indian even as he allows him this attack. As on the earlier occasions when Mohegan appeared, he recalls the tribal bargain:

> All this, and all that grew in it, and all that walked over it, and all that fed there, they gave to the Fire-eater—for they loved him. He was strong, and they were women, and he helped them."[79]

Once again we are reminded that the Indians, in this reading, have surrendered their own land, even if to a White with perhaps some Indian connection. But this is, in a sense, a litany of past evils, a fate which Mohegan soon acquiesces to by refusing to flee the forest fire about to threaten them. Mohegan next discusses his idyllic prospects in the next world:

> He will go to the country where his fathers have met. The game shall be plenty as the fish in the lakes. . . . and all just red-men shall live together as brothers.[80]

This undermines his earlier description of his world before the fall, implying that not all red men are just. It raises the possibility that Cooper is once again celebrating appropriate behaviour on both sides, as he appeared to do in places in *The Spy*. However, as there, the underdog, here the Indian, is compromised. Mohegan now reveals a completely new piece of information:

> I have no son but the Young Eagle, and he has the blood of a White man.[81]

Elizabeth responds with a general enquiry about Edwards' origins, presumably because the earlier remarks of Mohegan, and Jones's contentions spun from them convinced her of Edwards' mixed blood. What follows is a curious fire which threatens all with death, only to allow the unhardy Reverend Grant safe passage to them. Mohegan, already compromised by his surrender of land to the Edwards family, surrenders himself to death in the flames. Here, like Cooper, we must postpone consideration of the revelation of Edwards' true nature, to deal with Natty's response to this death.

Despite his friendship with Mohegan, Natty has, at various points, shown an implicit racism. In one of his early descriptions of his past, he stated:

> I am a plain, unlarned man, that has sarved the king [*sic*] and his country . . . ag'in the French and savages.[82]

In the tavern, he tries to whip Mohegan into action on Edwards' behalf, but when violence is threatened, has to restrain him:

> This is the way with all the savages; give them liquor, and they make dogs of themselves.[83]

A case might be made that these savage attributes are the fault of the Whites, the French, for bringing the savages into their war, although, of course, Natty was fighting for the English who were doing precisely the same, or the Whites in general for bringing in the liquor. But Natty is contaminated by the same faults. His presence in the wilderness is part of the march that brought those evils. Nor do his concerns or creed suggest a man really concerned with the fate of the savages, excepting perhaps Mohegan, and his concern for him seems more that he should perform the necessary act of ensuring Edwards' inheritance than anything deeper. This ambivalence is cemented by his attitude at the death scene. Mohegan's speech to Elizabeth welcomed his looming demise. Natty clarifies it:

> Now he thinks he shall travel where it will always be good hunting; where no wicked or unjust Indians can go; and where he shall meet all his tribe ag'in.[84]

Natty's whole attitude to this has a critical strain; he refers to the act as typical of these "wilful creatures."[85] Natty's attitude is a curious mingling of the critical and complementary:

> There's not much loss in that, to a man whose hands be hardly fit for basket-making. Loss! if there be any loss, 'twill be to me. I'm sure after he's gone, there will be but little left for me to do but to follow.[86]

Natty's grief here seems almost selfish, another reflection of a key attribute of his creed. Now, in fairness to the scene, Natty also acknowledges the White role in this event:

> Flesh isn't iron, that a man can live for ever, and see his kith and kin driven to a far country, and he left to mourn, with none to keep him company.[87]

Yet, although the text displays these confusions, here, as in *The Spy*, Cooper endorses the rising glory. Here he does so by a revelation concerning Edwards' heritage, which seriously questions the half-hearted Indian sympathy scenes of the earlier narrative. This much-delayed revelation occurs as a result of Elizabeth's near-death experience in the fire and Mohegan's death, but the reader may well agree with Edwards' half-apology to Elizabeth, "I shall remove a veil that perhaps it has been weakness to keep around me and my affairs so long."[88]

This revelation is, unsurprisingly, further delayed by a final assault of the dubious law upon the cave where Natty is now holed up. This assault is halted at the crucial moment by the arrival of Edwards, who now reveals that the cave contains his grandfather, the lost Major Effingham. Significantly, the dying man emerges in the manner of Rip, speaking a rambling language of loyalty:

> Each one who loves a good and virtuous king, will wish to see these colonies continue loyal.[89]

Of course, this is not an Irving fantasy, but a Cooper attempt at history, and here Effingham cannot go home. Significantly, his mind, unlike Rip's, is hopelessly decayed. His only function in the narrative is to provide this revelation, surrendering rightful tenancy of the lands to his son and "lie by the side of old Mohegan."[90] The revelation is not the mere fact of his life, but the true nature of his Indian connection. He saved Mohegan's life, and Mohegan admitted him an honorary member of the tribe. Edwards' father was named Eagle, though whether actually given the same tribal membership is unclear, and Edwards, himself, has been extended the same title. His blood is pure; he can be married to Elizabeth without the slightest difficulty. This revelation is shocking, especially if one comes to *The Pioneers* anticipating a writer who was profoundly troubled by the fate of the Indians. Cooper has, throughout the narrative, persistently implied that Edwards's Indian heritage was considerably more than this. It is by this act, more than any other in the novel, that Cooper permits that maintenance of his readers' illusions perceived by Rans.[91] Edwards wistful longing for some deeper connection is as feeble and false a protest as Elizabeth's earlier mournful comment on Mohegan:

> I have no other Indian blood or breeding; though I have seen the hour, Judge Temple, when I could wish that such had been my lineage and education.[92]

That hour is gone, perhaps from the moment Edwards first sights Elizabeth. The appropriate American order is descisively fulfilled through them. They respect the Indian heritage, but they recognise, as the reader recognises, that it is necessary for civilisation to march. There could scarcely be a happier outcome of such a march than so appropriate a marriage, reconciling the conflicts of the various wars of America's past. Nor is this all. A final coup de grace at the hands of Natty awaits. This is delivered in several ways. He, as much as Mohegan, has desired to bring about the appropriate union, and been an unconscionably long time about it. He and Edwards now show the depth of their ambivalence concerning the Indians, as they stand over Mohegan's grave:

> "He was the last of his people who continued to inhabit this country; and it may be said of him, emphatically, that his faults were those of an Indian, and his virtues those of a man."
> "You never said a truer word, Mr Oliver . . ."[93]

Natty has already acquiesced in the very march of civilisation he so deplores. That march, it seems, is perfectly acceptable provided that the right people, in this case Edwards and Elizabeth, are the agents of it. Having consigned his friend to his appropriate place in the racial hierarchy, he calls God's witness that, although things may not be entirely as we might wish them here on Earth (and it is by no means clear that Natty or Cooper do wish them any other way), they will be better in another place:

> There is one greater than all, who'll bring the just together ag'in at his own time, and who'll whiten the skin of a black-moor, and place him on a footing with princes.[94]

Natty will similarly postpone resolution of the Red–White conflict whose troubling aspects he is either complicit in or has endorsed in what is almost his last speech.[95] But, as in the rest of the novel, that conflict is not his prime concern. His last speeches are dominated by restatements of his creed, his love of the wilderness, his desire for solitude. Of course he must go west, but the degree of price to America intended in this seems questionable. Once again, Natty is functioning as agent for the march of civilisation. As Cooper, as narrator, puts it forcibly in the final sentence:

> He had gone far towards the setting sun,—the foremost in that band of Pioneers, who are opening the way for the march of our nation across the continent.[96]

It is not necessarily civilisation driving him out, but Natty choosing to go. Nor is he whole-heartedly opposed to that civilisation, having battled for much of the novel to ensure the establishment of its key symbols, Elizabeth and Edwards. In the face of this conclusion, it is not only unsurprising that Cooper's contemporaries saw this as a patriotic celebration, but it seems highly contentious to suggest that Cooper intended anything else.

Consider, in contrast, the end of Irving's *History* where the empire falls and Knickerbocker is vanished, or the end of Brackenridge's novel where the eternal struggle between aristocrat and democrat is set to play out anew upon a European stage. They saw no need for marriages of convenience; they did not permit the comfortable illusion. Cooper may have recognised the illusions, but he ended in endorsing them.

A NICE NEAT ENDING

The second and third novels of the Leather-Stocking series largely maintained the playing field established by *The Pioneers*. This is particularly the case with *The Prairie*, written and published after Cooper left for Europe on a grand tour bearing little similarity to Irving's troubled departure. Cooper left more popular with his countrymen than he was ever to be again, and *The Prairie* did not upset that apple-cart.

The *Last of the Mohicans* is a little more complex. Again, Cooper's historical framing was precise:

> The incidents we shall attempt to relate occurred, during the third year of the war which England and France . . . waged, for possession of a country, that neither was destined to retain.[97]

This locates the story in a far more distant world, implying a futility given the different and, Cooper's other writings imply, brighter future round the corner. Natty is closer to the Indians than in either of the other novels, declaring an unparalleled kinship to Chingachgook (Mohegan) in his final speech, and one that is not altogether reflected in *The Pioneers*:

> The gifts of our colours may be different, but God has so placed us as to journey on the same path. I have no kin, and I may also say, like you, no people.[98]

Yet although it is a kinship between White and Red, it is almost more a kinship between two friends. Natty's "no people" rejects both races, and elsewhere, he constantly stresses his pure blood:

> Tis strange that an Indian should understand White sounds better than a man, who, his very enemies will own, has no cross in his blood, although he may have lived with the red skins long enough to be suspected.[99]

Uncas is a nobler Indian than any encountered in *The Pioneers*, or even than Hard-Heart in *The Prairie*, but this nobility consists in the closeness to which he approaches

White modes of behaviour, "Uncas, denying his habits, we had almost said his nature, flew with instinctive delicacy, accompanied by Heyward to the assistance of the females."[100]

It is also notable that Cora is open to his attractions but certainly not to those of Magua. While this might be ascribed to Magua's treatment of the sisters, there is the distinct sense that it arises from Magua's natural Indian characteristics, which Uncas transcends. Even if Uncas is to represent the possibility of the Indians, and it is a fairly questionable one since it implies that an Indian may only be praised the closer he attains to Whiteness, it is destroyed by the twin deaths of Uncas and Cora. The interracial relationship remains impossible; there is still no way out. Thus, although the manner implies a more sympathetic attitude to the Indians than that portrayed in *The Pioneers*, the ending closes the door upon it.

The Prairie moved further in the same direction. This novel describes the pioneering experience in which Natty, at the conclusion of *The Pioneers*, was poised to be a leading participant. Again, the novel takes a long time over an unnecessarily tangled plot, although not quite as severely as in the constant capturings and recapturings of *The Last of the Mohicans*. An unimpressive family of settlers, named Bush, are proceeding through the prairie lands. They are led by Ishmael, a squatter and general law unto himself and his. Ostensibly in quest of land, Ishmael, led astray by his brother Abiram, is engaged in the white slave trade, bearing a captive Spanish woman by the name of Inez. An orphan member of the family, Ellen Wade, is being pursued by her lover, Paul Hover. It is also, regrettably, necessary to mention Middleton, Inez's husband, who is likely fuelled by deep sexual frustration since his gorgeous bride was abducted on their wedding night. Into this tangled web come two groups of Indians, noble and ignoble, a repeat of the pairing in the previous novel, and Natty Bumppo, now an ancient man, here designated "the trapper."

The parallels between this and other novels are numerous. Again, it is contained history, here the early settlement of the Louisiana Purchase:

> The incidents and scenes which are connected with our present legend, occurred in the earliest periods of the enterprises which have led to so great and so speedy a result.[101]

Natty's lack of Indian blood and his lament for the lost Delaware, coupled to his obliviousness of his role in the processes of their destruction, are familiar themes.[102] His true attitude is damningly exposed when Hard-Heart, the noble Indian, asks that Natty notify his people of the circumstances of his death and slay his colt on the grave so that it may bear Hard-Heart to the blessed prairies. Natty claims his "traditions" forbid him to carry the words and compels a change of message. Nobody questions his right to force that change.[103]

The narrative focused on the various rights to the purchased lands. Natty has travelled here to escape civilisation but, as usual, affects to believe that nobody else should be allowed this escape. Or rather, only those he considers suitable, and distinctly not the Bush family. But the designation of Bush as a squatter upon his previous land shows how narrow is the divide between them, for that designation was applied to Natty back in upstate New York. Indeed, in one exchange with Bush, Natty admits as much, despite Cooper's attempt to ascribe that similarity to wholly different motivations:

> "Can you tell me, stranger, where the law or the reason is to be found which says that one man shall have a section, or a town, or perhaps a country, to his use, and another have to beg for earth to make his grave in. This is not nature, and I deny that it is law. That is, your legal law."
>
> "I cannot say that you are wrong," returned the trapper, whose opinions on this important topic, though drawn from very different premises, were in singular accordance with those of his companion, "and I have often thought and said as much, when and where I believed my voice could be heard."[104]

For all their similarities, the fading Natty cannot side with these men; instead, he now sides with the law, represented by Middleton. This is a law determinedly allied to the past. For Middleton is revealed as the grandson of Duncan, the flawed British soldier in *Mohicans*, whose racial prejudices forbade him to consider marriage to Cora, and here redeemed in a quite unnecessary fashion.[105] For, Middleton recounts:

> When the war took place between the crown and her colonies, my grandfather did not forget his birthplace, but threw off the empty allegiances of names, and was true to his proper country; he fought on the side of liberty.[106]

Natty, already in paroxysms of joy at this encounter, proceeds to ally the two worlds: "There was reason in it; and what is better, there was Natur'!"[107]

Nor is this all; Duncan was so transformed that he bequeathed both the names of Nathaniel and, crucially, Uncas to his descendants. Thus, symbolically, are the races united. There was no reason to expect this transformation at the conclusion of *Mohicans*. It is a quite unnecessarily fulsome endorsement of the dream. Middleton is defiant proof that all has worked out for the best in the best of all possible worlds, and Natty, for all his equivocations, endorses his ascendancy at his death.

The trapper's approaching death is the centre of the novel, a death which, dissatisfied with his inability to hunt, he longs to embrace. In that death, there is the clear implication of a loss of a world. As with Loyalists and Patriots, or the fate of Uncas and Cora, the drama is balanced. Natty does show a greater awareness of the flaws of his race than in either of the other novels. In a long exchange with the naturalist, a comic figure, Natty grants the New World equality of status with the Old:

> Now if man is so blinded in his folly as to go on, ages on ages, doing harm chiefly to himself, there is the same reason to think that he has wrought his evil here as in the countries you call so old.[108]

There is, in this exchange, a rare echo of Irving, "It is the fate of all things to ripen, and then to decay."[109] But Natty's sense of his mortality, of the evils of his world is qualified by an acquiescence in whatever may come:

> If I could choose a change in the orderings of Providence—which I cannot and which it would be blasphemy to attempt, seeing that all things are governed by a wiser mind than belongs to mortal weakness. . . . [110]

Any weakening of the racial lines is firmly tempered by the appropriate ending. Natty has already softened his defence of frontier life by urging Paul back to settled lands, since Ellen could not survive its rigours. He shows further contempt for the Amer-Indians by departing in such a manner that Hard-Heart cannot glimpse any tears he may shed. His death and the accounts of those companions only cement this. Paul, one endorsed heir, has arisen to the rank of a state legislator. Middleton, the other, is a high-ranking general, clearly ready to open fire on Hard-Heart's tribe at the slightest excuse. Natty, dying, is still resolutely the man without a taint of Indian blood:

> "Let the wise chief have no cares for his journey . . . a hundred Loups shall clear his path from briars."
> "Pawnee, I die as I have lived, a Christian man . . . as I came into life, so will I leave it. Horses and arms are not needed to stand in the presence of the Great Spirit of my people."[111]

At his moment of death, Natty performed a remarkable impression of Thomas Jefferson, holding two ideas in his mind at the same time. He divides his bequests equally, giving the traps to the Indian, but sending the more significant gift, the rifle, east to Edwards. He expresses the hope that he and Hard-Heart may, contrary to their beliefs, find themselves ultimately in the same heaven, but exclaims with relief to Middleton when he arrives:

> Captain . . . I am glad you have come; for though kind, and well meaning according to the gifts of their colour, these Indians are not the men, to lay the head of a White man in his grave.[112]

At the end, as at the beginning of the Leather-Stocking's narrative, the question remained whether Cooper was engaged in an act of deep subversion. Perhaps he intended a self-condemning depiction of the contradictions of the American character. But if this is subversion, it is significantly undermined by Cooper's persistent endorsement of the ascendant White position, an endorsement accomplished most significantly by Natty himself. He may attempt equal bequests to Hard-Heart and the distant Edwards, but his support of Edwards's claim, of Middleton's ancestry, made him utterly complicit in the approaching Indian disaster. Neither author nor creator can go further than this half-hearted funeral alliance, and the balance of the evidence suggests that they did not comprehend their own failure.

Conclusion
A Nice Derangement of Epitaphs

"Is it the Fourth?"

"Thomas Jefferson still survives."[1]

The story of the deaths of Adams and Jefferson on the fiftieth anniversary of the Declaration of Independence (4 July, 1826) is a familiar one.[2] A return to it here is justified by its meaning for the quest in which this study has been engaged. 1826 marked a pause in that literary journey. Irving, Neal, and Cooper were all in Europe. Both Irving and Neal were drifting away from the direct engagement with questions of American character which occupied their early work; Cooper was about to craft a culminating illusion, *The Prairie* (1827). The next wave of writers had yet to emerge.

Yet the questions of national character which preoccupied those uneasy voices of the early republican period remained as pertinent in 1826 as in 1776. The place of Indians and slaves; the relative merits of savage versus civilised, of Old versus New Worlds; the relative political power of aristocrat or democrat; the danger of the tyranny of the one versus the tyranny of the many: all these questions remained open to debate. Nor, in 1826, had there been a conclusive answer to Crèvecoeur's grand question. Perhaps there could never have been. Perhaps it was the quest and not the answer that mattered. But this study has shown that it was precisely that quest which was not permitted. Instead, time and again, insistent, fixed answers were confidently proclaimed by, most prominently of all, Thomas Jefferson.

At his death, he was at it again. Unable to attend the Fourth of July celebrations, he penned a eulogy to the American dream he had done so much to craft:

> May it [the Declaration] be to the world, what I believe it will be, (to some parts sooner, to others later, but finally to all,) the signal of arousing men to burst the chains under which monkish ignorance and superstition had persuaded them to bind themselves, and to assume the blessings and security of self-government. . . . All eyes are opened or opening to the rights of men.

It was the old illusion written afresh, an illusion the endurance of which Adams' dying words obliquely recognised. That illusion, personified in Jefferson, would survive; those other views whose validity it denied and obscured would be forgotten. Whether or not Adams fully recognised in 1800 that had been the meaning of his defeat, a meaning anticipated by the defeats of Crèvecoeur and Brackenridge, further demonstrated in the exile of Irving. In 1826, the event repeated itself, with fresh irony. In reality, Adams was mistaken, Jefferson was already dead. But that factual error contained a larger historical truth.

It was the myths of Jefferson and Cooper, not the satire of Brackenridge and Irving, or the warnings of Adams, that would survive. Yet all of them were Americans, all their experiences facets of the American character. At this end, as at the beginning, both still demanded recognition.

That recognition needed to run deeper than mere eulogies. Adams hinted at it with the toast he offered to his local declaration committee. Unusually, he was briefer than his old friend, giving two words only: "INDEPENDENCE forever."[3] This implied what Adams and his fellow worriers sought, beneath the temporary temptations of ambition. What they wanted was not a blind switching of Americans from allegiance to Jefferson's dream to allegiance to theirs. They sought the independence of thought implied by Crèvecoeur's question which possessed so many possible answers. They recognised, because they witnessed it in action, the persistent existence of a multitude of Americas and Americans. They also recognised, because they were on the receiving end of it, the tendency to deny this. But the worriers, despite those denials, did not forsake America. Crèvecoeur tried to return. Brackenridge persisted in chronicling his warnings. Irving and Neal would both come back, Irving to end his life working on the greatest American symbol of all, his namesake George Washington; Neal opposing slavery. And Adams, the "Atlas of Independence," went to his death reiterating a broader independence than Jefferson's flowery rhetoric acknowledged. In 1826, as in 1776, Jefferson's Fourth remained illusory. America still needed writers prepared to say so.

This study has charted a sequence of writers who did say so. They expose the undertow of doubt and unease beneath the familiar optimism of Jefferson's Declaration. They show that American national character was born and remained in debate, despite frequent attempts to close down the question. The endurance of the debate showed it to be as significant to an understanding of American character as the prevailing optimistic strain it challenged. In 1826, that contest continued. In keeping Crèvecoeur's question open, the worriers enjoyed a triumph, even if they could not recognise it.

Notes

NOTES TO THE INTRODUCTION

1. This was an adopted name; his full name was Michel-Guillaume Jean de Crèvecoeur. The complexities of Crèvecoeur's identities are explored in detail in Chapter 1.
2. J. Hector St. John de Crèvecoeur, "Letter III," in *Letters from an American Farmer and Sketches of Eighteenth-Century America* (ed.) Albert A. Stone, 69 (Harmondsworth, Middlesex: Penguin, 1986). Hereafter, *Letters and Sketches*.
3. According to the National Library of Scotland on-line catalogue—consulted 28/12/05.
4. Michael Kammen, *People of Paradox: An Inquiry Concerning the Origins of American Civilisation* (New York: Oxford University Press, 1980), xi–xii.
5. Gordon S. Wood, *The American Revolution* (London: Weidenfeld & Nicholson, 2003), xxiii.
6. Henry Adams, *History of the United States of America During the Administrations of Thomas Jefferson and James Madison 1800–1817*, 2 volumes (New York: Library of America, 1986). This is the kind of point for which it is difficult to give specific references. It depends for its overall effect on long sections of the entire history. But for indications, see 1:125 (the end of the chapter "American Ideals, 1800") and, indeed, the whole of that chapter. This also indicates the multiplicity of visions then existing. Also, 1:23–4. This section indicates that Adams saw the question of national character as intrinsically bound up with the question of national government—a point of view also evidenced by Wood.
7. For the detailed analysis and supporting evidence, see the opening of Chapter 3.
8. Thomas Jefferson to John Dickinson, March 6, 1801. Quoted in Adams, *History*, 1:141. Henry Adams was acutely conscious that it was his illustrious ancestor, second president John Adams, whose steering Jefferson here attacked.
9. Henry Adams' thesis throws a sidelight on the question. His main argument that the Republicans then failed to live up to their own rhetoric, adopting many Federalist policies, is an oblique reflection on the illusions constructed in Jefferson's inaugural and election campaign.
10. The absence of women from this discussion may be criticized. A number of women writers were examined, but their work did not engage with the key questions explored in this study. Additionally, there is plenty of ongoing work examining the situation of women in the revolutionary era, and exploring their portrayal in the literature of the period. Good starting points are

Davidson, *"Revolution"* for the literary perspective, eds. Ronald Hoffman and Peter Albert, *Women in the Age of the American Revolution* (Charlottesville, VA.: Published for the United States Capital Historical Society by the University Press of Virginia, 1989) and Mary Beth Norton, *Liberty's Daughters: The Revolutionary Experience of American Women 1750–1800* (Ithaca, NY: Cornell University Press, 1980).

11. The reasons for these framing dates are explained in the following.

12. See Andrew Burstein, *Sentimental Democracy: The Evolution of America's Romantic Self-Image* (New York: Hill & Wang, 1999); Joseph J. Ellis, *After the Revolution: Profiles of Early American Culture* (New York, London: Norton, 1979); Marcus Cunliffe, *The Literature of the United States* (Harmondsworth, UK: Penguin, 1968), Chapter 3; Russel B. Nye, *The Cultural Life of the New Nation 1776–1830* (New York: Harper and Brothers, 1960); Kenneth B. Silverman, *A Cultural History of the American Revolution* (New York: Thomas Y. Crowell Co., 1976), 232–5; Emory Elliott, *Revolutionary Writers: Literature and Authority in the Early Republic 1725–1810* (New York; Oxford: Oxford University Press, 1982), particularly Chapter 1, 19–54; ed. Gordon S. Wood, *The Rising Glory of America 1760–1820* (New York: George Braziller, 1971). The thesis draws on interpretations of key literary texts including Paine's, Crèvecoeur's, and centrally Hugh Henry Brackenridge and Philip Freneau's epic poem, *The Rising Glory of America* (1771). The latter is discussed in Chapter 2.

13. See work on the High Federalists including William C. Dowling, *Literary Federalism in the Age of Jefferson: Joseph Dennie and The Port folio 1801–1812* (Columbia: University of South Carolina Press, 1999); David Hackett Fischer, *The Revolution of American Conservatism: The Federalist Party in the Era of Jeffersonian Democracy*, (New York: Harper 1965); Stephen Kurtz, *The Presidency of John Adams: The Collapse of Federalism 1795–1800* (Philadelphia, 1957); Linda Kerber, *Federalists in Dissent: Imagery and Ideology in Jeffersonian America* (Ithaca, NY: Cornell University Press, 1970).

14. See work on African-Americans and Indians cited as evidence for the failings of the Revolution in particular Edward Countryman et. al., "Forum: Rethinking the American Revolution—Indians, the Colonial Order, and the Social Significance of the American Revolution", in *William and Mary Quarterly*, 3rd Ser., Vol. 53, No. 2. (April, 1996), 342–62. This acknowledges both the "rising glory" and the price and that the two are inseparable but his focus on the price is still the exclusion of the Indians. The various responses (*ibid.*, 363–78) then take up this issue, commenting on other exclusions—blacks, women etc. We might note that the loyalists are rarely considered in this context, a point explored in Chapter 1.

15. 1760 also saw the ascension to the British throne of George III, whose view of a strengthened royal power would play its role in what followed. See Linda Colley, *Britons: Forging the Nation 1707–1837* (London: Pimlico, 2003), 204–8.

16. The starting dates of the following studies are only noted when not evident from the title. Wood, *The American Revolution* begins around 1760. Francis D. Cogliano, *Revolutionary America 1763–1815: A Political History* (London: Routledge, 2000); R.R. Palmer, *The Age of the Democratic Revolution 1760–1800*, 2 volumes (Princeton, NJ: Princeton University Press, 1959); Edmund S. Morgan, *The Birth of the Republic, 1763–1789* (Chicago: University of Chicago Press, 1956). Literary studies tend not to recognise the significance of the period suggested by this study. Cathy N. Davidson, *Revolution and the Word: The Rise of the Novel in America* (New York; Oxford:

Oxford University Press, 1986) covered 1790–1820, omitting important sources. Jane Tompkins, *Sentimental Designs: The Cultural Work of American Fiction 1790–1860* (New York; Oxford: Oxford University Press, 1985).

17. See first quotation, 10, in the following.

18. Steven Watts, *The Republic Reborn: War and the Making of Liberal America 1790–1820* (Baltimore, London: Johns Hopkins University Press, c1987), 42–3, made a magnificent case against this narrow-minded view in the course of introducing his discussion of Hugh Henry Brackenridge. "Novels can be an interesting and richly rewarding source for the study of history. Compared to conventional documents such as speeches, diaries, and tax records, literature often speaks with more imagination and less restraint to the cultural and social sensibility of an age. Although one should not deny the independent integrity of the creative writer, neither can it be forgotten that the novelist is partly a product and a reflection of his time. He often deliberately explores important cultural tendencies and social pressures in the world around him. . . . The imaginative author can open for the historian windows on the past too often left shuttered by the politician, the minister, or the census-taker."

19. A parallel example would be Walter Scott's invention of social history in his fiction, which had considerable influence on early American writers, particularly Cooper. See Andrew Hook, *Scotland and America 1750–1835* (Glasgow: Blackie and Son Ltd., 1975).

20. See also Washington Irving's observations on the relative truth of many "experienced writers," in Washington Irving, "A History of New York", in *History, Tales and Sketches*, (New York: Library of America, 1983), 511–12.

NOTES TO CHAPTER 1

1. John Adams to Thomas Jefferson, August 24, 1815, in *The Adams–Jefferson Letters: The Complete Correspondence Between Thomas Jefferson and Abigail and John Adams*, ed. Lester J. Cappon, 2 Vols. 2:415 (Chapel Hill, NC: Published for the Institute of Early American History and Culture at Williamsburg, VA by the University of North Carolina Press, 1959). This was only one instance of an Adams obsession during his retirement, see also John Adams to Hezekiah Niles, February 13, 1818, ed. Lyman H. Butterfield, in *An American Primer*, ed. Daniel Boorstin, (New York: New American Library, 1968), 246–57. Two other points are notable there, the awareness of the difficulties attendant in making the Revolution a success, and of the price paid in the process.

2. Attrib. Benjamin Franklin (hereafter BF), "Right, Wrong and Reasonably" from *The Gazetteer and Daily Advertiser*, London, April 18, 1767 in, *The Papers of Benjamin Franklin*, 14:131, eds. Leonard W. Labaree et. al. (New Haven; London: Yale University Press, 1959), hereafter *PBF*. Emphasis in original. Assuming it was by Franklin, his intention here was to attack the mistaken views of America held by many Britons. This particular paper was responding to another satire attacking the Americans on the back of a petition from New York merchants regarding trade restrictions.

3. The date of first publication given here for Franklin's *Autobiography* refers to Part 1 only. For an account of the vexed publication history of that work see the following, 31. The significance of both their contributions was recognised by D. H. Lawrence, *Studies in Classic American Literature* (London:

Penguin Books, 1971), 15–39; and Crèvecoeur's by Larzer Ziff, *Writing in the New Nation* (New Haven, CT: Yale University Press, 1991), 18–33.

4. Leonard W. Labaree, Ralph L. Ketcham, Helen C. Boatfield and Helene E. Fineman eds., "Introduction" in Benjamin Franklin, *The Autobiography of Benjamin Franklin* (New Haven, London: Yale University Press, 1964, reprint 2003), 16. Hereafter, *Autobiography One.*

5. The *Sketches* went unpublished in Crèvecoeur's lifetime, and long afterwards. A complete uncut edition was only published in 1995, *More Letters from the American Farmer: An Edition of the Essays in English Left Unpublished by Crèvecoeur.* Ed. Dennis D. Moore. Athens: Univ. of Georgia. The *Journey* was published in French in 1801, and subsequently translated into German. An English translation was only published in 1964.

6. "Examination before the Committee of the Whole of the House of Commons," February 13, 1766, in *PBF*, 13:135.

7. Gordon S. Wood, *The Creation of the American Republic 1776–1787* (Chapel Hill: University of North Carolina Press, 1969). Bernard Bailyn, *The Ideological Origins of the American Revolution* (Cambridge, MA: Belknap Press of Harvard University Press, 1967).

8. Bailyn, *Ideological Origins*, 20. See also "A New People for a New World" in Wood, *Creation*, 46–8.

9. For Berkeley see Ellis, *Revolution*, 6–7. See the following, Chapter Two, esp. 98–104.

10. BF to Charles Wilson Peale, July 4, 1771, in *PBF*, 18:163. Reprinted by permission of the American Philosophical Society. See also the letter to which Franklin was replying, 80–1. Franklin's concern for learning in America is also evidenced in his numerous letters to the officers of the Library Company of Philadelphia organising the delivery of books or recommending purchases. See also BF to his son William Franklin, from London, November 3–[4], 1772, *PBF*, 19:361.

11. Crèvecoeur, *Letters and Sketches*, 70. The various letters cannot be precisely dated, it is assumed that the majority were composed between 1769 and 1778, see the following, 48–9.

12. Jeremy Belknap to Ebenezer Hazard, February 4, 1780, quoted in Ralph Ketcham, *From Colony to Country: The Revolution in American Thought 1750–1820* (New York: Macmillan, 1974), 155

13. Contemporaries recognised this. See in particular James Kirke Paulding, *Letters from the South* (New York: AMS Press, 1973, reprint of 1817 edition), 249–51.

14. Gordon S. Wood, "Introduction", in *Rising Glory*, ed. Wood, 10.

15. John Adams, "A Dissertation on the Canon and Feudal Law No.3", September 30, 1765, eds. Robert J. Taylor, Mary-Jo Kline, and Gregg L. Lint, *The Adams Papers: Papers of John Adams, Volume 1* (Cambridge, MA.: The Belknap Press of Harvard University Press, Copyright © 1977 by the Massachusetts Historical Society), p. 120. Reprinted by permission of the publisher. Obviously his comparisons would have been questionable for Maryland or North Carolina, and were limited to Massachusetts in sources.

16. BF to David Hume, September 27, 1760, in *PBF*, 9:230. See also similar comments in, attrib. BF, "To the Printer of the London Chronicle," May 9, 1759, in *ibid.*, 8:342.

17. Ellis, *After the Revolution*, 80–1. Saul Cornell, *The Other Founders: Anti-Federalism and the dissenting tradition in America, 1788–1828* (Chapel Hill: Published for the Omohundro Institute of Early American History and Culture, Williamsburg, VA, by the University of North Carolina Press, 1999), p. 26, ftnote 11.

18. See the following, 32.
19. William B. Willcox, et. al, Introduction, *PBF*, 21:xlii.
20. Benjamin Franklin, 'The Interest of Great Britain Considered,' in *ibid.*, 9:47–99.Attrib. BF, "To the Printer of the London Chronicle," (Defence of the American) May 9, 1759, in *ibid.*, 8:340–56. The piece concludes with a firm assertion of the colonies' British–American identity.
21. The story of Franklin's role in the dispute is traced in detail in several studies. Robert Middlekauff, *Benjamin Franklin and his Enemies* (Berkeley: University of California Press, 1996); Daniel D. Morgan, *Devious Dr. Franklin, Colonial Agent: Benjamin Franklin's years in London* (Macon, GA: Mercer University Press, 1996); Francis Jennings, *Benjamin Franklin, politician* (New York: Norton, 1996)
22. Benjamin Franklin to an unidentified correspondent, from London, November 28, 1768 (printed in part in the *The Gentleman's Magazine* 49[supplement, 1779]), *PBF*, 15:273. The letter only survives in the periodical, so it is unclear whether a real correspondent existed.
23. Benjamin Franklin, "The Interest of Great Britain Considered", *PBF*, 9:62–3.
24. *Ibid.*, 65. Crèvecoeur came to similar conclusions about frontiersmen, see the following, 61.
25. *Ibid.*, 71. It is of note that George II was still on the throne when the pamphlet was published (though he would die a few months later) and the Newcastle–Pitt administration still formed the government.
26. *Ibid.*, 77.
27. *Ibid.*, 72.
28. *Ibid.*, 79.
29. *Ibid.*, 90.
30. *Ibid.*, 90–1.
31. BF to David Hume, September 27, 1760, *ibid.*, 229.
32. *Ibid.*, 230.
33. Franklin use of national descriptors ("British" or "English") varies, as will be clear from the quotations here and on page 25. This reflects the contemporary problem created by the emergence of a strongly patriotic British identity which, despite the appropriation of that adjective, was dominated by the English, leaving groups on the periphery confused about their place within it. This confusion is another thread in Franklin's engagement with the problem of imperial relationships and American national character.
34. BF to Lord Kames, February 25, 1767, *PBF*, 14:69–70. See also BF to Thomas Cushing, London, January 5, 1773, *PBF*, 20:10 and BF to Thomas Cushing, March 9, 1773, *ibid.*, 99.
35. Attrib. BF, Homespun, "Further Defence of Indian Corn", January 15, 1766, *PBF*, 13:48.
36. Benjamin Franklin, "The State of the Trade with the Northern Colonies", *The London Chronicle* November 1–3, 1768, *PBF*, 15:P252. See also BF to William Strahan, November 29, 1769, *PBF*, 16:247 where, discussing the possibility of separation, BF argues that because of the actions of parliament, "the Sameness of Nation, the Similarity of Religion, Manners and Language" will avail nothing to prevent it. Also "The Colonists Advocate III," *The Public Advertiser*, January 11, 1770, *PBF*, 17:21. "The Rise and Present State of our Misunderstandings", *The London Chronicle* November 6–8, 1770, *PBF*, 17:268–9, reiterated Franklin's belief in the Americans as a "growing" and soon to be "a great people."
37. BF to Mary Stevenson, March 25, 1763, *PBF*, 10:232–3. This quotation also shows Franklin alive to the idea of *translatio studii*, discussed earlier.

38. BF to William Strahan, July 20, 1762, *PBF*, 10:133.
39. BF to William Strahan, August 23, 1762, *PBF*, 10:149.
40. BF to William Franklin, January 30, 1772, *PBF*, 19:53. Reprinted by permission of the American Philosophical Society.
41. BF to William Franklin, August 19–[22], 1772, *PBF*, 19:258–59.
42. *Ibid.*
43. BF to Pierre Samuel du Pont de Nemours, October 2, 1770, *PBF*, 17 :234–5. Courtesy, Winterthur Library, Joseph Downs Collection of Manuscripts and Printed Ephemera.
44. N.N. "First Reply to Vindex Patriae", in *The Gazeteer*, December 28, 1765, *PBF*, 12:414. See also, "'Pacificus:' Pax Queritur Bello," *The Public Advertiser*, January 26, 1766, *PBF*, 13:56, for a similar description which does confine itself to the Northern Colonies.
45. BF to Joseph Galloway, January 11, 1770, *PBF*, 17:24. See BF to Jane Mecom, December 30, 1770, 17:314–15 for a similar use of "my Country." Again it is unclear what that country is.
46. Owen Dudley Edwards, "The Writers of the American Revolution: Variations on a theme by Auden" in *America and Ireland 1776–1976: The American Identity and the Irish Connection*, eds. David Noel Doyle and Owen Dudley Edwards, (Westport, CT: Greenwood Press, 1980), 15–43. Lawrence, *Studies*, 14–27. We also see it in his relations with his wife, who never mattered enough to bring him home, and his relations with his illegitimate son, cast off in the Revolution. On father and son see Sheila Skemp, *Benjamin and William Franklin: father and son, patriot and loyalist* (Boston: Bedford Books of St. Martin's Press, 1994).
47. See *Autobiography One*, 25–36.
48. Benjamin Franklin, "The Autobiography," in *Writings*, ed. J.A. Leo Lemay, (New York: Library of America, 1987), 1307. Hereafter "Autobiography Two."
49. See William Strahan to William Franklin, April 3, 1771, *PBF*, 18:65 and William Franklin's response.
50. *Autobiography Two*, 1338.
51. *Ibid.*
52. *Ibid.*, 1355–56.
53. *Ibid.*, 1357.
54. *Ibid.*, 1358.
55. *Ibid.*, 1358.
56. *Ibid.*, 1353.
57. The James letter is undated, but scholars have subsequently dated it to 1782. The Vaughan letter is dated January 31, 1783. Abel James (c. 1726–1790) was a prominent Philadelphia merchant and member of the American Philosophical Society. Benjamin Vaughan (1751–1835), born in Jamaica and raised in London, served as an unofficial British diplomat at the 1782 Paris peace negotiations. A sympathiser with the French Revolution, he was hounded by the British, imprisoned by the French and finally escaped to the United States in 1797 to settle in Maine. Further evidence of Vaughan's conviction of the importance of Franklin is that he edited the first edition of Franklin's political writings published in 1779. See "Bibliographical Notes," in *Autobiography One*, 287, 299. See also Alexander DeConde, "Benjamin Vaughan" in *American National Biography*, gen. eds. John A. Garraty and Mark C. Carnes, (New York, Oxford: Oxford University Press, 1999), 22:289–290. (Hereafter *ANB*).
58. *Autobiography Two*, 1373.
59. *Ibid.*, 1374.

60. *Ibid.*, 1378.
61. BF to Lord Kames, London, May 3, 1760, *PBF*, 9:103–5.
62. *Autobiography Two*, 1372.
63. *Ibid.*, 1383.
64. Benjamin Franklin, Plan of Conduct, *PBF*, 1:100.
65. *Autobiography Two*, 1385.
66. See D. H. Lawrence in particular, and his bald statement in his essay on Franklin's *Autobiography*: "I do not like him" in Lawrence, *Studies*, 19.
67. *Autobiography Two*, 1384.
68. Both quotations, *Ibid.*, 1390.
69. *Ibid.*, 1391.
70. *Ibid.*, 1392.
71. Both Quotations, *Ibid.*, 1393.
72. BF to Benjamin Vaughan, October 24, 1788 in *Benjamin Franklin's Autobiography*, eds. J. A. Leo Lemay and P. M. Zall, (London: W.W. Norton and Company Inc., 1986), 206.
73. *Ibid.*, 1411.
74. *Ibid.*, 1412.
75. *Ibid.*, 1413.
76. *Ibid.*, 1415.
77. *Ibid.*, 1416.
78. *Ibid.*, 1417.
79. *Ibid.*, 1431.
80. *Ibid.* Emphasis in original.
81. Jefferson's original tombstone noted his authorship of the Declaration of Independence and the Virginia Statute of Religious Liberties, and his foundation of the University of Virginia—items which all Americans (except the long excluded loyalists) could cheer. It made no reference to his role as a partisan politician in the 1790s, or to his presidency.
82. BF to Samuel Mather, July 7, 1773, *PBF*, 20:289. Emphasis in original.
83. Crèvecoeur, "Letter XII", in *Letters and Sketches*, 204–5. Exact dates of composition of these essays are not known. Given the tone of Letter XII, with its acknowledgement of the necessity of choice between Patriots and Loyalists, it seems likely that it was written once war had broken out between Britain and the colonists, and before Crèvecoeur fled to Europe in 1778. See the following, 48–50, for further discussion of the dating issue.
84. Albert E. Stone, "Introduction," in *ibid.*, 7. Andrew Burstein, *Sentimental Democracy*, Chapter 1.
85. Susan Manning, "Introduction," in *Letters from an American Farmer*, ed. Susan Manning, (Oxford: Oxford University Press, 1997), viii.
86. Jeffrey H. Richards, "Revolution, Domestic Life and the End of 'Common Mercy' in Crèvecoeur's 'Landscapes'", *William and Mary Quarterly*, 55 (April, 1998), 296.
87. Palmer, *Democratic Revolutions*, 1:185–90.
88. Richards, Revolution, is the latest to claim Crèvecoeur as a loyalist. William H. Nelson, *The American Tory* (Oxford: Clarendon Press, 1961) and Wallace Brown, *The King's Friends* (Providence, Rhode Island: Brown University Press, 1965) use selective quotations from the *Letters* and *Sketches* to claim Crèvecoeur as reluctant loyalist. Robert M. Calhoon, *The Loyalists in Revolutionary America 1760–1781* (New York: Harcourt, Brace, Jovanovich, 1973) does not mention Crèvecoeur.
89. The available biographies of Crèvecoeur remain problematic. Some of the best work is in French: Robert de Crèvecoeur (Crèvecoeur's great-grandson), *Saint John de Crèvecoeur: sa vie et ses ouvrages* (Paris, 1883) and Howard C.

Rice, *Le cultivateur americain: Etude sur l'oeuvre de Saint John de Crève-coeur* (Paris: H. Champion, 1933). In English, Thomas Philbrick, *St. John de Crèvecoeur* (New York: Twayne Publishers, 1970) is the best brief biographical sketch. Julia Post Mitchell, *St. John de Crèvecoeur* (New York: Columbia University Press, 1916) should be used for in depth study. The most recent biography, Gay Wilson Allen and Roger Asselineau, *St. John de Crèvecoeur* (New York, London: Viking, 1987) has been shown to be littered with factual errors and inadequate referencing. See Bernard Chevignard, "St. John de Crèvecoeur: A Case of Arrested Bibliographic Development," *Early American Literature*, 23, no. 3 (1988), 319–327. Its literary analysis is severely limited (the *Journey* is largely ignored). There remains scope for a full-length modern biographical study which would require a Francophone historian.

90. Crèvecoeur, *Letters and Sketches*, 36. A. W. Plumstead, "Hector St. John de Crèvecoeur", in *American Literature 1764–1789, The Revolutionary Years*, ed. E. Emerson, (Madison: University of Wisconsin Press, 1977), 213–31, contains the best discussion of this important point.

91. I have found details thus far of a 1782 Belfast edition and a 1783 Dublin edition in *United States Government Publications an Author Index Representing Pre-1956 Holdings in American Libraries Reported to the National Union Catalogue in the Library of Congress* (London: Mansell, 1980; hereafter, *National Union Catalogue*).

92. The French editions, which differ substantially from the original English version, have not been translated into English. I have not, therefore, been able to consider them. The limited quotations and analysis available suggests that they support the thesis here presented, i.e., that they show him moving from the despair of the end of *Letters* and the unpublished essays towards the re-forging attempt of *Journey*.

93. According to the *National Union Catalogue*, copies of this edition were to be found in 34 libraries. Given the likely loss of books, and Carey's known financial acumen, it seems reasonable to assume that this 1793 edition was a fairly sizeable one. It is also clear that copies of earlier editions made their way to America, although in lesser numbers. This includes the second French edition of 1787, with its altered authorial nomenclature.

94. The relevant section in this Advertisement, printed in the 1783 edition reads: "Since the [first] publication of this volume, we hear that Mr. St. John has accepted a public employment at New York." Crèvecoeur, *Letters and Sketches*, 36.

95. In the Irish case, see R. B. McDowell, *Irish Public Opinion 1750–1800* (London: Faber and Faber, 1944), 48–49. McDowell cited Crèvecoeur and Franklin ("Information to those who would remove to America") as the most influential texts for prospective Irish emigrants, rather than, perhaps equally obvious texts like the preamble to the Declaration of Independence or *Common Sense*. He apparently took the book's title page at face value, reproducing Crèvecoeur's description of himself as a "Pennsylvania farmer" (48), and gave no hint that the darker hues of Letter XII had any impact on those emigrants.

John Bristed, *The Resources of the USA* (1818), 6, provides further evidence,

> Gilbert Imlay and M. St. John de Crèvecoeur, author of "The American Farmer" and of pretended "Travels in Upper Pennsylvania and the State of New York" have exceedingly exaggerated the excellencies of the United States, by misrepresenting them as the abode of more than all the perfections of innocence, happiness, plenty, learning, and wisdom, than can be allotted to human beings to enjoy.

This is a difficult statement to interpret. It suggests that confusion over Crèvecoeur was early established. It also suggests an additional authorial confusion not indicated elsewhere. Percy G. Adams, "The Historical Value of Crèvecoeur's Voyage," *American Literature* 25 (1953–4), 152–168, Bristed quotation at 159. Adams also states that Crèvecoeur in all his writings was an optimist. This is questionable, but it may indicate the illusion under which Bristed was labouring.

96. The reasons for this deliberate confusion are examined in the following, as are the complicated narrators of the *Journey.*
97. Crèvecoeur, "Letter II", in *Letters and Sketches,* 51.
98. *Ibid.,* 52.
99. See for example, BF, "Positions to be Examined," April 4, 1769, *PBF,* 16:109.
100. Crèvecoeur, "Letter II", in *Letters and Sketches,* 54.
101. *Ibid.,* 51.
102. "Letter III", in *ibid.,* 67.
103. Both quotations, *Ibid.,* 66.
104. *Ibid.,* 67.
105. Thomas Jefferson to Henry Lee, May 8, 1825, in Thomas Jefferson, *Writings* (New York: Library of America, 1984), 1501. Hereafter *TJW.*
106. Crèvecoeur, "Letter III", in *Letters and Sketches,* 67.
107. All three quotations, *Ibid.,* 68.
108. All three quotations, *Ibid.,* 168–9.
109. *Ibid.,* 70.
110. Both quotations, *Ibid.,* 72.
111. All four quotations, *ibid.,* 73.
112. All four quotations, *ibid.,* 82.
113. Both quotations, *Ibid.,* 82–83.
114. *Ibid.,* 81.
115. It is interesting to note that the Quakers come out of these descriptions quite well, in striking contrast to Franklin's attitude to them.
116. Crèvecoeur, "Letter IV", in *Letters and Sketches, ibid.,* 107.
117. "Letter VIII", in *ibid.,* 161.
118. "Letter IX", in *ibid.,* 167.
119. *Ibid.,* 167–8.
120. Both quotations, *Ibid.,* 168.
121. *Ibid.,* 172.
122. *Ibid.,* 171.
123. *Ibid.,* 178.
124. Both quotations, *Ibid.,* 173.
125. *Ibid.,* 174. Note Crèvecoeur's recognition of the weakest giving way to the strongest. This was an idea that resurfaced when he discussed the Revolution in his writings, and argued that history would be determined by the winning side.
126. *Ibid.*
127. *Ibid.,* 176–177.
128. Note that it is Bartram, and not Franklin, who is selected for this purpose, although Franklin's electrical inventions are commented on in one of the *Sketches,* 299–300, and was instrumental in supporting Bartram's career.
129. Both quotations, "Letter XI", in *ibid.,* 193.
130. Both quotations, "Letter XII", in *ibid.,* 200.
131. *Ibid.,* 201.
132. *Ibid.,* 201–2.
133. *Ibid.,* 201.

134. Both quotations, *Ibid.*, 204.
135. Both quotations, *Ibid.*, 203.
136. *Ibid.*, 204.
137. Both quotations, *Ibid.*, 203.
138. *Ibid.*, 204.
139. *Ibid.*, 203.
140. *Ibid.*, 204.
141. All three quotations, *ibid.*, 205.
142. *Ibid.*, 210.
143. In sharp contrast to the *Sketches* and the *Journey*.
144. Crèvecoeur, *Letters and Sketches*, 120.
145. *Ibid.*, 119.
146. *Ibid.*, 222.
147. This is another theme which runs through much of the fiction of the period examined in this study. James Fenimore Cooper, in the Leatherstocking novels, is the best-known example, but it crops up on many other occasions.
148. Crèvecoeur, *Letters and Sketches*, 214. This blind spot is strikingly reminiscent of Cooper both in *The Pioneers* (1823) and *The Last of the Mohicans* (1826). See Chapter Five.
149. Crèvecoeur, *Letters and Sketches*, 215.
150. *Ibid.*, 227.
151. *Sketches of Eighteenth Century America* was first published in 1925 by Yale University Press. The editors were Henri L. Bourdin, Ralph H. Gabriel, and Stanley T. Williams. They attempted a volume imitative of the *Letters*. Thus, the ordering of the *Sketches* was theirs, not Crèvecoeur's. Further, they omitted a total of five essays and amalgamated another two, all without fully referencing what they had done. Dennis D. Moore, "Introduction", in *More Letters From an American Farmer, an Edition of the Essays in English Left Unpublished by Crèvecoeur*, ed. Dennis D, Moore, (Georgia:, 1995) is the best discussion of these important editorial questions, and also does exactly what it says in the title regarding the pieces excluded from *Letters*.
152. Crèvecoeur, *Letters and Sketches*, 381.
153. *Ibid.*, 344.
154. *Ibid.*, 347.
155. *Ibid.*, 352.
156. *Ibid.*, 422.
157. *Ibid.*, 420.
158. *Ibid.*, 431
159. *Ibid.*, 432
160. *Ibid.*, 463. The final tableau sees a repetition of these sentiments. See exchange between Mrs M. (wife of a fled loyalist) and the Deacon, 480.
161. Both quotations, *ibid.*, 447.
162. *Ibid.*, 448
163. This included a two-year period of leave in France between 1785 and 1787, when he worked on the revised French editions of *Letters*.
164. J. Hector St. John de Crèvecoeur, *Journey into Northern Pennsylvania and the State of New York* (Ann Arbor, 1964), 445, trans. Clarissa Spencer Bostelmann. This is the only complete English translation of the work, and all further page references are taken from this edition.
165. Adams, "Historical Value", has the best discussion on this. The extent of the borrowing, especially in the footnotes, should not obscure the centrality of Crèvecoeur's voice to the main text. This should be read in conjunction with Percy G. Adams, "Introduction", in *Crèvecoeur's eighteenth-century travels in Pennsylvania and New York*, trans, & ed. Percy G. Adams, (Lex-

ington: University of Kentucky Press, 1961). This is the only source identified which agrees that Crèvecoeur attempted to remain neutral during the Revolution. It does not consider the issue of the nonpublication of the *Sketches* or the relationship between the *Journey* and Crèvecoeur's other writings.

166. Crèvecoeur, *Journey*, xviii.
167. *Ibid.*, 84, 94, 237. These are only a selection from the large number of possible examples.
168. *Ibid.*, 78
169. *Ibid.*, 79
170. See, particularly, the comparison between American and French Revolutions. *Ibid.*, xvi.
171. *Ibid.*, 38
172. *Ibid.*, 371. The speaker is a member of the New York legislature.
173. *Ibid.*, 380. The speaker is the New Haven college president.
174. *Ibid.*, 367. The speaker is a member of the New York legislature.
175. Franklin observed these in action during a treaty negotiation, see Autobiography Two, 1421–22.
176. *Ibid.*, 10.
177. *Ibid.*, 154. (footnote.)
178. *Ibid.*, 56.
179. *Ibid.*, 63. It is also worth noting that Crèvecoeur retells several Indian stories in the course of his narrative, a preservation which I have yet to come across elsewhere and in striking contrast to Cooper, as will be seen.
180. Indian use of the phrase "Imagine my chagrin" seems rather unlikely. *Ibid.*, 268.
181. *Ibid.*, 266.
182. All three quotations, *ibid.*, 533. Compare third with final paragraph in Adams, *History*, 2:1345.
183. *Ibid.*, 264.

NOTES TO CHAPTER 2

1. Hugh Henry Brackenridge and Philip Freneau, *A Poem, on the Rising Glory of America* (Cambridge: ProQuest Information and Learning Company, American Drama Full-Text Database, 2003) [1771], 13. Hereafter Brackenridge and Freneau, *Rising Glory.*
2. Quotation from Elizabeth Bowen, *The House in Paris* (London, 1946), 144. Originally published 1936.
3. John Murrin, "A Roof without Walls: The Dilemma of American National Identity", in *Beyond Confederation: Origins of the Constitution and American National Identity*, eds. Richard Beeman, Stephen Botein, and Edward C Carter II (Chapel Hill: Published for the Institute of Early American History and Culture, Williamsburg, Virginia, by the University of North Carolina Press, c.1987). is excellent on this limitation of the Constitution. James Roger Sharp, *American Politics in the Early Republic: The New Nation in Crisis* (New Haven: Yale University Press, 1993) challenged the claim that the constitution established a consensus, arguing that that consensus was only established following the Republican attainment of ascendancy, post-1800. We may note here that this consensus takes no account of the Burr Conspiracy or the Hartford Convention. Sharp also saw the Revolution as a point of unity, again a highly questionable assertion (18). What Sharp did recognise is the

second American need identified here—for "some principle, tradition, myth, purpose, or code of behaviour" to bind them together (19–20).

4. Benjamin Franklin submitted a draft proposal in 1775. Richard Henry Lee renewed the question simultaneous with the resolution on independence (June 7, 1776). The Articles, as eventually ratified, were accepted by Congress on November 15, 1777, and ten states rapidly followed suit. Maryland, in dispute with Virginia over western land claims, only ratified on March 1, 1781 barely two months before Yorktown.

5. Quotation from "The Constitution of the United States of America, 1787", in Henry Steele Commager (ed.), *Documents of American History* (New York, 1973), 138–149.

6. Alexander Hamilton, John Jay, James Madison, *The Federalist Papers* (New York: New American Library Inc., 1961), 38.

7. George Washington, "First Inaugural Address", in *Inaugural Addresses of the Presidents of the United States* (Washington, DC: US Government Printing Office, 1961), 4.

8. See Douglass Adair, "'That Politics May Be Reduced to a Science': David Hume, James Madison and the Tenth Federalist," in *Fame and the Founding Fathers: Essays by Douglass Adair*, ed. Trevor Colbourn (New York: Published for the Institute of Early American History and Culture at Williamsburg, VA, by Norton, 1974), 93–106. Also Drew McCoy, *The Last of the Fathers: James Madison and the republican legacy* (Cambrige: Cambridge University Press, 1989), 42–3, esp. footnote for a good summary of recent scholarship. Ralph Ketchum, *James Madison* (New York: Macmillan, 1971), 241–2. See Footnote 238 for additional referencing on the development of factions in the new nation.

9. Hamilton et. al., *The Federalist Papers*, 80.

10. Adams expressed this opinion in a letter to another Pittsburgh judge, Wilson McCandless, who had sent him a copy of a new edition of *Modern Chivalry* in 1847, taking the opportunity to recall a conversation they had had about the book when Adams visited Pittsburgh in 1843. Adams noted the Don Quixote connection, but commented on Farrago and Teague as "illustrations of life and manners peculiar to the times," rather than on the political aspects of the book. See Claude M. Newlin, *The Life and Writings of Hugh Henry Brackenridge* (Princeton: Princeton University Press, 1932), 190–1.

11. The book is divided into Part One, encompassing four volumes (two appearing in 1792, and one each in 1793 and 1797 respectively), and Part Two, encompassing three volumes (published in 1804, 1805, and 1815 respectively). Each volume is subdivided into books and chapters. See Hugh Henry Brackenridge, *Modern Chivalry* (New York: American Book Company, 1937, reprinted 1962), ed. Claude M. Newlin, xxiii–xxviii deals with publication schedule. This is the only complete modern edition. All references hereafter are to that edition. The rough date of each episode discussed, according to this schedule, is given in the footnotes the follow.

12. Hugh Henry Brackenridge, *Gazette Publications* (Carlisle, PA: Alexander and Phillips, 1806), 3.

13. Claude M. Newlin, *Life and writings*. Daniel Marder, *Hugh Henry Brackenridge* (New York: Twayne Publishers, 1967). Daniel Marder also edited a useful collection of Brackenridge's writings: ed. Daniel Marder, *A Hugh Henry Brackenridge Reader 1770–1815* (Pittsburgh: University of Pittsburgh Press, 1970).

14. Henry M. Brackenridge, the author's son, was the first to note the central impact of the Whiskey Rebellion on Brackenridge's career in his "Biographical Notice of H. H. Brackenridge", in *Southern Literary Messenger*, 8:1,

(January, 1842), 4–16. Cathy N. Davidson, *Revolution and the Word: The Rise of the Novel in America* (New York: Oxford University Press, 1986), 173–178. Robert Lawson-Peebles, *Landscape and Written Expression in Revolutionary America* (Cambridge; New York: Cambridge University Press, 1988), 122–134. Christopher Looby, *Voicing America : Language, Literary Form, and the Origins of the United States* (Chicago: University of Chicago Press, 1996), 203–266. Lewis Leary, *Soundings: some early American writers* (Athens: University of Georgia Press, 1975), 161–174. Ellis, *After the Revolution*, 73–110. Watts, *Republic Reborn*, 42–58. Of these works, Ellis alone shows real awareness of the interconnected nature of Brackenridge's political and literary endeavours. Without this, a full understanding of *Modern Chivalry* is not possible, nor should that work be seen as necessarily the central factor in a study of Brackenridge. Watts gave some excellent context for the book, and noted the defining impact of the Whiskey Rebellion upon Brackenridge, but he is centrally concerned to fit the book into his examination of the struggle of individual Americans with a burgeoning capitalist society. Lawson-Peebles noted some of the crucial aspects of Brackenridge's career, in particular the effect of the Whiskey Rebellion, and drew some interesting literary comparisons, particularly with Crèvecoeur, but paid insufficient attention to the deep interconnections between Brackenridge's whole political experience and the satire of *Modern Chivalry*.

15. The original manuscript was lost in a fire at Princeton in 1802. Book III, copied by another classmate William Bradford (later U.S. Attorney General) survived in a Bradford notebook now in the Historical Society of Pennsylvania collection. From that, Chapter 1 (Brackenridge) appeared in Newlin, *Life and writings*, 15–21, and Chapters II, III, and the Conclusion (Freneau), edited by Lewis Leary, in *The Pennsylvania Magazine of History and Biography*, 66 (1942), 459–478. A complete copy of the work was then discovered in the hand of John Blair Smith (another Princeton classmate) by a couple from Lexington, Kentucky in 1957. See Michael Davitt Bell, "Introduction", in Hugh Henry Brackenridge and Philip Freneau, *Father Bombo's Pilgrimage to Mecca 1770*, ed. Michael Davitt Bell (n.p., 1975), xi–xiii.

16. Brackenridge and Freneau, *Father Bombo's Pilgrimage*, 83–87. On Freneau, see Lewis Leary, *That Rascal Freneau: A Study in Literary Failure* (New York: Octagon Books, 1971 reprint of 1941). He discussed *Rising Glory*, 33–39; Mary Weatherspoon Bowden, *Philip Freneau* (Boston: Twayne Publishers, 1976), 25–29, is useful on the differences between the 1772 and 1786 versions.

17. Brackenridge and Freneau, *Father Bombo's Pilgrimage*, 74.

18. See Introduction, 6 (footnote 11).

19. See, most recently, Eric Wertheimer, "Commencement Ceremonies: history and identity in The Rising Glory of America 1771 and 1786", *Early American Literature* 29:1 (1994:1), 35–58. This article makes an excellent case, in miniature, for the complexities of the evolving American identity but, in doing so, demonstrates the need for a new history of the literature of this period which will embrace these scattered texts. See also Susan Castillo, "Imperial Pasts and Dark Futurities: Freneau and Brackenridge's 'The Rising Glory of America'", *Symbiosis: A Journal of Anglo-American Literary Relations*, 6:1 (2002:April), 27–43.

20. Brackenridge and Freneau, *Rising Glory*, 5.

21. *Ibid.*, 10. A similar past for America had earlier been crafted by, among others, John Adams in *A Dissertation on Canon and Feudal Law* (1765).

22. *Ibid.*, 7.

23. *Ibid.*, 8. See the following, 120, for further discussion of Solon.

24. Probably a reference to Sir William Johnson (1715–1774), a benevolent figure in white-Indian relations in New York State from 1738 who eventually became Superintendent of the Northern Indians. See Francis Jennings, "William Johnson" in *ANB*, 12:138–140.
25. In the 1786 revised text, only Franklin survives, joined by Washington. Franklin is celebrated for his scientific contribution, which is regrettable as it gives no clue as to how the two authors viewed his political position in 1772. Given that two of the other three are closely tied to the Empire, it suggests a similar view of Franklin's position, and supports the argument that, in 1772, Freneau and Brackenridge were still tentatively thinking of the rising glory of America as occurring in conjunction with some kind of relationship to the British. The 1786 text is reproduced in Philip Freneau, *Poems*, ed. Harry Hayden Clark (New York: Hafner Publishing, 1929), 3–17.
26. Brackenridge and Freneau, *Rising Glory*, 13.
27. *Ibid.*, 13–14. In the 1786, text "America" is substituted for "Britain."
28. *Ibid.*, 18.
29. Both quotations, *Ibid.*, 20.
30. *Ibid.*, 21.
31. *Ibid.*, 23.
32. These references further date the poem. Russia and Babylon would soon be viewed distinctly less favourably.
33. *Ibid.*, 22.
34. *Ibid.*, 27.
35. Hugh Henry Brackenridge, *The Battle of Bunkers-Hill* (Temecula, California: Reprint Services Corporation, 1989; Originally published Philadelphia: R. Bell, 1776), 2. Emphasis in original.
36. Hugh Henry Brackenridge, *The Death of General Montgomery in Storming the City of Quebec: A Tragedy* (S.1: Reprint Services, 1989; Orginally published Philadelphia: R. Bell, 1777), 6.
37. Hugh Henry Brackenridge, "The Bloody Vestiges of Tyranny", in *Reader*, ed. Marder, 63.
38. *Ibid.*, 69.
39. *Ibid.*, 68.
40. Frank Luther Mott, *A History of American Magazines* (Cambridge: Harvard University Press, 1938–68), 5 vols., 1:27.
41. Hugh Henry Brackenridge, *The United States Magazine* (Philadelphia: F. Bailey, 1779), Vol. 1, no issue no. (January, 1779), 9.
42. *Ibid.*
43. *Ibid.*, 19. Italics in original. These are signed "Sidney." It is not clear whether this is a pseudonym (potentially for Brackenridge himself) or lifted from another source.
44. Ibid., Vol. 1, no issue no. (December, 1779), 483.
45. Hugh Henry Brackenridge, "The Bloody Vestiges of Tyranny", in *Reader*, ed. Marder, 69.
46. Hugh Henry Brackendge, *Incidents of the Insurrection in the Western Parts of Pennsylvania in the Year 1794* (Philadelphia: Printed and sold by John M'Culloch, 1795), 3 vols., 1:41–2.
47. See Richard Hofstadter, *The Idea of a Party System; The Rise of Legitimate Opposition in the United States 1780–1840* (Berkeley: University of California Press, 1969), Chapter 1. Hofstadter is not precise as to when Monroe made these statements, but these quotations capture a significant strain in contemporary views on party, and Monroe's presidency enshrined this kind of illusion with the coining of the phrase 'the era of good feelings. See Chapter 4. John C. Miller, *The Federalist Era 1789–1801* (New York: Harper,

1960), 99ff. noted the Founders' disbelief in political parties, but did not deal with the evolution of that belief in response to their appearance. Stanley Elkins and Eric McKitrick, *The Age of Federalism* (New York; Oxford, UK: Oxford University Press, 1993), specifically 263–270. Sharp, *American Politics*, esp. "Introduction," is the most recent survey of the development of political parties. Sharp is too favourable to Jefferson and too critical of Hamilton. He neglects the case of Adams. See also Ron Chernow, *Alexander Hamilton* (New York: Penguin Press, 2004), 391–2.

48. On Monroe, see Hofstadter, *Party System*, 22–23, 188–198. Also Wood, *Creation*, 561.

49. On Madison, see, in addition to sources already cited, Wood, *Creation*, 499–506.

50. See Gordon S. Wood, "The Relevance and Irrelevance of John Adams", in Wood, *Creation*, 567–592, which is a brilliant treatment of Adams' ideas. In particular, Wood's recognition that Adams placed himself in the path of the developing American myth is crucial. See also Elkins and McKitterick, *Age of Federalism*, 529–537 on Adams and "Balance." C. Bradley Thompson, *John Adams and the Spirit of Liberty* (Lawrence: University of Kansas, 1998) is an immensely valuable exploration of Adams' political theories. It convincingly demonstrates that the Democratic Republicans, whether deliberately or not, misunderstood him. There is more to be done on similarities between Brackenridge and Adams, and on their importance to the Adams Presidency.

51. See Elliott, *Revolutionary Writers*, 180–1. Lawson-Peebles, *Landscape*, 124–5.

52. Owen S. Ireland, *Religion, Ethnicity, and Politics: Ratifying the Constitution in Pennsylvania* (Pennsylvania: The Pennsylvania State University Press, 1995) and Harry M. Tinkcom, *The Republicans and Federalists in Pennsylvania 1790–1801: A Study in National Stimulus and Local Response* (Harrisburg: Pennsylvania Historical and Museum Commission, 1950) refer to Brackenridge only in passing.

53. William Findley, *Pittsburgh Gazette*, February 10, 1787, in Marder, *Hugh Henry Brackenridge*, 37.

54. Hugh Henry Brackenridge, *Pittsburgh Gazette*, April 21, 1787, in Newlin, *Life and Writings*, 83–4, Ellis, *After the Revolution*, 90–1.)

55. A Farmer, *Pittsburgh Gazette*, April 14, 1787, in Newlin, *Life and Writings*, 82. It is at least possible, however, that this could have been Brackenridge himself adopting the common pseudonym. That would chime with his desire to be accepted into the Easterners' ranks and with the viciousness of his reaction to Findley's position—the latter's stock is no higher than Brackenridge's, yet he enjoys greater position.

56. John Caldwell, *William Findley From West of the Mountains: A Politician in Pennsylvania, 1783–1791* (Gig Harbor, WA: Red Apple Publishing, 2000) is an important reconsideration of the Findley–Brackenridge feud. See especially Chapters 9–12, quotation at 122. Newlin, *Life and Writings*, 76–85, discusses it but omits reference to Brackenridge's more unpleasant turns of phrase.

57. Hugh Henry Brackenridge, *Pittsburgh Gazette*, December 1, 1787, in *ibid.*, 96–97.

58. *Ibid.*, 3:13–14.

59. Thomas Slaughter, *The Whiskey Rebellion: Frontier Epilogue to the American Revolution* (New York; Oxford, UK: Oxford University Press, 1986) is the best recent study of the topic. Elkins and McKitrick, *Age of Federalism*, 466ff., contains an excellent summary of recent and less-recent scholarship

on the subject. Steven R. Boyd, *The Whiskey Rebellion: Past and Present Perspectives* (Westport, CT: Greenwood Press, 1985) is a useful collection of primary sources and recent scholarship. Saul Cornell, *The Other Founders: Anti-Federalism and the Dissenting Tradition in America, 1788–1828* (Williamsburg, VA: Omohondro, 1999), 195–218, considers the rebellion in the wider context of the anti-Federalist tradition. See also Terry Bouton, "A Road Closed: Rural Insurgency in Post-Independence Pennsylvania", *Journal of American History*, 87 (December 2000), 855–887.

60. Joseph J. Ellis is excellent on the book, but draws slightly different conclusions.
61. Hugh Henry Brackenridge, *Incidents*, 1:5.
62. *Ibid.*, 2:63.
63. This section includes an intriguing moment when one building is spared because the man's negro servants protest that it contains their bacon.
64. Brackenridge, *Incidents*, 1:16.
65. Both quotations, *ibid.*, 1:41.
66. Both quotations, *ibid.*, 1:42.
67. *Ibid.*, 2:54.
68. Brackenridge was, indeed, arrested and went through two days of interrogation at the hands of Hamilton and his subordinates before they accepted his story. He seems to have suffered from their conviction of a strong rebel leadership, with Brackenridge the most plausible figure on the spot to fill the role. See especially, Slaughter, *Whiskey Rebellion*, 218–219.
69. All three quotations from *ibid.*, 2:73.
70. Hugh Henry Brackenridge, "Volume IV, Chapter XII" in *Modern Chivalry*, 300. Hereafter "*MC*". This volume was published in 1797, which enables us to identify the President as Washington. On the publication schedule of *Modern Chivalry* see footnote 11.
71. *Ibid.*, 304.
72. "Chapter XIV," in *ibid.*, 310.
73. "Chapter XV," in *ibid.*, 315.
74. Newlin, *Life and Writings*, 198–240, is a good narrative account of Brackenridge's political involvement at this period, but cannot precisely account for Brackenridge choosing to turn back to politics at this point. His full motivation remains to be discovered.
75. Hugh Henry Brackenridge, *Gazette Publications*, 3.
76. Hugh Henry Brackenridge, *MC*, 614–15.
77. In addition to studies already mentioned see Emory Elliott, *Revolutionary Writers*, 171–217. David Simpson, *The Politics of American English* (New York: Oxford University Press, 1986), 113–118, discussed Brackenridge's use of dialect. Looby, *Voicing America*, quotation at 245, is particularly flawed, largely ignoring Part II and dismissing the narrator's observations across the book as "flat, repetitive, and boring".
78. The dilemma, encapsulated in the phrase "To please or to instruct," was a common problem for a number of writers in this period. The actual phrase is drawn from Washington Irving, "Christmas Books," in "The Sketch Book," in *History, Tales and Sketches*, Washington Irving (New York: The Library of America, 1983), 961. Its implications will, therefore, be considered in detail in Chapter 3. Here it is simply important to note its applicability to Brackenridge.
79. William Findley (1742–1821) was one of Brackenridge's political rivals in western Pennsylvania. He also wrote a history of the Whiskey Rebellion. See John Caldwell, *William Findley From West of the Mountains*, 2 Vols. (Gig Harbor, Washington: Red Apple, 2000–2002). Also Rodger C. Henderson,

"William Findley", in *ANB*, 7:918–919. Brackenridge reprinted the poem in *Gazette Publications*, 311–340.

80. *Ibid.*, 319.
81. Intriguingly, it is Traddle the Weaver's wife who is most furious with the Chevalier for trying to persuade her husband, her domineering manner perhaps anticipating that of van Winkle's wife in Irving.
82. Hugh Henry Brackenridge, *Gazette Publications*, 316.
83. *Ibid.*, 324.
84. Farrago anticipates Irving's unfulfilled plan to do the same to produce his next work after *A History of New York*. See the following, pp. 204–205.
85. Hugh Henry Brackenridge, *MC*, 21.
86. *Ibid.*
87. *Ibid.*, 134.
88. *Ibid.*
89. *Ibid.*, 135.
90. *Ibid.*, 135.
91. *Ibid.*, 136.
92. *Ibid.*, 138–9.
93. *Ibid.*, 139.
94. The narrator also addresses slavery in a section (117–118) where he proposes, in more humorous terms, that the explanation for their being different colours of mankind is due to Adam having been White and Eve having been Black. It is clear from the tone of these sections, and from his writings on the Indians elsewhere, that Brackenridge did not consider Indians or slaves equal to the White race. Yet his censures on the White race confuse the issue somewhat, since that race hardly occupies the exulted plinth normally to be expected in such a racial pyramid. Nor is he unaware of the absurdities of the slavery system, as the example in the main text shows.
95. *Ibid.*, 6.
96. *Ibid.*, 56.
97. *Ibid.*
98. *Ibid.*, 86.
99. *Ibid.*, 350.
100. *Ibid.*, 334.
101. *Ibid.*
102. *Ibid.*, 405.
103. *Ibid.*, 403.
104. *Ibid.*, 509. Emphasis in original.
105. *Ibid.*, 553.
106. *Ibid.*, 554–5.
107. *Ibid.*, 638–639.
108. *Ibid.*, 676.
109. *Ibid.*, 747.
110. *Ibid.*, 751–2.
111. *Ibid.*, 712.
112. *Ibid.*, 712. Emphasis in original.
113. *Ibid.*, 754.
114. *Ibid.*, 611.
115. *Ibid.*
116. *Ibid.* Adams' similar views can be seen in his *Defence of the Constitution of the United States*. See the mix of quotations and analysis in Wood, *Creation*, 571–4.
117. Hugh Henry Brackenridge, *MC*, 783. Emphasis in original.
118. *Ibid.*, 786. Emphasis in original.

119. *Ibid.*, 786.
120. *Ibid.*, 787.
121. *Ibid.*, 743.

NOTES TO CHAPTER 3

1. Thomas Jefferson, "First Inaugural Address," in *TJW*, 493. Joseph J. Ellis, *American Sphinx: The Character of Thomas Jefferson* (New York: Alfred Knopf, 1998), 182, notes that the capitals were added in newspaper transcriptions and that the two factions were not capitalised in Jefferson's handwritten text. He extrapolates this to a convoluted argument that Jefferson meant that everybody accepted "a republican form of government and a federal bond among the states." Whether or not this is accurate, it does not change the fact, which Ellis does not comment on, that Jefferson was proclaiming a unity which did not exist. Since Ellis argued that TJ was referring to all Americans here, the point also ignores the fact that the Republicans had spent much of the preceding administration asserting that it was tainted by monarchism. Lance Banning, *The Jeffersonian Persuasion: Evolution of a Party Ideology* (Ithaca, London: Cornell University Press, 1978), 274–75, argued that Jefferson's desire for reconciliation was genuine and a matter of detaching the body of the people from their former leaders. We might also note that this was a spoken address, however inaudibly delivered; his hearers would have understood him to be unifying the parties.
2. Washington Irving (hereafter WI), "A History of New York", in *History, Tales and Sketches*, Washington Irving, (New York: Library of America, 1983), 547. Hereafter *HTS*.
3. Jefferson, "First Inaugural", in *TJW*, 492.
4. *Ibid.*, 494.
5. *Ibid.*, 495. See Marshall Smelser, *The Democratic Republic 1801–1815* (New York: Harper & Row, 1968), 17.
6. Adams, *History*, 1:138–140 recognised this contradiction with typical perspicuity.
7 Jefferson, "First Inaugural, in *TJW*, 493.
8. *Ibid.*, 493.
9. Thomas Jefferson to John Dickinson, Mar 6 1801, in *TJW*, 1084.
10. See C. Bradley Thompson, *John Adams and the Spirit of Liberty* (Lawrence: University of Kansas, 1998). See previous, 110, ftnote. 46.
11. R. B. Bernstein, *Thomas Jefferson* (Oxford: Oxford University Press, 2003), 136 touched on this interpretation in discussing the First Inaugural Address. Sharp, *American Politics* gave a fuller account, see especially, 276–288, but failed to properly deal with Adams' role. See also Footnote 312.
12. WI, "Salmagundi No.VII", Saturday April 4, 1807, in *HTS*, 143.
13. WI, "Salmagundi No.XIII", August 14, 1807, in *ibid.*, 249.
14. The standard biography of Irving remains Stanley T. Williams, *The Life of Washington Irving*, 2 Vols. (New York: H. Milford, 1935). The most recent biography is Andrew Burstein, *The Original Knickerbocker: The Life of Washington Irving* (New York: Basic Books, 2007). Two studies of Irving's early career are useful: William L. Hedges, *Washington Irving: An American Study 1802–1832* (Baltimore, MD: The Johns Hopkins Press, 1965); Martin Roth, *Comedy and America: The Lost World of Washington Irving* (Port Washington, N.Y.: Kennikat Press, 1976).

15. Williams, *Life*, 1–22, covers Washington Irving's childhood years in rather purple prose.
16. *Ibid.*, 1:14.
17. WI to William Irving, Jr., July 1, 1804 in *Letters of Washington Irving*, eds. Ralph M. Aderman et. al., 4 Vols. (Boston: Twayne Publishers, 1978–82), 1:13. Hereafter *LWI*. From Letters: Volume I [1], 1802–1823, The complete works of Washington Irving, Volume XXIII [23] by Washington Irving (Author), Ralph M. Aderman (Editor), Herbert L. Kleinfield (Editor), Jenifer S. Banks (Editor). 1979. Reprinted with permission of Gale, a divsion of Thomson Learning: www.thomsonrights.com. Fax 800–730–2215.
18. WI to Peter Irving, July 10, 1804, in *ibid.*, 1:22.
19. WI to Amos Eaton, December 15, 1802, in *ibid.*, 1:5–6.
20. *Ibid.*, 1:7. The author of this comment has not been identified by the editors.
21. See Burstein, *Original Knickerbocker*, 18–20.
22. Williams, *Life*, 1:93.
23. WI to James Kirke Paulding, June 22, 1807, in *LWI*, 1:239.
24. WI to [Mary Fairlie?], July 7, 1807, in *ibid.*, 1:245.
25. See WI to Gouverneur Kemble, July 1, 1807, in *ibid.*, 1:242, and accompanying footnote 5.
26. Williams, *Life*, 1:96–7.
27. WI to [Mary Fairlie?], in *LWI*, 244.
28. The work was subsequently published as a book in London in 1811 (with some excisions by the pirating publisher) and finally in New York in 1814 with some minor removal of sections by Irving. See discussion in Washington Irving, *The Complete Works of Washington Irving*, eds. Henry A. Pochman et. al. (Boston, Massachusetts: Twayne Publishers, 1970–1989), 30 vols., 6:319–326. (Hereafter *CWWI*).
29. Thus it appears in the Library of America edition cited throughout this chapter and in the modern collected edition of Irving's works. Notably, Irving excluded it from his collected edition of 1848. Paulding included it in a collected edition of his works in 1835, acknowledging that it had been produced in collaboration with the Irvings.
30. Paulding is considered in detail in Chapter 4.
31. Bruce Granger, "Assignments of Authorship", in *CWWI*, 6:327–336. This gives a table of existing critical views to that date.
32. This problem is demonstrated by the insistence of other early novelists such as Hannah Webster Foster (*The Coquette*), William Hill Brown (*The Power of Sympathy*), and Susannah Rowson (*Charlotte Temple*) that their novels were based on true stories. A similar pressure can be glimpsed in the various scientific references present in Charles Brockden Brown's fictions, such as that on biloquism in *Wieland, or the Transformation*.
33. WI, "Salmagundi No.I", January 24, 1807, *HTS*, 49.
34. *Ibid.*, 52.
35. *Ibid.*, 56.
36. WI, "Salmagundi No.II", February 4, 1807, *ibid.*, 63–76.
37. *Ibid.*, 67/67–8.
38. Both quotations, *ibid.*, 67.
39. Roth, *Comedy*, the only full length study of *Salmagundi* and *A History*, acknowledged the possibility of a snipe at the Hemmings question, although not in connection with this set of remarks. Where he does mention it, he dismisses the scandal as a "piece of scurrility." I have located no other critical comment on this specific point. *CWWI*, 6:341, simply stated that the line was drawn from William Shakespeare, *As You Like It*. The speech in

question is spoken by Jacques, who is reporting a speech of Touchstone's. The Arden Introduction—William Shakespeare, *As You Like It*, ed. Agnes Latham, (London: Methuen, 1975), 49–50, suggests that the whole section aims at a bawdy reading. See also the Oxford Shakespeare edition, ed. Alan Brissenden (Oxford: Clarendon Press, 1993), 144.

40. WI, "Salmagundi No.II," in *HTS*, 75.
41. WI, "Salmagundi No.III," February 13, 1807, in *ibid.*, 83.
42. "Salmagundi, No.XIII," August 14, 1807, in *ibid.*, 252. "Slang-whanger" is specifically defined as "A noisy or abusive talker or writer" in *Oxford English Dictionary* (1989), and Irving's *Salmagundi* is given as an example of the word in use. It is derived from "slangwhang," "[t]o assail with, to make use of, violent language, abuse, or vituperation." This in turn is derived from "slang," "[t]he special vocabulary used by any set of persons of a low or disreputable character; language of a low and vulgar type," and "whang," "[t]o make a loud resounding noise, as of a heavy blow or explosion, of shot flying through the air." See *OED Online Edition* (http://dictionary.oed.com) consulted 15/02/06.
43. Roth, *Comedy*, is, most unfortunately, among those who take this position.
44. Both quotations from "Salmagundi, No.XIV," September 19, 1807, in *HTS*, 256.
45. "Salmagundi No.III", in *ibid.*, 80–1.
46. *Ibid.*, 81.
47. WI, "Salmagundi No.V", March 7 1808, in *ibid.*, 113.
48. *Ibid.*, 115.
49. *Ibid.*, 116.
50. See Smelser, *Democratic Republic*, 57–61 for a good brief summary of US–Barbary relations.
51. WI, "Salmagundi No.VII," April 4, 1807, in *ibid.*, 143.
52. See previous, Chapter One, 14–17.
53. *Ibid.*, 145.
54. Monroe produced a lengthy self-justificatory account of his 1790s diplomatic mission to France: James Monroe, *A View of the Conduct of the Executive, in the Foreign Affairs of the United States, Connected With the Mission to the French Republic, During the Years 1794, 5 & 6* (1797).
55. *Ibid.*, 147.
56. *Ibid.*, 148.
57. *Ibid.*, 150.
58. Irving returned to this theme under the name of Will Wizard in "Salmagundi No. XIII" (238–244), and again in the *History*.
59. A similar argument occurs in the sixth Mustapha Letter in "Salmagundi XIV," where William Irving complains that in the face of fresh insults from Great Britain, all the people can do is talk endlessly. See 257–8.
60. WI, "Salmagundi No. XI," June 2, 1807, in *ibid.*, 202.
61. *Ibid.*, 203.
62. *Ibid.*, 205.
63. *Ibid.*, 206.
64. *Ibid.*, 207.
65. Both quotations in *ibid.*, 208.
66. Both quotations from *ibid.*, 209. Emphasis in original.
67. Both quotations from *ibid*, 209. Emphasis in original.
68. WI, "Salmagundi No. IV," February 24, 1807, in *ibid.*, 96.
69. WI, "Salmagundi No. XIV," September 19, 1807, in *ibid.*, 255. Emphasis in original.
70. *Ibid.*, 255–6.

71. Both quotations from *ibid.*, 259. Emphasis in original.
72. All three quotations from, *ibid.*, 260. Emphasis in original.
73. Both quotations from, *ibid.*, 261.
74. *Ibid.*, 292–3.
75. *Ibid.*, 296.
76. The most serious flaw in Davidson, *Revolution*, is her total neglect of Irving.
77. Michael L. Black and Nancy B. Black, "Introduction" in *CWWI*, 7:xxxiv–lxviii, details the process of revision. The Editors of the *Complete Works* chose to reprint the final 1848 edition.
78. WI, "A History of New York", in *HTS*, 379.
79. Irving also applied this dictum to the reputations of great men, see *ibid.*, 563–4.
80. *Ibid.*, 383.
81. *Ibid.*, 379–380.
82. *Ibid*, 381. Italics in original.
83. *Ibid.*, 380–381.
84. *Ibid*, 374.
85. *Ibid*, 373.
86. All three quotations from *ibid.* 412.
87. *Ibid.* 412.
88. *Ibid.* 413.
89. Washington Irving, "Traits of Indian Character" and "Philip of Pokanoket" in *HTS*, 1002–1028.
90. The Vanegas in question appears to be M. Venegas, author of the *History of California*. See *CWWI*, 7:314, note 42.28–35.
91. Both quotations from Irving, *History*, in *HTS*, 414.
92. *Ibid.*, 416 (first quotation); 417 (second quotation).
93. *Ibid.*, 419.
94. Both quotations, *ibid.*, 420. Emphasis in original.
95. *Ibid.*, 421.
96. *Ibid.*, 423. The argument is very briefly recalled in discussing the Swedish threat to the colony, 534.
97. *Ibid.*, 468. See the following for further discussion of this point.
98. There is no consistent critical view as to who the other two governors are intended to represent. The editors of the modern collected works skirted the question, noting only the William/Jefferson connection, *CWWI*, 7:xxvi–xxvii. Williams, *Life*, 117–118 took a similar view. Loschkey apparently argued that the governors represented the first four American presidents, raising something of a numerical problem as there are only three governors: Helen M. J. Loschkey, *Washington Irving's Knickerbocker's History of New York: Folk History as Literary Form*, Dissertation Abstracts International 31 (1971) 6559A, cited in *Washington Irving—a reference guide*, ed. Haskell Springer (Boston: G.K. Hall, 1976). Philip McFarland, *Sojourners* (New York: Atheneum, 1979), 109, equates Stuyvesant with Washington because he places himself above party (a somewhat problematical ascription) and Twiller with Adams because of the Golden Age. Adams' administration does deserve a better press than it usually receives, but this is to carry it a little far.
99. Washington Irving, *HTS*, 454.
100. One can see this both purely in terms of the repudiation of their rules, and in the dismissal of their ideas—on Jefferson, see Adams, *History*, 1:1239–1252.
101. *Ibid.*, 474.
102. *Ibid.*, 474. Emphasis in original.

103. *Ibid.*, 474.
104. *Ibid.*, 492.
105. *Ibid.*, 465. See Marcus Cunliffe, *George Washington: Man and Monument* (Boston: Little, Brown, 1958), esp., 11–14, and Henry Adams, *History*, 1:188–189—the latter is one of the most perceptive comments on Jefferson in existence.
106. Washington Irving, *HTS*, 492.
107. See John Adams, *A Dissertation on Canon and Feudal Law* (1765), in *Papers of John Adams*, 1:103–28. Adams connects the liberty of thought to both politics and religion. Again, it would be fascinating to know if Irving had encountered this work. Whether or not he did so, it does demonstrate, again, the commonality of literary concerns in this era.
108. Washington Irving, *HTS*, 493.
109. *Ibid.*, 494. Emphasis in original.
110. Though he does later; see *ibid.*, 547–8.
111. *Ibid.*, 495–6. Emphasis in original.
112. The object being satirised is clear here, since Knickerbocker described Kieft's second proclamation as "a kind of non-intercourse bill, forbidding and prohibiting all commerce and connection", *ibid.*, 520.
113. *Ibid.*, 519.
114. *Ibid.*, 544–45.
115. *Ibid.*, 559.
116. *Ibid.*, 564.
117. *Ibid.*, 565.
118. *Ibid.*, 566–7.
119. *Ibid.*, 567. A possible argument against this identification is that Stuyvesant also loves war (607–8).
120. *Ibid.*, 574–578.
121. *Ibid.*, 558, where Kieft is compared to King Arthur.
122. *Ibid.*, 722.
123. *Ibid.*, 722.
124. *Ibid.*, 454. See also the curious prefiguring of this in "Salmagundi No. XIII," in *ibid.*, 247.
125. Jeffrey Rubin-Dorsky, *Adrift in the Old World: The Psychological Pilgrimage of Washington Irving* (Chicago: University of Chicago Press, 1988) has examined this period of Irving's life in most detail. But he focused on the period after Irving's departure for Europe in 1815 and made little comment on Irving's early work, or the turmoil he was already wrestling with after 1809. Williams, *Life*, 119–144, gave more consideration to that earlier period but again, principally because he saw *The Sketch Book* as Irving's first masterpiece, downplayed the political concerns of the *History* and consequently any relevance the continuance of such concerns might have to Irving's activities in this decade.
126. WI to Mrs. Josiah Ogden Hoffman, February 12, 1810, *LWI*, 1:282.
127. WI to Mrs. Josiah Ogden Hoffman, February 26 1810, in *ibid.*, 284.
128. WI to John E. Hall, September 26 1810, in *ibid.*, 290.
129. *Ibid.*, 291. In the light of this, it is interesting to note Irving's admonitions on the same subject to Edwin C. Holland, a minor poet, in his review of the latter's work in the *Analectic Magazine* of March, 1814. See the following.
130. In an intriguing claim, that demonstrates again, this time on a rather petty level, the interconnection of literature and politics in this period, Pierre M. Irving, Irving's nephew, literary executor, and first biographer, stated that Irving was rejected because Joel Barlow, then the minister designate, believed he had been critical of the latter's epic poem *The Columbiad*, see

Pierre M. Irving, *The Life and Letters of Washington Irving* (London: R. Bentley, 1862–1864), 1:305, note.2.

131. WI to William Irving Jr., February 9, 1811, in *ibid.*

132. WI to Henry Brevoort, January 13, 1811, *ibid.*, 297. This is the same letter in which Irving gives his famous description of Madison as being "but a withered little apple-John."

133. WI to William P. Van Ness, February 20, 1811, *ibid.*, 307.

134. WI to Henry Brevoort, June 8, 1811, *ibid.*, 323.

135. The name adopted by Washington Irving's circle of male friends from the early 1800s. Their reasons for adopting it are not clear.

136. Hedges, *American Study*, is alone among Irving's biographers in trying to tease out themes from the contents of the *Analectic Magazine* (107–115) but he dismisses Irving's own contributions as "patriotic potboilers" (114). He does make some interesting suggestions regarding the magazine as showing Irving's awareness of new trends in thought.

137. Paulding's career is discussed in Chapter 4. The important point to note here is the fact of their continued collaboration through to the end of 1814.

138. On Verplanck, see Robert W. July, *The Essential New Yorker: Gulian Crommelin Verplanck* (Durham, NC: Duke University Press, 1951), esp. 97–102.

139. This choice of subject bears an interesting similarity to Charles Brockden Brown's *Monthly Magazine and American Review* (1799–1800) and *American Review and Literary Journal* (1801–1802) both of which often began issues with such biographical sketches from Brown's pen.

140. Brown, in his early periodical ventures, produced a considerable number of reviews of contemporary American publications. William Wirt (1772–1834) served as U.S. attorney general (1817–1829). The *Letters* were originally published in 1803. He also wrote a biography of the patriot hero Patrick Henry. published in 1817. See Michael L. Oberg, "William Wirt," *ANB*, 23:675–676.

141. Amos Stoddard (1762–1813) served in the U.S. Army and oversaw the transfer of the Louisiana Purchase from Spain to France to America. As he was representing both France and America at the time, that meant transferring the lands from himself to himself. *Sketches* was published in 1812, and Stoddard was killed the following year at the siege of Fort Meigs. See Smelser, *Democratic Republic*, 101, on the transfer. See also entry in *Dictionary of American Biography* (ed.) Dumas Malone, 18:51–52.

   There is no entry on Stoddard in the *ANB*, but see *Webster's American Literary Biographies*, ed. Robert McHenry (Springfield, Massachusetts: G. & C. Merriam Company, 1978), 415–416.

142. "They are a creditable example of the progress of Americans in elegant literature," "Review of *The Letters of the British Spy*" (reprinted from the *British Critic*), in *Analectic Magazine* (Vol.1, February 1813), 146.

143. The following quotation is an illustration of the kind of questions these pieces discuss—"It is entreated that the reader will determine with himself, whether he consider it to be the duty of a king to prefer the welfare of his people to every other consideration, or the duty of the people to disregard the obvious interests of their country, and to sacrifice their lives and fortunes to the personal resentments of the monarch." Quotation from "Historical Sketch of the Last Years of the Reign of Gustavus the 4th" (original periodical source unrecorded), *Analectic Magazine*, October 1813, 266.

144. "De La Litterature by Madame de Stael-Holstein" (original periodical source unrecorded), *Analectic Magazine*, September 1813, 180 (Vol.2?).

145. *Ibid.*, 183.

146. All of Irving's original contributions are reprinted in Washington Irving, *Miscellaneous Writings: Volume 1*, ed. Wayne R. Kime (Boston: Twayne Publishers, 1981), Volume 28 in *The Complete Works of Washington Irving*. All page references to these pieces are taken from that edition. References to other articles in the *Magazine*, including the original pieces by Paulding and Verplanck are taken from the original magazine editions. There is no modern collection of Paulding's various periodical contributions.

147. Robert Treat Paine, Jr. (1773–1811) was the son of one of the signers of The Declaration of Independence. He began writing poetry in the 1790s, including fiery nationalist pieces during the war fever of 1798 which caught the attention of John Adams. Like many contemporary artists he failed as a professional writer, in his case because of habits of drinking and dissolute living, the principal causes of his death in 1811. See Winfred E.A. Bernhard, "Robert Treat Paine, Jr.," in *ANB*, 16:923–5.

148. Washington Irving, "Review of the works of Robert Treat Paine," in Washington Irving, *CWWI*, 28:50.

149. *Ibid.*, 63.

150. Irving, "Odes, Naval Songs, and other occasional poems by Edwin C. Holland Esq., Charleston," in *ibid.*, 107–8.

151. Irving also published two sketches on Indian subjects—("Traits of Indian Character;" February, 1814; and "Philip of Pokanoket," June, 1814). They were republished in *The Sketch Book* and are discussed in the following.

152. Irving noted Lawrence's famous dying words as "don't surrender the ship" (*ibid.*, 71). These, transmuted to "Don't give up the ship" became a Navy motto. It is not clear whether Irving was the first to record the words but, if so, it was an ironically important contribution to the post-War optimistic strain of national character with which he was so uncomfortable.

153. Washington Irving, "Biographical Memoir of Commodore Perry," in *ibid.*, 104.

154. *Ibid.*, 92.

155. *Ibid.*, 93.

156. *Ibid.*, 93–4.

157. Watts, *The Republic Reborn*. It is striking, in a book centred on the cultural effects of the war, and the responses of leading cultural figures to it, that Watts omits any extended discussion of Irving who would seem to illuminate many of the themes he discussed.

158. Washington Irving, "Biography of Captain James Lawrence," in Washington Irving, *CWWI*, 28:76.

159. Washington Irving, "Biographical Memoir of Commodore Perry," in *ibid.*, 94.

160. WI to Ebenezer Irving, October 3, 1814, *LWI*, 1:377.

161. WI to Henry Brevoort, Jr., May 25, 1815, in *ibid.*, 394.

162. M. A. Weatherspoon, "1815–1819: Prelude to Irving's *Sketch Book*," *American Literature* 41 (1969–1970), 566–571. She listed the then extant explanations for this departure: Stanley T. Williams argued that Irving was troubled about his career, did not like the success standards of the present generation of Americans and was feeling his age (1:143–4); William Hedges simply suggested "for want of anything better to do, he drifted to Europe" (12). Weatherspoon then argued that he was in love with Serena Livingston, was tricked into believing she was to marry someone else, and left partly under the effects of this. Hedges and Williams do not consider the question in sufficient detail. Weatherspoon's evidence is inconclusive, and it seems suggestive that Irving made no attempt to rush back when he discovered the deception. Williams also reproduced (2:255–262) a manuscript fragment by Irving describing his early life probably written in May

or June 1823 to explain that life to Emily Foster, then possibly the object of his affections. It corroborates key features of the crisis—his misery over Matilda Hoffman's death, his inability to write, the hopes engendered in him by the War of 1812 and the horrors of the business world. But, it doesn't deal with the content of his literary works, or with his editorship of the *Analectic* except to state that they happened. The interconnection was important. Jeffrey Rubin-Dorsky has given the most detailed analysis of the departure (see 199, ftnote 121 previous) but as already indicated, he does so only in the context of Irving's life in 1815. As will be clear from my analysis, I do not believe Irving's departure for Europe in 1815 can be satisfactorily explained without a full examination of the period 1809–1815 and a detailed consideration of the aims and themes of his earlier literary works.

163. I suggest that Irving was, ultimately, unhappy with the world that emerged from the War of 1812, whose development has been most ably described by Watts, *Republic Reborn*.

164. WI to Henry Brevoort, July 8–9, 1812, in *LWI*, 1:340.

165. WI to Henry Brevoort, May 9, 1816, in *ibid.*, 446.

166. WI to Henry Brevoort, July 16, 1816, *ibid,*, 449. See also letters to Brevoort of October 17, 1815 and March 15, 1816 which trace the development of the crisis.

167. *Ibid.*, 450. Emphasis in original.

168. *Ibid.*, 449.

169. See for example, WI to Henry Brevoort, August 28, 1817, *ibid.*, 495. This discusses the possibilities for getting Thomas Campbell to visit America to deliver his lectures on poetry and belles letters. Irving had earlier produced a biographical sketch of Campbell for an 1810 American edition of his poems, reprinted in March, 1815 as his final contribution to the *Analectic*. He argued here that Campbell could give a "proper direction" to American literature. The fact that Irving noted specifically, in his sketch, the significance to Americans of Campbell having written on American themes (specifically, his poem *Gertrude of Wyoming*) suggests that this may also have been a significant factor—a notable Old World poet who recognised the validity of New World themes.

170. WI to Washington Allston, Birmingham, May 21, 1817, *ibid.*, 478. Reprinted by permission of the Houghton Library, Harvard University, call number *MS am 1588 (15)*. Allston was then in London, having travelled over in 1811. He was at work on an enormous painting depicting *Belshazzar's Feast*. He was still at work on the canvas at his death in 1843. He was frequently frustrated by the lack of financial support for American artists, but in the case of *Belshazzer* benefited from a $10,000 trust fund established by ten Boston gentlemen. See A. Kristen Foster, "Washington Allston", in *ANB*, 1:372–4.

171. See the "Introduction" and "Textual Commentary" in *CWWI*, 8:xi–xxxii, 340–364, for such composition dates as are known and a detailed publication history. It is of particular significance that each issue was to be distributed by booksellers in New York, Philadelphia, Boston, and Baltimore, indicating his desire for a national audience. For the two essays from the *Analectic* see below, 238.

172. See *ibid.*, for full publication history. What is clear is the rapid popularity of the book which enjoyed an initial print run in the U.S. for Numbers I and II of 2000 copies (xvi–xvii). It seems probable that the number was the same for the later installments, and the work went fairly rapidly through three further editions. In Britain, the initial print run was 1000. Rubin-Dorsky cited Luther Mott, *Golden Multitudes* (72) and Hart, *The Popular Book* (83) both of whom believed the book to have been a bestseller in America.

There are slight discrepancies of order between original periodical editions and first book editions (table, 355) but these do not materially affect the arguments made here regarding content.

173. Intriguingly, Richard Henry Dana, Sr. in the *North American Review* (September, 1819), found fault with the increased "elegance" of Irving's style, quoted in *CWWI*, 8:xxvii. He seems to have been almost alone in taking this position.

174. *The Sketch Book* does afford a glimpse of the later Crayon in "The Spectre Bridegroom" subtitled "A Travellers Tale" with its German setting.

175. Washington Irving, "The Sketch Book", in *HTS*, 743.

176. All quotations in *ibid.*, 744.

177. All three quotations in *ibid.*, 746.

178. *Ibid.*, 747.

179. *Ibid.*, 750. My emphasis.

180. *Ibid.*, 751.

181. Both quotations in *ibid.*, 787.

182. *Ibid.*, 787–8. There is a hint of Voltaire's *Candide* to this passage. A journal entry for August 21, 1822, *CWWI*, 3:12 indicates that by that date he had read the work.

183. This section also includes a poignant little comment on the supposed influence of literature, which is deeply ironic, considering the sense, already examined, that Irving felt his articles in the *Analectic Magazine* had been ignored, and the extended comment at the end of the Christmas sketches, discussed in the following. It may, of course, be a fair comment as to the influence of English writers:
    "Every one knows the all pervading influence of literature at the present day, and how much the options and passions of mankind are under its control." *Ibid.*, 789–90.

184. Both quotations in *ibid.*, p.793.

185. Critics tend to underestimate the importance of the American quality of Rip van Winkle and his experience (Rubin-Dorsky in the third chapter of his study is an honourable exception). Hedges, having been diverted into an unhelpful phallic metaphor (140) argued that, in employing the soubriquet of Knickerbocker, "Irving was merely trying to capitalize on his earlier reputation in order to stimulate sales of The Sketch Book" (141). M. W. Bowden, in her biography, argues that Rip is simply a story of financial failure. Critics have also focused on the Germanic origins of the tale (see, for example, Philip Young, "Fallen from Time: The Mythic 'Rip van Winkle'" in *Washington Irving: The Critical Reaction* [New York: AMS Press, 1993], ed. James W. Tuttleton, 67–84, originally published in *The Kenyon Review*, 22 [1960], 547–573) and referred to generally in the biographies and introductions to modern editions. Young argued that Rip, in fact, falls asleep in Valhalla, a somewhat far-fetched assertion. It seems more likely that Irving drew on the Ossian legends knowledge possibly acquired during his 1817 tour in Scotland and meeting with Walter Scott, although the work was in circulation in America long before that (see on Irving's Scottish trip and Ossian in America, Hook, *Scotland and America*). Undeniably, Irving borrowed from existing literature here, as elsewhere in the work, but, particularly in the two American tales, he fashioned it into something quite different. Finally, it seems important to take issue with another aspect of the critical debate—the argument that Irving was using these two tales to fashion an American mythology, an American past which did not exist (see Hedges [115] and Terence Martin, "Rip, Ichabod and the American Imagination", in Tuttleton, *Critical Heritage*, 56–66, originally published in *American Literature* 31 [1959],

137–149). It should be remembered that Irving had already crafted precisely that past in the *History*, and that two more examples of it, written earlier, were present in *The Sketch Book* in the forms of the Indian sketches. To be quite clear, it is not that these analyses are necessarily wrong, or entirely irrelevant, but simply that the American dimension is much more central to the experiences of Rip and Ichabod than these writers have allowed.

186. Irving, "The Sketch Book", in *HTS*, 776.
187. All three quotations in *ibid.*, 779.
188. *Ibid.*, 780.
189. All quotations in *ibid.*, 783.
190. *Ibid.*, 783.
191. Paraphrase, *ibid.*, 778.
192. Paraphrase of *ibid.*, 783.
193. *Ibid.*, 783.
194. *Ibid.*, 903.
195. *Ibid.*, 961–2.
196. *Ibid.*, 970–1.
197. *Ibid.*, 973.
198. *Ibid.*, 974.
199. *Ibid.*, 977.
200. Both quotations in *ibid.*, 978.
201. *Ibid.*, 982.
202. *Ibid.*, 1003–4.
203. Rubin-Dorsky, *Adrift*, 118, made a precisely opposite case, arguing that we understand Ichabod's story but what happened to Rip will remain always a mystery. I don't agree, but Rubin-Dorsky's expression of this point "we will always be awed, mystified, and continually disturbed by Rip's expression of overwhelming loss" upon his return does hint at a facet of Irving's underlying message. Rip does not understand the Revolution—can anybody understand the Revolution?
204. *Ibid.*, 1060.
205. *Ibid.*, 1059–1060.
206. "Many dismal tales were told about funeral trains, and mournful cries and wailings heard and seen about the great tree where the unfortunate Major André was taken . . .", *ibid.*, 1078. André haunts a number of the writers in this study: Irving here and Cooper in *The Spy*, while one of Paulding's cousins assisted at André's capture. André's fate aroused a great deal of American sympathy and it seems likely that he lingered in minds as the most obvious symbol of the darker side of the Revolution. For biographical information on André see, Paul David Nelson, "John André," in *ANB*, 1:486–7. See also Caleb Crain, *American Sympathy: Men, Friendship and Literature in the New Nation* (New Haven/London: Yale University Press, 2001), 1–15.
207. *Ibid.*, 1063.
208. *Ibid.*, 1086.
209. *Ibid.*, 1087.

NOTES TO CHAPTER 4

1. James Madison, "Seventh Annual Message to Congress", December 15, 1815, in *Writings*, James Madison (New York: Library of America, 1999), 715.
2. Jonas Clopper, *Fragments of the History of Bawlfredonia* (Baltimore: n.p., 1819), 12.

3. Three modern biographies exist of Paulding, Larry J. Reynolds, *James Kirke Paulding* (Boston: Twayne Publishers, 1984); Lorman Ratner, *James Kirke Paulding: The Last Republican* (Westport, CT: Greenwood Press, 1992); Ralph M. Aderman and Wayne R. Kime, *Advocate for America: James Kirke Paulding* (Selinsgrove, PA: Susquehanna University Press, 2003). None of them contain detailed literary analysis. Two biographies exist of Neal, Benjamin Lease, *That wild Fellow John Neal and the American Revolution* (Chicago: University of Chicago Press, 1972); Donald A. Sears, *John Neal* (Boston: Twayne Publishers, 1978). The only work on Jonas Clopper uncovered are two brief introductions to a 1970 reprint of the *Fragments* in 'The American Humorists' series published by Lost Cause Press. These are a general series introduction written by Professor Clarence Gohdes and an introduction specifically on *Fragments* signed F.C.S (it has not been possible to identify the writer). General surveys also neglect them, notably Davidson's. Several long poems by Neal and Paulding were omitted from consideration.
4. The phrase was first coined in the July 12, 1817 edition of the Boston *Columbian Centinel*. See George Dangerfield, *The Era of Good Feelings*, (London: n.p. 1953), 95–104.
5. James Monroe, "First Inaugural Address," in *Inaugural Addresses*, 29–37 passim. Hofstadter, *Party System*, 194–197, is extremely perceptive concerning the First Inaugural Address, and its connection to Monroe's view of parties which was noted in Chapter 2. Monroe's Inauguration is briefly considered in Harry Ammon, *James Monroe: The Quest for National Identity* (Charlottesville: University of Virginia Press, 1971), 369–371, and in W. P. Cresson, *James Monroe* (Chapel Hill: The University of North Carolina Press, 1946), 282–284. Both are more concerned with the stances on specific policies suggested by the document than in the presence of an underlying thesis of rising glory. This is particularly intriguing in Ammon's case since his "Introduction" makes detailed reference to the utopian vision of the revolutionaries which, he argues, it was the central concern of Monroe's life to bring to fruition.
6. John Neal, "Advertisement", in John Neal, *Errata* (New York: published for the 'proprietors,' 1823), Consulted on-line at *Early American Fiction Full Text Database*, 2 vols. (Charlottesville: University of Virginia, 2000), 1:x. (Hereafter, *EAFTD*).
7. John Neal, *American Writers: A Series of Papers Contributed to Blackwood's Magazine 1824–1825*, ed. Fred Lewis Pattee (Durham, NC: n.p., 1937), 153.
8. Lease, *Wild Fellow*, 48–66.
9. This position was taken by Arthur Hobson Quinn, *American Fiction: An Historical and Critical Survey* (New York: n.p., 1936) and followed by Lease and Sears, neither of whom have much to say about the novel. Quinn at least noted the importance of the Indian theme.
10. Neal, *American Writers*, 161.
11. John Neal, *Keep Cool*, 2 vols. (Baltimore, Md.: Joseph Cushing, 1817), 1:52.
12. *Ibid.*, 1:x (Unless otherwise indicated, all italicised words in quotations in this chapter are so printed in the original source.).
13. *Ibid.*, 1:xv.
14. *Ibid.*, 1:xv–xvi.
15. *Ibid.*, 1:viii.
16. This rather mirrors the confused political situation. Everybody, in the aftermath of military victory and the failed attempt at New England sucession, was a Republican—the question was, were they a John Quincy Adams, Cal-

houn, Clay, Crawford, or Jackson Republican? In other words politics was a matter of personal success as much as personal principle.

17. *Ibid.*, 1:xvi–xvii.
18. *Ibid.*, 1:xvii.
19. *Ibid.*, 1:131.
20. *Ibid.*, 1:117.
21. *Ibid.*, 1:114–5.
22. Among Echo's other railings, the most intriguing is the section subsequent to this (116–7) where he argues that "we can never know the whole of a man's merit even as a *writer*, unless familiar with his general character."
23. *Ibid.*, 1:90.
24. *Ibid.*, 1:222.
25. *Ibid.*, 1:222–3.
26. *Ibid.*, 1:225.
27. *Ibid.*, 1:231.
28. This list is a curious one into which it would, perhaps, be dangerous to read too much, but he was with Wellington at Waterloo, combating insurgents in Russia and the colonial powers in South America.
29. *Ibid.*, 2:36.
30. *Ibid.*, 2:38.
31. *Ibid.*, 2:47.
32. *Ibid.*, 2:40.
33. *Ibid.*, 2:42.
34. *Ibid.*, 2:43.
35. *Ibid.*, 2:43.
36. *Ibid.*, 2:146.
37. *Ibid.*, 2:154.
38. *Ibid.*, 2:163.
39. Neal, *American Writers*, 168, footnote, details the rapidity of composition. Neal claimed a total of 102 days for *Randolph, Errata*, and *Seventy-Six*. *Brother Jonathan* alone underwent significant revisions in Neal's attempt to convince Blackwood's to publish it, which they eventually did, losing heavily on the investment. See Lease, *Wild Fellow*, 55–64.
40. Neal, *American Writers*, 168.
41. John Neal, *Logan*, 2 vols. (Philadelphia: H.C. Carey & I. Lea, 1822), consulted on-line at *Early American Fiction Full-Text Database* (Charlottesville: University of Virginia, 2000). On religion, see 1:186–91. On love, see 2:45–6. Its justification of men being in love with different women at different times anticipated some of the preoccupations of *Randolph*. The section on the arts (2:184–88) recalled *Keep Cool*.
42. Neal, *Logan*, 1:69.
43. *Ibid.*, 1:68.
44. *Ibid.*, 1:110.
45. *Ibid.*, 1:220.
46. *Ibid.*, 1:140–1.
47. *Ibid.*, 1:141.
48. *Ibid.*, 1:141.
49. *Ibid.*, 1:266.
50. Oscar is something of a Brownian amalgam. He claims to have killed a man as the avenging agent of God in a sequence with distinct overtones of *Wieland* (2:232ff), and turns out to be a sleepwalker (316) referencing *Edgar Huntly*.
51. *Ibid.*, 2:288.

52. The use of "Jonathan" to denote American is a familiar device, most conspicuously deployed by Paulding in his several satirical works (e.g. *The Diverting History of John Bull and Brother Jonathan* [New York: Inskeep & Bradford, 1812]).

53. John Neal, *Seventy-Six*, 2 vols. (Baltimore: Joseph Robinson, 1823), in *EAF-TYD*, 1:14–15.

54. *Ibid.*, 1:15.

55. *Ibid.*, 1:16.

56. WI to Henry Brevoort, Washington, January 13 1811, in *LWI*, 297.

57. *Ibid.*, 1:16.

58. *Ibid.*, 1:29.

59. *Ibid.*, 1:23. See also 1:247–8.

60. See in *ibid.*, 1:258ff.

61. See *ibid.*, 1:209ff for successive attacks on the law, the church, the speaking of French and Italian, and the meddling of women. See also 2:228–9 on novel writing.

62. *Ibid.*, 2:191.

63. See for example *ibid.*, 1:79, 1:134.

64. *Ibid.*, 2:16–17.

65. *Ibid.*, 1:25–6.

66. The novel ends abruptly with Archibald's death. The fate of the narrator, Jonathan, is left unclear.

67. Neal, *American Writers*, 71.

68. See Vernon Louis Parrington Jnr, *American Dreams: A Study of American Utopias* (Providence, RI: Brown University, 1947), 12–13.

69. Clopper, *Fragments*, 12.

70. *Ibid.*, 13. Given the date of publication, and Clopper's location in Baltimore, this is probably also a sneer at the Panic of 1819, which originated in Maryland.

71. *Ibid.*, 15.

72. *Ibid.*, 23.

73. *Ibid.*, 25.

74. *Ibid.*, footnote, 26.

75. *Ibid.*, 28.

76. *Ibid.*, 32.

77. *Ibid.*, footnote, 39.

78. All three quotations from *ibid.*, 40.

79. *Ibid.*, 68.

80. *Ibid.*, 48.

81. *Ibid.*, 59.

82. *Ibid.*, 63.

83. Monroe, First Inaugural, 35.

84. Clopper, *Fragments*, 63–5. The term 'asylumorians' suggests at least two interpretations—the mad house, or lunatic asylum, or this locale as an asylum of liberty or freedom and a satire thereon. It may also be recalling Paine's characterisation of America in *Common Sense* as an "asylum for mankind."

85. This most likely derives from "Bacchus," presumably intended to imply that only the drunk would attempt such a task.

86. *Ibid.*, 79.

87. *Ibid.*, 80.

88. *Ibid.*, 82.

89. *Ibid.*, 104.

90. *Ibid.*, 105.

91. The satire of Jefferson is carried forward in "Fragment V" in *ibid.*, 122ff.

92. *Ibid.*, 113.
93. *Ibid.*, 114.
94. *Ibid.*, 117.
95. *Ibid.*, 120.
96. *Ibid.*, 156–7. Alexander refers to Alexander Hamilton, Federalist leader and Washington's Treasury Secretary. Timothy refers to Adams's Secretary of State, Timothy Pickering.
97. *Ibid.*, 156. The phrase "hypocritical friend" clearly suggests Jefferson is the intended target, given his and Adams' earlier relationship. However, this is muddled by the use of "Tammany," which implies New York and Burr, and may well be Clopper's dig at the uneasy Burr–Jefferson electoral alliance in 1800.
98. *Ibid.*, 159.
99. Paulding, *Letters*, 1:204.
100. A further interesting connection—Paulding's cousin, John, was one of André's captors.
101. He escaped after several months' imprisonment when the jail caught fire. The authorities chose not to recapture him. See Aderman and Kime, *Advocate for America*, 21–25.
102. James Kirke Paulding, *Diverting History*, 96. This directly recalls Irving's attacks on them in the *History*. Paulding repeated this opening in *Letters from the South*.
103. *Ibid.*, 98.
104. *Ibid.*, 7.
105. *Ibid.*, 14.
106. *Ibid.*, 119.
107. *Ibid.*, 67.
108. *Ibid.*, 68.
109. The poetry review was by John Wilson Croker, the Ingersoll review by John Barrow (then Second Secretary of the Admiralty), although Paulding thought that Robert Southey had written it. See Aderman, *Advocate for America*, 56–59; Hill Shine and Helen Chadwick Shine, *The Quarterly Review Under Gifford: Identification of Contributors* (Chapel Hill: The University of North Carolina Press, 1949), 40–41.
110. James Kirke Paulding, *The United States and England* (New York: A. H. Inskeep, 1815), 6–7.
111. Only in discussing literature is there a substantial paean to American achievements, here the diffusion of knowledge among all parts of the population. *Ibid.*, 82–3.
112. *Ibid.*, 95.
113. James Kirke Paulding, *Letters*, 1:214.
114. *Ibid.*, 1:216. See also James Kirke Paulding, *Salmagundi: 2ⁿᵈ series*, 3 vols. (New York: Haley and Thomas, 1819–20), 3 Vols., 1:141–2. Hereafter *Salmagundi 2*.
115. Paulding, *Letters*, 2:62 (on speculation, the need to farm) and 2:156–7, 167–8, 81–2, 144–5 (charitable institutions), 100–101 (the wonders of agriculture.)
116. *Ibid.*, 25.
117. *Ibid.*, 1:119–120. On Paulding and slavery see Larry E. Tise, *Proslavery: A History of the Defence of Slavery in America 1701–1840* (Athens: University of Georgia Press, 1987.)
118. *Ibid.*, 1:120.
119. *Ibid.*, 1:126.
120. *Ibid.*, 1:130–1.
121. Paulding, *Salmagundi 2*, 1:167.
122. *Ibid.*, 1:190.

123. James Kirke Paulding, *A Sketch of Old England* (New York: Charles Wiley, 1822), (*EAFFTD*), 99.
124. James Kirke Paulding, *Letters*, 1:99–100.
125. Paulding, *United States*, 87, 89. Also Paulding, *Salmagundi 2*, 1:32.
126. James Kirke Paulding, *Koningsmarke*, 2 vols. (New York: AMS Press, 1971), 1:32.
127. *Ibid.*, 1:44–5.
128. *Ibid.*, 1:46–7.
129. See particularly the description of the councillors in *ibid.*, 1:83ff.
130. *Ibid.*, 1:99.
131. *Ibid.*, 2:107
132. *Ibid.*, 1:149.
133. *Ibid.*, 1:121.
134. *Ibid.*, 2:102.
135. *Ibid.*, 2:127–8.
136. Both quotations in *ibid.*, 2:214.
137. *Ibid.*, 2:215.

NOTES TO CHAPTER 5

1. Daniel Webster, "Speech [commemorating Cooper]" delivered February 25, 1852, in ed. William Cullen Bryant, *Memorial of James Fenimore Cooper* (New York: G. P. Putnam, 1852), 24. Consulted on-line at The James Fenimore Cooper Society Web site:—http://www.oneonta.edu/external/cooper/biographic/memorial.html in August 2005.
2. Lawrence, "Fenimore Cooper's Leatherstocking Novels" in *Studies*, 52–69, quotation at 54.
3. *The Red Rover* (1827) is excluded as it falls after the project's cut off date of 1826. An exception is made in this case for *The Prairie* (1827) because of its place in the Leather-Stocking sequence.
4. The Conclusion discusses the significance of this moment.
5. The term "vagueness" was employed by James Grossman, *James Fenimore Cooper* (London: Methuen and Co., 1950).
6. See, for example, Robert E. Spiller, *Fenimore Cooper: Critic of his Time* (New York: Russell & Russell, 1963), 73.
7. See Alan Taylor, *William Cooper's Town: Power and Persuasion on the Frontier of the Early American Republic* (New York: A. A. Knopf, 1995).
8. James Fenimore Cooper, quoted in Grossman, *Cooper*, 12.
9. John P. McWilliams, *The Last of the Mohicans: Civil Savagery and Savage Civility* (New York: Twayne Publishers, 1995), 5–6, firmly viewed Cooper's literary career as based on a financial imperative.
10. John P. McWilliams, *Political Justice in a Republic: James Fenimore Cooper's America* (Berkeley: University of California Press, 1972), sees Cooper's attitude to the Revolution as being much more ambivalent, and specifically contrasts him with Neal (48). The corpses with which Neal concludes *Seventy-Six* and the general bloodiness throughout make such a view questionable.
11. Mark Twain, "Fenimore Cooper's Literary Offences", in eds. George Dekker and John P. McWilliams, *Fenimore Cooper: The Critical Heritage* (London: Routledge and Kegan Paul, 1973), 276–287, quotation, 277; article originally published in *North American Review*, clxi (June 1895), 1–12.
12. *Ibid.*, 276.

13. Robert Lawson-Peebles, "Fenimore Cooper's First Novel, Family Property, and the Battle of Waterloo", in *Symbiosis*, 8:2, (October, 2004), 124–139, quotation, 126.
14. James Fenimore Cooper, *Precaution*, 2 vols. (New York: A.T. Goodrich and Co., 1820), 1:29.
15. *Ibid.*, 2:311.
16. Wayne Franklin, "Introduction," in James Fenimore Cooper, *The Spy* (Harmondsworth, Middlesex: Penguin Books, 1997), xvi–xvii.
17. James Fenimore Cooper, *The Spy* (New York: AMS Press, 2002), 23. All subsequent references taken from this edition. See also James Fenimore Cooper, *The Prairie* (Albany, NY: SUNY Press, 1985), 156. Reprinted by permission from *The Prairie: A Tale* by James Fenimore Cooper, the State University of New York Press ©1985, State University of New York. All rights reserved.
18. All three quotations in *ibid.*, 92. The reference is to the threatened confiscation of his estate by the rebels.
19. *Ibid.*, 39–40.
20. *Ibid.*, 40.
21. *Ibid.*, 41.
22. *Ibid.*, 180.
23. *Ibid.*, 182.
24. All three quotations in *ibid.*, 183.
25. All three quotations in *ibid.*, 184.
26. *Ibid.*, 185.
27. *Ibid.*, 33.
28. Both quotations in *ibid.*, 54.
29. Sumpter is not referred to again, an illustration of the irrelevancies into which the two Whites are permitted to digress to avoid the slavery issue.
30. Both quotations in *ibid.*, 50.
31. *Ibid.*, 99.
32. *Ibid.*, 356–7.
33. See, for example, in *ibid.*, 94, 101, 140.
34. *Ibid.*, 140.
35. James Fenimore Cooper, *The Pilot* (Albany, NY: SUNY Press, 1986), 351–2, contains one curious slavery vignette. Col. Howard (representing the loyalists) has two Black slaves who are captured in the course of the narrative and mocked by the American sailors. An officer intervenes before they come to too serious harm. The incident does suggest a capacity in Cooper for mockery when he comments on their reaction to their capture, "both occupied in mournful forebodings on the results that were to flow from this unexpected loss of their liberty." Yet the incident is appropriately resolved, and Cooper on this occasion affects to imply that the situation really has improved since then and, in any case, it is a fault of the lower Whites, who are of dubious worth in any case.
36. Cooper, *Spy*, 33.
37. *Ibid.*, 298.
38. *Ibid.*, 379–80.
39. *Ibid.*, 368. See also the similar ringing endorsement of American funeral practices, 341.
40. *Ibid.*, 420.
41. *Ibid.*, 421.
42. Cooper, *Pilot*, 411.
43. *Ibid.*, 11.
44. Ian Dennis, *Nationalism and Desire in Early Historical Fiction* (Basingstoke, UK: Macmillan, 1997), 136–153, makes this case.

45. See particularly Taylor, *William Cooper's Town* on *The Pioneers*. Taylor's analysis of the novel as an attempt by James Fenimore Cooper to "revive and reclaim his lost property and position," and the fact that Fenimore Cooper "indulged his pleasing memories and exorcised his painful ones" is telling, but I believe Taylor underplays the significance to that attempt of the treatment of the Amer-Indian and Loyalist dimensions.

46. Francis Parkman to [the Cooper Memorial Committee] n.d., 1852 in Dekker and McWilliams, *James Fenimore Cooper*, 249, originally published in Bryant, *Memorial of James Fenimore Cooper*, 34–35.

47. Geoffrey Rans, *Cooper's Leather-Stocking Novels—A Secular Reading* (Chapel Hill: University of North Carolina Press, 1991), 43. McWilliams, *Mohicans*, 6–7, argued that Cooper reflected the perplexities of his time. However, as Chapter 4 shows, contemporaries like Paulding and Neal did not see the need to muddy their portrayals of American society to anything like the same extent.

48. Rans, *Leather-Stocking*, 5.

49. James Fenimore Cooper, *The Pioneers* (SUNY Press: Albany, 1980), 3. Reprinted by permission from *The Pioneers or the Sources of the Susquehanna: A Descriptive Tale* by James Fenimore Cooper, the State University of New York Press © 1980, State University of New York. All rights reserved.

50. *Ibid.*, 15–16.

51. *Ibid.*, 34.

52. *Ibid.*, 45.

53. *Ibid.*

54. *Ibid.*

55. *Ibid.*, 45–6.

56. *Ibid.*, 46.

57. *Ibid.*, 70.

58. See Charles Swann, "Guns mean Democracy: *The Pioneers* and the Game Laws", and Richard Godden, "Pioneer Properties, or 'What's in a hut?'", both in *James Fenimore Cooper: New Critical Essays*, ed. Robert Clark (London: Vision Press, Ltd., 1985), 96–142.

59. *Ibid.*, 266.

60. See the following.

61. *Ibid.*, 356.

62. *Ibid.*, 160.

63. Kay Seymour House, *Cooper's Americans* (Columbus: Ohio State University Press, 1965), 48.

64. Cooper, *Pioneers*, 83.

65. *Ibid.*, 84.

66. *Ibid.*, 85.

67. *Ibid.*

68. *Ibid.*, 86.

69. *Ibid.*, 138. See similar comments on 165 and 290.

70. *Ibid.*, 143.

71. *Ibid.*, 214.

72. *Ibid.*, 215.

73. *Ibid.*, 280.

74. *Ibid.*

75. *Ibid.*

76. See the discussions on 165–6, 185–6 (in this case, a discussion between Edwards and Mohegan with Natty as spectator) and 291.

77. *Ibid.*, 401.

78. *Ibid.*

79. *Ibid.*
80. *Ibid.*, 403.
81. *Ibid.*
82. *Ibid.*, 134.
83. *Ibid.*, 166.
84. *Ibid.*, 420.
85. *Ibid.*, 418.
86. *Ibid.*, 420. There is, in fact, another good novel to be got out of what Natty does, despite the death of his friend.
87. *Ibid.*, 419.
88. *Ibid.*, 424.
89. *Ibid.*, 437.
90. *Ibid.*, 442.
91. It may be argued that this kind of revelation was frequent in Cooper's models, most notably Walter Scott (for example, the supposedly Irish hero of his poem *Rokeby*), but that does not diminish its implications in terms of Cooper's portrayal of the United States.
92. *Ibid.*, 441.
93. *Ibid.*, 452.
94. *Ibid.*, 451.
95. *Ibid.*, 455.
96. *Ibid.*, 456.
97. James Fenimore Cooper, *The Last of the Mohicans* (Albany, NY: SUNY Press, 1983), 12. All further references are to this edition.
98. *Ibid.*, 349.
99. *Ibid.*, 35. See also Natty's reactions on 119, 121, 126, 183, 189. The killing of the French sentinel (138) is a particularly glaring example.
100. *Ibid.*, 114–5.
101. Cooper, *Prairie*, 11.
102. For the first see *ibid.*, 76, for the second, 57.
103. *Ibid.*, 280–1.
104. *Ibid.*, 61.
105. See Cooper, *Mohicans*, Chapter XVI.
106. *Ibid.*, 112.
107. *Ibid.*
108. *Ibid.*, 240.
109. *Ibid.*, 241.
110. *Ibid.*, 249–250. See also 306.
111. *Ibid.*, 380–381.
112. *Ibid.*, 383.

NOTES TO THE CONCLUSION

1. The last words of Thomas Jefferson and John Adams, quoted in Joseph J. Ellis, *Passionate Sage: The Character and Legacy of John Adams* (New York: W. W. Norton and Co., 1993), 205.
2. See Merrill D. Peterson, *The Jefferson Image in the American Mind* (New York: Oxford University Press, 1960, rpt 1985), 3–14. Ellis, *Passionate Sage*, 205–232. Ellis is excellent on the meaning of Adams for Americans. Andrew Burstein, *America's Jubilee: How in 1826 a Generation Remembered Fifty Years of American Independence* (New York: Alfred A. Knopf, 2001), 262–286. Burstein queries whether Adams uttered the word "survived." He argues that the Adams Family would not have wished to disseminate such a

myth, but this is only so if one takes it as a patriotic statement (268). It seems much more likely, given their past relationship, that Adams, at death, was haunted by the knowledge that Jefferson would outlive him, both physically and in memory.

3. Both quotations in Ellis, *Passionate Sage*, 206.

Bibliography

PERIODICALS

Monthly Magazine and American Review (1799–1800)
Literary Review and American Register (1801–1802)
Analectic Magazine (1813–1815)

PRINTED PRIMARY SOURCES

Allen, Paul. *Life of Charles Brockden Brown*, introd. Charles E. Bennett (Delmar, NY: Scholar's Facsimiles & Reprints, 1975)

Brackenridge, Hugh Henry. *Gazette Publications* (Carlisle, PA: Alexander and Phillips, 1806)

———. *Incidents of the Insurrection in the Western Parts of Pennsylvania in the Year 1794* (Philadelphia: John M'Culloch, 1795)

———. *Modern Chivalry*, ed. Claude M. Newlin (New York: American Book Company, 1937, reprinted 1962)

———. *The Battle of Bunkers-Hill* (Temecula, CA: Reprint Services Corporation, 1989; Originally published Philadelphia: R. Bell, 1776)

———. *The Death of General Montgomery in Storming the City of Quebec: A Tragedy* (S.1: Reprint Services, 1989; Orginally published Philadelphia: R. Bell, 1777)

Brackenridge, Hugh Henry and Freneau, Philip Morin. *A Poem, on the Rising Glory of America* (Cambridge: ProQuest Information and Learning Company, American Drama Full-Text Database, 2003)

———. *Father Bombo's Pilgrimage to Mecca 1770*, ed. Michael Davitt Bell (Princeton: University Library, 1975)

Brown, Charles Brockden. *An Address to the Congress of the United States on the Utility and Justice of Restrictions Upon Foreign Commerce: With Some Reflections on Foreign Trade in General and the Future Prospects of America* (Philadelphia: C & A Conrad and Co., 1809)

———. *An Address to the Government of the United States, on the Cession of Louisiana to the French* (Philadelphia: J. Conrad & Co., 1803)

———. *British Treaty: With an Appendix of State Papers: Which are now First Published* (America: n.p., 1808)

———. *The Rhapsodist and Other Uncollected Writings*, ed. Harry R. Warfel (New York: Scholars Facsimiles and Reprints, 1943)

———. *Somnambulism and Other Stories*, ed. Alfred Weber (Frankfurt am Main: P Lang, 1987)

————. *The Novels and Related Works of Charles Brockden Brown* (Kent, OH: Kent State University Press, 1977–1987)

Clopper, Jonas. *Fragments of the History of Bawlfredonia* (Baltimore, MD: n.p., 1819)

Crèvecoeur, J. Hector St. John de. *Journey into Northern Pennsylvania and the State of New York*, trans. Clarissa Spencer Bostelmann (Ann Arbor, MI: University of Michigan Press, 1964)

————. *Letters From an American Farmer and Sketches of Eighteenth Century America*, ed. Albert E. Stone (New York: Penguin Books, 1986)

Cooper, James Fenimore. *Lionel Lincoln* (New York: Charles Wiley, 1825), Consulted on-line at *Early American Fiction Fiction Full Text Database* (Charlottesville: University of Virginia, 2000)

————. *Precaution* (New York: A. T. Goodrich and Co., 1820), Consulted on-line at *Early American Fiction Fiction Full Text Database* (Charlottesville: University of Virginia, 2000)

————. *The Last of the Mohicans* (Albany, NY: SUNY Press, 1983)

————. *The Pilot* (Albany, NY: SUNY Press, 1986)

————. *The Pioneers* (Albany, NY: SUNY Press, 1980)

————. *The Prairie* (Albany, NY: SUNY Press, 1985)

————. *The Spy* (New York: AMS Press, 2002)

Dickinson, John. *Letters from a Farmer in Pennsylvania* (Eaglewood Cliffs, NJ: Prentice Hall, 1962)

Franklin, Benjamin, *Writings* (New York, NY: Library of America, 1987).

Hamilton, Alexander, and Jay, John, and Madison, James. *The Federalist Papers* (New York: New American Library Inc., 1961)

Inaugural Addresses of the Presidents of the United States, (Washington, DC: US Government Printing Office, 1961)

Irving, Washington. *The Complete Works of Washington Irving*, eds. Henry A. Pochman et. al., 30 vols. (Boston, MA: Twayne Publishers, 1970–1989)

————. *History Tales and Sketches* (New York: Library of America, 1983)

————. "Bracebridge Hall," in *Bracebridge Hall, Tales of a Traveller, The Alhambra* (New York: Library of America, 1984)

————. "Tales of a Traveller," in *Bracebridge Hall, Tales of a Traveller, The Alhambra* (New York: Library of America, 1984)

Jefferson, Thomas. *Writings* (New York: Library of America, 1984)

Journals and Notebooks of Washington Irving, ed. Nathalia Wright et. al. (Madison: University of Wisconsin Press; Boston: Twayne Publishers, 1969–1986)

Madison, James. *Writings*, (New York: Library of America, 1999)

More Letters From an American Farmer, An Edition of the Essays in English Left Unpublished by Crèvecoeur, ed, Dennis D, Moore (Athens, GA: University of Georgia Press, 1995)

Neal, John. *American Writers: A Series of Papers Contributed to Blackwood's Magazine 1824–1825*, ed. Fred Lewis Pattee (Durham, NC: Duke University Press, 1937)

————. *Brother Jonathan, or, The New-Englanders* (Edinburgh, U.K.: W. Blackwood, 1825)

————. *Errata:, The Works of Will Adams* (New York: published for the 'proprietors,' 1823), Consulted on-line at *Early American Fiction Fiction Full Text Database* (Charlottesville: University of Virginia, 2000)

————. *Keep Cool* (Baltimore, MD: Joseph Cushing, 1817)

————. *Logan: A Family History* (Philadelphia: H.C. Carey & I. Lea, 1822), consulted on-line at *Early American Fiction Full-Text Database* (Charlottesville: University of Virginia, 2000)

————. *Otho: A Tragedy* (Boston, MA: West, Richardson and Lord, 1819), consulted on-line at *American Drama Full-Text Database*, (Cambridge, U.K.: Proquest Information and Learning company, 2003)

————. *Randolph* (Baltimore, MD: n.p., 1823), consulted on-line at *Early American Fiction Full-Text Database* (Charlottesville: University of Virginia, 2000)

————. *Seventy-Six.* (Baltimore, MD: Joseph Robinson, 1823) Consulted online at Early American Fiction Full-Text Database (Charlottesville: University of Virginia, 2000).

————. "Late American Books," in *Blackwood's Magazine*, XVIII (September, 1825), 316–334

————. "Review of 'A Summary View of America," in *Blackwood's Magazine*, XVI (December, 1824), 617–652

————. "Sketches of the Five American Presidents, and of the Five Presidential Candidates, From the Memoranda of a Traveller," in *Blackwood's Magazine*, XV (May, 1824), 508–513.

Paine, Thomas, *Common Sense*, (Hammondsworth, U.K.: Penguin, 1986) [1776].

Paulding, James Kirke. *A Sketch of Old England* (New York: Charles Wiley, 1822), consulted on-line at *Early American Fiction Full-Text Database*, (Charlottesville: University of Virginia, 2000)

————. *John Bull in America; or, The New Munchausen* (New York: Charles Wiley, 1825), consulted on-line at *Early American Fiction Full-Text Database* (Charlottesville: University of Virginia, 2000)

————. *Koningsmarke; or, Old Times in the New World* (New York: AMS Press, 1971)

————. *Letters From the South* (New York: AMS Press, 1973, reprint of 1817 edition)

————. *Salmagundi: 2nd series* (New York: Haley and Thomas, 1819–20)

————. *The Diverting History of John Bull and Brother Jonathan* (New York: Inskeep & Bradford, 1812)

————. *The History of the Little Frenchman and His Bank Notes. Rags! Rags! Rags!* (Philadelphia: Edward Earle, 1815)

————.*The United States and England* (New York: A.H. Inskeep, 1815)

Shakespeare, William, *As You Like It,* ed. Agnes Latham (London: Methven, 1975).

————. *As You Like It,* ed. Alan Brillenden (Oxford, U.K.: Clarendon Press, 1993).

The Adams–Jefferson Letters: The Complete Correspondence Between Thomas Jefferson and Abigail and John Adams, ed. Lester J. Cappon (Chapel Hill, NC: Published for the Institute of Early American History and Culture at Williamsburg, VA by the University of North Carolina Press, 1959)

The Letters and Journals of James Fenimore Cooper, ed. James Franklin Beard (Cambridge, MA: Belknap Press of Harvard University Press, 1960–1968)

The Letters of James Kirke Paulding, ed. Ralph M. Aderman (Madison: University of Wisconsin Press, 1962)

Letters of Washington Irving, eds. Ralph M. Aderman et. al (Boston: Twayne Publishers, 1978–1982)

The Papers of Benjamin Franklin, eds. Leonard W. Labaree et. al., (New Haven; London: Yale University Press, 1959–)

The Papers of John Adams, ed. Robert J. Taylor et. al. (Cambridge, MA: The Belknap Press of Harvard University Press, 1977–)

The Papers of Thomas Jefferson, eds. Julian P. Boyd et. al. (Princeton: Princeton University Press, 1950–)

Weems, Mason Locke. *The Life of Benjamin Franklin With Many Choice Anecdotes and Admirable Scenes of This Great Man Never Before Published by any of his Biographers*, (Philadelphia: M. Carey, 1817)

SECONDARY SOURCES

Adams, Henry. *History of the United States of America during the Administrations of Thomas Jefferson and James Madison*, 2 vols. (New York: Library of America, 1986)

Adams, Percy G. "Introduction" in *Crèvecoeur's Eighteenth-Century Travels in Pennsylvania and New York*, trans. & ed. Percy G. Adams, (Lexington: University of Kentucky Press, 1961)

———. "The Historical Value of Crèvecoeur's Voyage," in *American Literature* 25 (1953–1954), 152–168

Aderman, Ralph M. and Kime, Wayne R. *Advocate for America: James Kirke Paulding* (Selinsgrove, PA: Susquehanna University Press, 2003).

Aderman, Ralph M. *Critical Essays on Washington Irving* (Boston, MA: G. K. Hall, 1990)

Allen, Gay Wilson, and Asselineau, Roger. *St John de Crèvecoeur* (New York, London: Viking, 1987)

Ammon, Harry. *James Monroe: The Quest for National Identity* (Charlottesville: University of Virginia Press, 1971)

Axelrod, Alan. *Charles Brockden Brown: An American Tale* (Austin: University of Texas Press, 1983)

Bailyn, Bailyn. *The Ideological Origins of the American Revolution* (Cambridge, MA: Belknap Press of Harvard University Press, 1967)

Becker, Carl. *Benjamin Franklin: A Biographical Sketch* (Ithaca, NY: Cornell University Press, 1946)

Becker, Carl. *The Declaration of Independence* (New York: Knopf, 1942)

Berkhofer, Robert F. *The White Man's Indian: Images of the American Indian From Columbus to the Present* (New York: Alfred A. Knopf, 1978)

Bouton, Terry. "A Road Closed: Rural Insurgency in Post-Independence Pennsylvania," in *Journal of American History* 87 (December, 2000), 855–887

Boyd, Steven R. *The Whiskey Rebellion: Past and Present Perspectives* (Westport, CT: Greenwood Press, 1985)

Brooks, Van Wyck. *The World of Washington Irving* (New York: E. P. Dutton and Co., 1944)

Brown, Wallace. *The King's Friends* (Providence, RI: Brown University Press, 1965)

Burstein, Andrew. *America's Jubilee: How in 1826 a Generation Remembered Fifty Years of American Independence* (New York: Alfred A. Knopf, 2001)

———. *Sentimental Democracy: The Evolution of America's Romantic Self-Image* (New York; Hill & Wang, 1999)

———. *The Original Knickerbocker: The Life of Washington Irving* (New York: Basic Books, 2007)

Buxbaum, Melvin H. *Critical Essays on Benjamin Franklin* (Boston, MA: G. K. Hall, 1987)

Calhoon, Robert M. *The Loyalists in Revoloutionary America 1760–1781* (New York: Harcourt, Brace, Jouanovich, 1973).

Castillo, Susan. "Imperial Pasts and Dark Futurities: Freneau and Brackenridge's 'The Rising Glory of America'," in *Symbiosis: A Journal of Anglo-American Literary Relations*, 6:1 (2002:April), 27–43

Charles, Joseph. *The Origins of the American Party System: Three Essays* (New York: Harper & Row, 1961)

Charvet, William. *Literary Publishing in America 1790–1850* (Philadelphia: University of Pennsylvania Press, 1959)

Chevignard, Bernard. 'St John de Crèvecoeur: A Case of Arrested Bibliographical Development,' *Early American Literature* 23:3 (1988), 319-327.

Christopherson, Bill. *The Apparition in the Glass: Charles Brockden Brown's American Gothic* (Athens, Ga.: University of Georgia Press, 1993)

Cogliano, Francis D. *Revolutionary America 1763–1815: A Political History* (London: Routledge, 2000)

Clark, Robert. *James Fenimore Cooper: New Critical Essays* (London: Vision Press, Ltd., 1985)

Conner, Paul W. *Poor Richard's Politicks: Benjamin Franklin and his new American Order* (New York: Oxford University Press, 1965)

Cowie, Alexander. *The Rise of the American Novel* (New York: American Book Company, 1948)

Crane, Verner W. *Benjamin Franklin and a Rising People* (Boston, MA: Little, Brown, 1954)

Cresson, W. P. *James Monroe* (Chapel Hill: The University of North Carolina Press, 1946)

Cullen, Jim. *The American Dream: A Short History of an Idea That Shaped America* (Oxford, U.K.: Oxford University Press, 2003)

Cunliffe, Marcus. *The Literature of the United States* (Harmondsworth, U.K.: Penguin, 1968)

———. *The Nation Takes Shape 1789–1837* (Chicago, IL: University of Chicago Press, 1959)

———. *George Washington: Man and Monument* (Boston: Little, Brown, 1958)

Cunningham, Noble E. *The Presidency of James Monroe* (Lawrence: University of Kansas Press, 1996)

Dangerfield, George. *The Era of Good Feelings* (London: Metheun & Co.. 1953)

Davidson, Cathy N. *Revolution and the Word: The Rise of the Novel in America* (New York; Oxford: Oxford University Press, 1986)

eds. Dekker, George, and McWilliams, John P. *Fenimore Cooper: The Critical Heritage* (London: Routledge and Kegan Paul, 1973)

Delbanco, Andrew. *The Real American Dream: A Meditation on Hope* (Cambridge, MA: Harvard University Press, 1999)

Dennis, Ian. *Nationalism and Desire in Early Historical Fiction* (Basingstoke, U.K.: Macmillan, 1997)

Dowling, William C. *Literary Federalism in the Age of Jefferson: Joseph Dennie and The Port folio 1801–1812* (Columbia: University of South Carolina Press, 1999)

Edwards, Owen Dudley. "The Writters of the American Revolution: Variations on a Theme by Auden." *America and Ireland 1776–1976: The American Identity and the Irish Connection*, ed. David Noel Doyle and Owen Dudley Edwards (Westport, CT: Greenwood Press, 1980)

Elkins, Stanley, and McKitrick, Eric. *The Age of Federalism* (New York; Oxford: Oxford University Press, 1993)

Elliott, Emory. *Revolutionary Writers: Literature and Authority in the Early Republic 1725–1810* (New York; Oxford: Oxford University Press, 1982)

Ellis, Joseph J. *After the Revolution: Profiles of Early American Culture* (New York, London: Norton, 1979)

———. *American Sphinx: The Character and Legacy of Thomas Jefferson* (New York: Alfred A. Knopf, 1997)

———. *Founding Brothers: The Revolutionary Generation* (New York: Alfred A. Knopf, 2001)

————. *Passionate Sage: The Character and Legacy of John Adams* (New York: W.W. Norton, 1993)

Emerson, Everett, *American Literature 1764–1789: The Revolutionary Years* (Madison: University of Wisconsin Press, 1977)

Fields, Wayne C. *James Fenimore Cooper: A Collection of Critical Essays* (Eaglewood Cliffs, NJ: Prentice-Hall, 1979)

Fliegelman, Jay. *Declaring Independence: Jefferson, Natural Language and the Culture of Performance* (Stanford, CA: Stanford University Press, 1993)

Franklin, Wayne. "Introduction," in James Fenimore Cooper, *The Spy* (Harmondsworth, Middlesex, U.K.: Penguin Books, 1997)

Freehling, William. "The Founding Fathers and Slavery," in *American Historical Review* 77:1 (Feb 1972), 81–93

Friedman, Lawrence J. *Inventors of the Promised Land* (New York: Alfred A. Knopf, 1975)

Garnett, Richard. "Alms for Oblivious: The Minor Writings of Charles Brockden Brown," in *Cornhill Magazine* 13 (1902), 494–506.

Giles, Paul. *Transatlantic Insurrections: British Culture and the Formation of American Literature, 1730–1860* (Philadelphia: University of Pennsylvania Press, 2001)

Gilreath, James. "Mason Weems, Mathew Carey and the Southern Booktrade 1794–1810," in *Publishing History* 10 (1981), 27–51

Granger, Bruce. *Benjamin Franklin: An American Man of Letters*, (Ithaca, NY: Cornell University Press, 1964)

ed. Greene, Jack P. *The American Revolution: Its Character and Limits*, (New York: New York University Press, 1987)

Greene, Jack P. *The Intellectual Construction of America: Exceptionalism and Identity From 1492 to 1800* (Chapel Hill: University of North Carolina Press, 1993)

Grossman, James. *James Fenimore Cooper* (London: Methuen and Co., 1950)

Hedges, William. "Charles Brockden Brown and the Culture of Contradictions," in *Early American Literature* 9 (1974), 107–141

Hedges, William L. "The Myth of the Republic and the theory of American literature," in *Prospects* 4 (1979), 101–120.

————. *Washington Irving: An American Study 1802–1832* (Baltimore, MD: The Johns Hopkins Press, 1965)

Hinds, Elizabeth Jane. *Private Property: Charles Brockden Brown's Gendered Economies of Virtue* (Newark: University of Delaware Press, 1997)

Hofstadter, Richard. *The American Political Tradition: And the Men Who Made it* (New York: Alfred A. Knopf, 1948)

————. *The Idea of a Party System; The Rise of Legitimate Opposition in the United States 1780–1840* (Berkeley: University of California Press, 1969)

House, Key Seymour. *Cooper's Americans* (Columbus: Ohio State University Press, 1965)

Huang, Nian-Sheng. *Benjamin Franklin in American Thought and Culture 1790–1990* (Philadelphia: American Philosophical Society, 1994)

Jennings, Francis. *Benjamin Franklin, Politician* (New York: Norton, 1996)

Kammen, Michael. *People of Paradox: An Inquiry Concerning the Origins of American Civilisation* (New York: Oxford University Press, 1980)

Kerber, Linda. *Federalists in Dissent: Imagery and Ideology in Jeffersonian America* (Ithaca, NY: Cornell University Press, 1970)

Ketcham, Ralph. *From Colony to Country: The Revolution in American Thought 1750–1820* (New York: Macmillan, 1974)

Kurtz, Stephen. *The Presidency of John Adams: The Collapse of Federalism 1795–1800* (Philadelphia: University of Pennsylvania Press, 1957)

Lawrence, D. H. *Studies in Classic American Literature* (London: Penguin Books, 1971)

Lawson-Peebles, Robert. "Fenimore Cooper's First Novel, Family Property, and the Battle of Waterloo" in *Symbiosis*, 8:2 (October 2004), 124–129.

———. *Landscape and Written Expression in Revolutionary America* (Cambridge; New York: Cambridge University Press, 1988)

Leary, Lewis. *Soundings: Some Early American Writers* (Athens: University of Georgia Press, 1975)

Lease, Benjamin. *That Wild Fellow John Neal and the American Revolution* (Chicago: University of Chicago Press, 1972)

Lemay, J. A. Leo. *Reappraising Benjamin Franklin: A Bicentennial Perspective* (Newark: University of Delaware Press, 1993)

Lemay, J. A. Leo, and Zall, P. M. *The Autobiography of Benjamin Franklin: A Genetic Text*, (Knoxville: University of Tennessee Press, 1981)

Levy, Leonard W. *Jefferson and Civil Liberties: The Darker Side* (Cambridge, MA: Belknap Press of Harvard University Press, 1963)

Lipset, Seymour Martin. *The First New Nation: The United States in Historical and Comparative Perspective* (London: Heinemann, 1964)

Looby, Christopher. *Voicing America: Language, Literary Form, and the Origins of the United States* (Chicago: University of Chicago Press, 1996)

Maier, Pauline. *American Scripture: How America Declared its Independence From Britain*, (London: Pimlico, 1999)

Manning, Susan. "Introduction," in *Letters from an American Farmer*, ed. Susan Manning (Oxford: Oxford University Press, 1997) vii–xxxvii

Marder, Daniel. *A Hugh Henry Brackenridge Reader 1770–1815* (Pittsburgh: University of Pittsburgh Press, 1970)

———. *Hugh Henry Brackenridge* (New York: Twayne Publishers, 1967)

Matthews, Jean V. *Toward a New Society: American Thought and Culture 1800–1830* (Boston: Twayne Publishers, 1990)

McDowell, R.B., *Irish Public Opinion 1750–1800* (London: Faber and Faber, 1944).

McFarland, Philip. *Sojourners* (New York: Atheneum, 1979)

McWilliams, John P. *Political Justice in a Republic: James Fenimore Cooper's America* (Berkeley: University of California Press, 1972)

———. *The Last of the Mohicans: Civil Savagery and Savage Civility* (New York: Twayne Publishers, 1995)

Middlekauff, Robert. *Benjamin Franklin and his Enemies* (Berkeley: University of California Press, 1996)

Miller, John C. *The Federalist Era 1789–1801* (New York: Harper, 1960)

Mitchell, Julia Post. *St John de Crèvecoeur* (New York: Columbia University Press, 1916)

Morgan, Daniel D. *Devious Dr. Franklin, Colonial Agent: Benjamin Franklin's Years in London* (Macon, Ga.: Mercer University Press, 1996)

Morgan, Edmund S. *Benjamin Franklin* (New Haven, CT: Yale University Press, 2002)

———. *The Birth of the Republic, 1763–1789* (Chicago: University of Chicago Press, 1956)

———. *The Meaning of Independence* (Charlottesville: University of Virginia Press, 1976)

Mott, Frank Luther. *A History of American Magazines* (Cambridge, MA: Harvard University Press, 1938–68)

Murrin, John. "A Roof without Walls: The Dilemma of American National Identity," in *Beyond Confederation: Origins of the Constitution and American*

National Identity, eds. Richard Beeman, Stephen Botein, and Edward C Carter II (Chapel Hill: Published for the Institute of Early American History and Culture, Williamsburg, VA, by the University of North Carolina Press, c.1987)

Nelson, William H. *The American Tory* (Oxford, U.K.: Clarendon Press, 1961)

Newlin, Claude M. *The Life and Writings of Hugh Henry Brackenridge* (Princeton, NJ: Princeton University Press, 1932)

Nye, Russel B. *The Cultural Life of the New Nation 1776–1830* (New York: Harper and Brothers, 1960)

Palmer, R.R. *The Age of the Democratic Revolution 1760–1800* (Princeton, NJ: Princeton University Press, 1959)

Philbrick, Thomas. *St John de Crèvecoeur* (New York: Twayne Publishers, 1970)

Quinn, Arthur Hobson. *American Fiction: An Historical and Critical Survey* (New York: D. Appleton-Century Co., 1936)

Petter, Henri. *The Early American Novel* (Columbus: Ohio State University Press, 1971)

O'Brien, Conor Cruise. *The Long Affair: Thomas Jefferson and the French Revolution 1785–1800* (London: Pimlico, 1998)

Orestano, Francesca. "The Old World and the New in the national landscapes of John Neal," in *Views of American Literaure*, eds. Mick Gidley and Robert Lawson-Peebles, (Cambridge: Cambridge University Press, 1989) 129–145.

Rans, Geoffrey. *Cooper's Leather-Stocking Novels—A Secular Reading* (Chapel Hill: University of North Carolina Press, 1991)

Ratner, Lorman. *James Kirke Paulding: The Last Republican* (Westport, CT: Greenwood Press, 1992)

Reynolds, Larry J. *James Kirke Paulding* (Boston: Twayne Publishers, 1984)

Richards, Irving T. "John Neal's Gleanings in Irvingiana," in *American Literature* 8 (1936), 170–179

Richards, Jeffrey H. "Revolution, Domestic Life and the End of "Common Mercy" in Crèvecoeur's "Landscapes," *William and Mary Quarterly*, 55 (April, 1998), 281–296.

Roth, Martin. *Comedy and America: The Lost World of Washington Irving* (Port Washington, NY: Kennikat Press, 1976).

Rubin-Dorsky, Jeffrey. *Adrift in the Old World: The Psychological Pilgrimage of Washington Irving* (Chicago: University of Chicago Press, 1988)

Sanford, Charles L. *Benjamin Franklin and the American Character* (Boston: Heath, 1955)

Sears, Donald A. *John Neal* (Boston: Twayne Publishers, 1978)

Seavey, Ormond. *Becoming Benjamin Franklin: The Autobiography and the Life* (University Park: Pennsylvania State University Press, 1988)

Sellers, Charles. *The Market Revolution: Jacksonian America 1815–1846*, (New York: Oxford University Press, 1991)

Sharp, James Roger. *American Politics in the Early Republic: The New Nation in Crisis* (New Haven, CT: Yale University Press, 1993)

Shaw, Peter. *The Character of John Adams* (Chapel Hill: Published for the Institute of Early American History and Culture, Williamsburg, VA, by the University of North Carolina, 1976)

Skemp, Sheila S. *Benjamin and William Franklin: Father and Son, Patriot and Loyalist* (Boston, MA: Bedford Books of St Martin's Press, 1994)

Slaughter, Thomas. *The Whiskey Rebellion: Frontier Epilogue to the American Revolution* (New York; Oxford: Oxford University Press, 1986)

Smelser, Marshall. *The Democratic Republic 1801–1815* (New York: Harper & Row, 1968)

Smith, Henry Nash. *Virgin Land: The American West as Symbol and Myth* (Cambridge, MA, 1950)

Spengemann, William C. *A New World of Words: Redefining Early American Literature* (New Haven, CT: Yale University Press, 1994)

Smith, Page. *John Adams* (Garden City, NY: Doubleday, 1962)

Spiller, Robert E. "The Verdict of Sydney Smith," in *The Third Dimension: Studies in Literary History* (New York: MacMillan, 1965) ed. Robert E. Spiller, 39–51.

Stourch, Gerald. *Benjamin Franklin and American foreign policy* (Chicago: University of Chicago Press, 1954)

Taylor, Alan. *William Cooper's Town: Power and Persuasion on the Frontier of the Early American Republic* (New York: A. A. Knopf, 1995)

Thompson, C. Bradley. *John Adams and the Spirit of Liberty* (Lawrence: University of Kansas, 1998)

Tompkins, Jane. *Sentimental Designs: The Cultural Work of American Fiction 1790–1860*, (New York; Oxford: Oxford University Press, 1985)

ed. Tuttleton, James W. *Washington Irving: The Critical Reaction* (New York: AMS Press, 1993)

Updike, John. "A Critic at Large: Many Bens," in *The New Yorker* 64 (2 February, 1988), 105–116

Van Doren, Carl. *Benjamin Franklin* (London: Putnam, 1939)

Verhoeven, W. M. *James Fenimore Cooper: New Historical and Literary Contexts* (Amsterdam; Atlanta, GA: Editions Rodopi B.V., 1993)

Waldstreicher, David. *In the Midst of Perpetual Fetes: The Making of American Nationalism 1776–1820* (Chapel Hill: Published for the Omohondro Institute of Early American History and Culture, Williamsburg, VA, by the University of North Carolina Press, 1997)

Wallace, James D. *Early Cooper and His Audience* (New York: Columbia University Press, 1986)

Watts, Steven. *The Republic Reborn: War and the Making of Liberal America 1790–1820* (Baltimore, MD; London: Johns Hopkins University Press, c.1987)

———. *The Romance of Real Life: Charles Brockden Brown and the Origins of American culture* (Baltimore, MD: Johns Hopkins University Press, 1994)

Wertheimer, Eric. "Commencement Ceremonies: History and Identity in The Rising Glory of America 1771 and 1786," in *Early American Literature* 29:1 (1994:1) 35–58.

Williams, Stanley T. *The Life of Washington Irving* (New York: H. Milford, 1935)

Winans, Robert B. "The Growth of a Novel Reading Public in Late Eighteenth Century America," in *Early American Literature* 9:3 (1975), 267–275.

Wood, Gordon S. *The American Revolution* (London: Weidenfeld & Nicholson, 2003)

———. *The Americanization of Benjamin Franklin* (New York: Penguin Press, 2004)

———. *The Creation of the American Republic 1776–1787* (Chapel Hill: University of North Carolina Press, 1969)

———. *The Radicalism of the American Revolution* (New York: Knopf, 1992)

ed. Wood, Gordon S. *The Rising Glory of America 1760–1820* (New York: George Braziller, 1971)

Ziff, Larzer. *Writing in the New Nation: Prose, Print and Politics in the Early United States* (New Haven, CT: Yale University Press, 1991)

Index